PROJECTIVE TESTING AND PSYCHOANALYSIS

PROJECTIVE TESTING AND PSYCHOANALYSIS

Selected Papers

ROY SCHAFER, PH.D

INTERNATIONAL UNIVERSITIES PRESS, INC.

NEW YORK   NEW YORK

Manufactured in the United States of America

To my Children:
Laurie, Amy, and Sylvia

CONTENTS

ACKNOWLEDGMENTS

The appearance of this book gives me another opportunity to acknowledge my indebtedness to the late David Rapaport for the example he set, the conceptualizations he hammered out, the interest and stimulation he provided, and the critical readings he offered of the papers reprinted here. I also wish to acknowledge that the writings, personal communications, and constructive criticisms of my work by Robert R. Holt and Ernst Prelinger were most useful to me in writing my later papers on testing. My wife, Sarah, helped me think through many of the principal points in my discussions. Finally, I wish to thank Mrs. Dorothy Ricker for her able, conscientious, and cheerful secretarial assistance, and my daughter, Laura, for preparing the bibliography of this book for publication.

PROJECTIVE TESTING AND
PSYCHOANALYSIS

INTRODUCTION

Bringing these papers on testing together in book form should, I think, be useful to students, teachers and practitioners of clinical psychology. I think so for three reasons, and I shall expand particularly on the third of them.

First, the demand for my two books on testing and reprints of my journal articles has remained high, and I take this demand to be a sign of the usefulness of the views and findings I have published. Republishing these papers in one place makes it easier and more convenient to study and refer to them.

Second, this group of papers represents my effort to apply contemporary Freudian psychoanalytic theory to a particular kind of clinical data in a systematic, disciplined, uncompromising way. From the beginning of its acceptance into clinical and theoretical thought, psychoanalysis has been subject to superficialization, distortion, unsystematic borrowing, wild application, and other abuses. Although these abuses have not hampered the growth of psychoanalysis itself, they have introduced confusion and poor practice into clinical psychology generally and psychodiagnostic work specifically. I believe that there is no other way than the one I have followed to find out how far psychoanalytic ideas are applicable in psychodiagnostic work or how illuminating their application will be. My adherence to this one point of view may seem to be rigid and doctrinaire compared to the "common-sense" eclecticism and idiosyncratic improvisation that one encounters in many publications. I submit, however, that it alone does not prejudge the issue; it alone tries to find out something. I do not mean "I alone": the psychodiagnostic work and publications of others—at the Menninger Foundation, the Austen Riggs Center, certain of the Yale psychiatric facilities, and the Research Center for Mental Health at New York University, to name only a few instances particularly familiar to me—represent the same basic position as mine. All of us are working within the psychoanalytic psychodiagnostic tradition crystallized by David Rapaport. Although Hermann Rorschach and Henry Murray stand out as significant predecessors of Rapaport in this connection, they never stood for the rigorous integration of psychoanalytic thought and diagnostic practice in the way and to the extent that Rapaport did. The field of psychodiagnostics owes much to him.

In this second regard, therefore, I think it will serve a useful purpose to present this collection of papers as a sample, not of flawless application, but of consistent and controlled application of psychoanalytic ideas in psychodiagnostic investigation.

I said before of this approach, "It alone tries to find out something." I was then referring to finding out about the rules, the limits, and the benefits of this integration of psychoanalysis and psychodiagnostics. There is, however, more to be found out than this, there is more that may be found out than this, through psychodiagnostic work. I come here to the third way in which this collection of papers will, I believe, be helpful. It is a way that is not easy to state and not possible for me to state concisely and without relying on a mode of expression familiar in literary criticism. It has to do with what I shall call clinical sensibility. The subject is large and complex; the following remarks do no more than sketch it.

As commonly used in the arts, the term sensibility refers to refined sensitivity in emotion and taste, quickness and acuteness of apprehension and feeling, and a readiness to feel compassion that is not pity but a complex blend of empathy and understanding. The terms I have just used are not operationally defined and do not lend themselves to instant validation studies or interjudge reliability checks; nevertheless, those in the arts who have sensibility recognize it in others when it is there. I maintain that the same is true in clinical work generally and in psychodiagnostic work specifically. Clinicians sense it in each other when it is there; they sense it through personal contact, conference discussions, reading of each other's reports or publications, and sometimes just looking at one another.

Clinical sensibility can be distinguished from its common imitations. It is not facile or confused high-flown conceptualization. It is not exaggerated empathy that is implicitly self-congratulatory and condescends to the patient. It is not undisciplined or "cookbook" finding of everything in everything. It is not unbridled countertransference or counteridentification responses to patients. It is more than sheer sensitivity and intuitiveness; the latter do not have the vocabulary, the comprehension of relevance, and the organizational capacity and scope that are necessary to arrive at meaningful communications concerning other persons. And it is certainly not that so-called hard-nosed empiricism or objective research-mindedness that approaches the study of human beings with the intent to prove the null hypothesis universally applicable. The last mentioned of these is not an imitation of sensibility, really; it is condemnation of sensibility in the name of being "sensible."

Clinical sensibility includes an unobtrusive, empowering recognition of the tragic in life—the life of nonpatients too, the life of the clinician too. This sense of the tragic implies that psychic development and organization inevitably have their arduous, painful, and self-limiting aspects; that conflict and subjective distress per se are not pathology, and naming them is not name-calling; that every adaptation has its price and leads into new areas of conflict; that many important experiences are inexpressible or, at best, expressible only indirectly and approximately; and that, as regards therapy and testing, the basic objective is not to unmask each patient or to dispose of him with diagnostic or psychodynamic labels, but to see how and at what cost he is trying to make the best of a bad internal situation—and is perhaps compelled to make the worst of a not-necessarily-so-bad external situation. The tragic sense is not despondent, inert, or self-pitying: it does not preclude zest and humor, and it certainly enhances the observer's interest and objectivity.

Clinical sensibility also carries an aura of wonder and puzzlement in the face of the strange, complex, often only dimly perceivable foundations and manifestations of specifically human subjective experience. It includes an excited yet patient confrontation of the new phenomena, or new patterns of familiar phenomena, that each person presents.

Clinical sensibility is neither antiscientific nor antilogical. At its best, it is rigorous in its implicit and explicit rules of evidence and relevance. These rules can be taught. It does not set itself beyond science, though it does recognize, without dismay, shame, or apology that most of its operations and its data are not subject to experimental manipulation. But neither is clinical sensibility antipoetic or antiesthetic: it accepts the challenge of defining the other person with full recognition of the fact that, in order to be able to attempt that definition, the clinician must engage in a far-reaching, imaginative, and esthetic participation of his self in the experience of that other person.

This sensibility does not confuse open-mindedness with naïveté. In clinicians who have any amount of experience, naïveté can only be an artificial and rigid posture. In contrast, clinical sensibility is an informed and expectant responsiveness that accepts its place in a professional tradition of understanding without being enslaved by that tradition.

I have been attempting to describe a configuration of qualities that has often gone under the name of psychological mindedness. As psychology has many sides, so that a good experimentalist or theoretician might also rightly be called psychologically minded, and as I do believe that clinical perception has much in common with artistic perception, though it is not the same thing, I prefer the term sensibility.

Clinical sensibility enters into psychodiagnostic work not only in contemplating the material gathered from the patient. It influences the kind and amount of material that is to be contemplated; although it does so more in some cases than others, it is always one variable in the psychodiagnostic process. According to my observation, the beginning student and the insensitive practitioner gather from patients somewhat different and clinically inferior types of response than does the tester (or therapist) with sensibility.

Although the foundations of clinical sensibility are not teachable—ultimately, it is a life sensibility—the sensibility that is there in the student may be enhanced by teaching that recognizes, welcomes, and respects it. Unfortunately, many university programs in clinical psychology do not devote themselves to this task, especially not when it comes to psychodiagnostic work. I shall not go into the complex and not altogether appealing reasons for this institutionalized negligence, blindness, or opposition. I mention it only as one of the considerations that led to my thinking this book might be useful. For the book is a record of a series of explorations—of increasing complexity, ambiguity, and difficulty—that have, I believe, heightened my own sensibility and may do the same for others. There cannot be too much speaking out for the clinical interest and potential of clinical psychology students. This then is my third reason for putting these papers together in book form.

As the reader progresses through these papers, he will find me paying increasing attention to relatively subtle and elusive aspects of subjective experience and the organization of personality. These aspects of experience and personality are both regressive and integrative. More and more I focus on bodily, sensory, and creative experience, and the configuration of fantasy systems, affects, attitudes, words, and other cognitive tools that seem to be the matrix of this experience. On the surface, the immediate clinical usefulness of these discussions may seem to diminish. I do not really think it does, but even if this appearance is valid, I would say that what can already

be defined as useful helps us only to perceive things in a familiar way and to respond to them in an accustomed way; it
is not useful in our finding new and better ways to perceive
and respond. Only experimenting in thought can do that.
This I have undertaken to do—not without trepidation about
where my interpretive leaps would land me.

There is no other world quite like that created by the process of responding to psychological tests. It is not the world of
dreams or daydreams; nor is it the world of everyday problem solving and human relations. Yet it shares many of the
properties of these other worlds and so is a basis for making
extrapolations or predictions from this world to the others.
It is in the leap from the one to the others that the psycho-
diagnostician encounters much of his work's difficulty and perplexity, and much of its satisfaction and value. Nevertheless,
after all is said and done, the test response remains a thing in
itself and can be valued as such. One may devote oneself to
the question, "What is it?" as well as to the more common and
comfortable question, "Of what use is it?" My last papers on
testing approach, but do not reach, the full confrontation:
"What is it?"

Today, clinical psychology is, like psychiatry and social
work, increasingly oriented toward groups, community problems, social change, and public policy. Even individual psychotherapy, not to speak of psychodiagnostics, is being called
into question. Perhaps this shift of emphasis away from the
private life, the inner life, is an unavoidable condition and
consequence of sorely needed social activism. I would urge,
however, that this activism, much of which is carried on in
the name of community mental health, needs a systematic yet
open concept of mind to guide it. The inner world can be an
extraordinarily uncomfortable place to spend much of one's
time and it is accessible most of all to those who can afford to
pause from action for long periods, meditate, and ask probing
questions. It is not so strange, therefore, that the subtleties
of mind are minimized, superficialized, and repressed with in-
stitutional sanction by some of those mental health profession-

als who are bent on making this a better world to be mindful of. If the republication of these essays contributes a little toward maintaining the interest of clinical psychologists in how the mind is put together and works, and if it demonstrates that psychodiagnostics, guided by psychoanalysis, is a way into this mind and is an approach worthy of a clinical psychologist's self-respect, it will seem to me all the more worthwhile.

Finally, a few remarks about selection. I have omitted the papers on testing I authored or coauthored between 1943 and 1951: the substance of these papers is contained in *Diagnostic Psychological Testing* by Rapaport, Gill, and Schafer (1945-46), *The Clinical Application of Psychological Tests* by me (1948), or, in condensed form, in the papers included here. Although several of the earlier papers in this collection center on matters that I have discussed at some length in my book *Psychoanalytic Interpretation in Rorschach Testing* (1954), they have been reprinted here for a number of reasons: they are relatively concise statements; they include points that are not in that book or are made from a somewhat different perspective; and they prepare some of the ground for the later papers. I would write these early papers somewhat differently now, and as the reader gets deeper into the book he should be able to see how I might do so. The reader will also encounter a certain amount of repetition: this fault is inevitable in a book of this sort, made up as it is of a number of papers conceived within the same point of view but written at different times, for different occasions, and about different tests or clinical problems. Some of the repetition should help make clear what I am aiming toward; for the rest, I must hope that the reader will bear with it.

New Haven, Connecticut
June, 1966

1

CONTENT ANALYSIS IN THE RORSCHACH TEST

Since the initial discussions must be brief, I would like to bypass specific references to the growing body of literature, beginning with Rorschach's monograph, which, I believe, supports the views I shall advance. Even so I shall be limited by time to headlines, and shall have to forego the pleasure and safety of obsessional ruminations pro and con and around these headlines.

I must first of all say that I do not think of the Rorschach test as containing its own system of psychology within itself. Rather, the test provides us with a sample of behavior to which we may put whatever questions we wish on whatever levels of abstractness we wish. If, for example, the concepts *introversion* and *extraversion* are important to us, we may ask which aspects of the test sample of behavior appear to reflect these propensities as we define them. If, however, the concepts that are important to us include repression, orality, authoritarian orientation, and the like, we may just as well ask which aspects of the sample of behavior appear to reflect these propensities. Of course, any individual sample of behavior answers some questions better than others, but this does not in any way invalidate the proposition that the psychological theory is not in the Rorschach test—it is in the mind of the interpreter, for better or for worse.

It follows that what is necessary is a continuous redefinition

Prepared for a panel discussion at the 1952 Annual Meeting of the Society for Projective Techniques. First published in the *Journal of Projective Techniques,* 17:335-339, 1953. See also Schafer (1954).

of all our concepts concerning Rorschach results, a redefinition that is in keeping with the best in current psychodynamic thinking. The first question must be: What about human beings matters to you? The second question: How well do the results clarify the significant variables? For the most part the concepts of Bleuler and Jung are no longer in the mainstream of personality theory, although they persist prominently in Rorschach work. It is also my belief that a great part of this redefinition is necessary in terms of contemporary Freudian psychoanalysis with its increasing interest in and clarification of ego problems (Erikson, 1950a; Kris, 1952; Rapaport, 1951b).[1] From this contemporary Freudian point of view such problems come to the fore as selective emphasis, relative strength, and interrelations between the id drives, the ego with its defenses, values, and effectiveness and style of perceiving and coping with reality, superego pressures, conscious and unconscious image of the self and of the surrounding world, identity problems in social context, varieties of ego states, and the like. Applying these views to the Rorschach test, we may, for a simplified example, infer strong efforts at establishing rapport from a strong emphasis on Form-Color responses, but then must ask whether this is primarily mature adaptivity, a manifestation of rigid reaction formations against hostility in an obsessional setting, a manifestation of a submissive, self-abasing, accusatory approach to others in a masochistic setting, or some other dynamic configuration. The meaning of *rapport* itself is established by our psychodynamic orientation.

All of these considerations apply, it seems to me, to content interpretation. Content often does suggest selective emphasis on certain drives, defenses, values, and the like. This is not restricted entirely or even mainly to the content of the human-movement responses: objects, animals, natural phenomena, and many other types of content may carry significant implications. For example, *a cradle, an open-mouthed baby bird, a stomach,* and *a waiter,* representing four different tradition-

[1] See also Hartmann (1964).

al content categories, all appear to have strong passive, oral-receptive connotations. On a certain level of abstraction they have one theme in common. Similarly, *a halo, the devil, the Decalogue,* and *fire and brimstone* all appear to have prominent connotations of guilt or superego pressure. Thus, different traditional classes of content may all be relevant to the same question. Moreover, different questions may often be profitably put to the same response. For example, the response "a bleeding, exhausted wolf dragging itself along" may have, with respect to drives, a strong oral-attacking emphasis; with respect to self-image, a masochistic emphasis on being defeated; with respect to interpersonal orientation, an emphasis on a need to attack to get what one needs accompanied by expectations and experiences of counterattack; and so on. The traditional content categories, such as animal, human, and object, are statically conceived and obviously inadequate for full content interpretation. What we may call *thematic analysis of content* seems to be required.

Thematic analysis requires us to approach content on certain levels of psychodynamic abstraction. Hierarchical conceptions are required to disentangle, interrelate, estimate the importance of, and give context to the themes we read out of the responses. We must have an idea, based on knowledge gathered outside the context of the test, about what goes together in people, before we can handle Rorschach themes meaningfully. Thematic analysis should be more than stringing themes like beads until we have a long sequence of gaudy and patternless interpretations.

In what follows I shall present some propositions regarding certain psychological intricacies of the process of Rorschach response. These propositions, derived mainly from psychoanalytic thinking, seem to me to afford a basis for putting fresh questions to our Rorschach data and for leading us out of the theoretical dead end of putting the same old questions to more and more Rorschach data.

(1) Each person carries within himself a network of imagery and imagery readiness, culled from bodily experience

and perception of the surrounding world, which ranges from primitive, diffuse, syncretic forms to highly differentiated, realistic forms. These images and image readinesses express in their formal and content aspects major adjustment problems and efforts of the person. These problems may pertain to all of the crucial personality variables with which we are currently concerned, such as defenses, self-image, and the like.

(2) The relative unstructuredness of the Rorschach test stimuli often brings out the selective imagery emphasis that reflects the person's adjustment problems and efforts.

(3) Each Rorschach response spreads out to a greater or lesser extent along a continuum extending from reality-oriented perception at the one end, through directed and undirected daytime imagery, to autistic and dreamlike imagery at the other end. Thus, one and the same Rorschach response may carry the imprint of the most highly developed ego functioning, as in very accurate form perception, and of the most primitive levels of unconscious processes, as in bizarre content. Such a response is "a man with a fang coming out of his mouth," at the bottom of Card IX. Some responses spread very little; for example, simply "an animal," with no further elaboration of detail or quality, to the side red area on Card VIII. A response with little spread, falling more at the autistic end of the continuum, is "a mouth" to the entirety of Card VII—a response with little differentiated perception in it and considerable diffuseness and autism.

(4) The spread across this continuum is facilitated by what Kris (1952), in his discussion of the preconscious and creativity, has called "temporary regression in the service of the ego," that is, a partial and fluctuating relaxation of ordinary ego controls and orientation to allow normally preconscious or unconscious material some access to consciousness in the interest of performing a certain creative task. Without this regression, subjects would do little more in the Rorschach situation than describe the blots or cling to the most obvious forms, as some indeed do if they experience their own equilibrium as too precarious to tolerate any degree of regression.

Among the important factors that bring about this partial and fluctuating ego regression during the Rorschach test appear to be the subject's wish to respond, the simultaneous encouragement of fantasy and reality testing by the test instructions, the opportunity afforded the subject to externalize responsibility for his responses, and the usual absence of autobiographical specificity in the responses.

(5) Some of the spread of the Rorschach responses over the continuum from autism to realistic perception must also be accounted for in terms of the expression of need in perception even when all of the subject's efforts are directed toward realistic perception. "Need" is used here very broadly, to include defenses, values, appetites, etc. The power of the perceptual search or readiness for need-satisfying objects has been well demonstrated in the various experiments which have been concerned with personal aspects of perception.

This gross framework, I believe, may help our theoretical understanding of what goes on during the Rorschach test, and may also have a beneficial effect on our interpretation of the Rorschach content. The interplay of the real inkblot, personal imagery, the defensive and need-implementing shifts of the ego in general and of what Klein (1951) has called perceptual style in particular, is complex and subtle, and in need of much clarification. But, by remaining alert to the type, direction, place, and time of shifts up and down the regressive continuum, we may observe crucial and characteristic aspects of the dynamics of the person and his maladjustment in actual operation before our eyes, just as we might in an active therapeutic session.

Areas of significant anxiety and emphasis on certain defense mechanisms may be seen especially clearly. Subjects not only differ among themselves in the degree to which they are capable of such regression; they also fluctuate considerably within their own records and sometimes even within single responses. Defenses may be very weak or thrown overboard, as in certain schizophrenic character problems, with the result that the record is flooded with regressive material; defenses may be rigidly maintained, as in certain compulsive and/or repressive characters, which do not permit going beyond banalities; the level typically shifts very rapidly in certain unstable hypomanic settings where cards or responses may be ugly or evil one moment and gay or angelic the next; such shifts often occur more slowly and/or moderately in the records of many neurotics and normals; and sometimes single responses contain within themselves expressions of various aspects of a major problem. For example, "a fascinating and amusing ghost" has both phobic and counterphobic qualities. Of course, many fluctuations occur because subjects also have an accumulation of readily available and conventional mental imagery which compellingly "fits" certain areas of the cards or on which the subject can fall back defensively when the regression touches off anxiety.

I would like to end on a cautious note. This approach obviously runs the risk of encouraging "wild psychoanalysis" of Rorschach content. This risk is partly offset, I believe, by the fact that we are dealing with a relatively standardized situation in which we have the opportunity to observe many persons respond to the same stimuli. We cannot rely entirely on the standardized situation, however. Additional safeguards should include the following: (1) using a battery of tests; (2) emphasizing themes and their interplay rather than isolated responses; (3) avoiding naïve interpretation of universals per se as in "there is evidence of repression"; interpretations must be given an individual context, placed in a hierarchically organized total personality picture, and must have a quantitative aspect, however gross; (4) being very careful not to read into the test results our genetic preconceptions; too often test reports are more interpretations of Fenichel's protean text than they are of the Rorschach record; (5) not setting up one-to-one relationships between certain individual responses or even certain classes of content and diagnostic categories; we must remember that meanings of content shift with context and that no one problem or trend is the exclusive property of any one group of patients.

In summary, I have emphasized that we must re-examine the questions we put to the Rorschach responses in the light of contemporary psychodynamic thinking; that contemporary psychoanalysis and particularly its emphasis on ego psychology can be of great service to us in this regard; that the traditional content categories are statically conceived and therefore inadequate; that to some extent Rorschach content involves highly charged personal imagery expressing major adjustment problems and efforts; that this imagery often has primitive and differentiated aspects side by side or in sequence; that this complex structure of the response and total record is the reflection of a temporary, partial, more or less fluctuating ego regression; that personal style of perception also plays a significant part in this process; that we may therefore observe crucial dynamic struggles being exhibited before our eyes in the Rorschach responses; and that psychoanalytic *thematic analysis of Rorschach content,* while it exposes us to many of the abuses of opportunistic or naïve psychoanalysis, opens up a most important aspect of the Rorschach test to systematic investigation.

2

SOME APPLICATIONS
OF CONTEMPORARY
PSYCHOANALYTIC THEORY
TO PROJECTIVE TESTING

This paper will be limited to a consideration of four prominent or promising emphases in contemporary Freudian psychoanalytic theory and their bearing on projective-test theory and interpretation. These four emphases constitute a small but representative sample of recent trends in psychoanalysis. From the psychoanalytic point of view these emphases seem particularly helpful in clarifying crucial dynamic aspects of projective-test response processes. Of course, these psychoanalytic trends can be only sketchily summarized here. Also, for simplicity, my remarks about testing will pertain only to testing psychiatric patients.

It will set the theoretical stage for the discussion proper if I explain briefly my stress on *contemporary* Freudian psychoanalysis. This stress indicates that the ego will occupy a central conceptual position in the following remarks.[1] It indicates that psychoanalysis long ago pushed beyond the theoretical and clinical point of fascination only with instinctual tendencies and associated primitive acts and fantasies, and the methodological point of persistent endeavor to demonstrate only the universality of these tendencies, acts, and fantasies. Today, for example, simply to identify a "phallic symbol"

First published in the *Journal of Projective Techniques*, 18:441-447, 1954.

[1] For a comprehensive discussion of psychoanalytic ego psychology see Rapaport (1951b, especially Part VII).

in a patient's productions is hardly more than an academic exercise—and a poor one at that. Psychoanalytic theory has become progressively more concerned with individual stylistic differences in the selective control, modification, and expression of these instinctual trends. At the same time, it has become more concerned with the origins of these individual differences—in culture and in constitutional predisposition as well as in early family experiences. The study of the origins and organization of individual differences in this light is essentially the psychoanalytic study of the ego. The concept "ego" is a broad one, subsuming such varied phenomena as control of and defense against impulses, reality testing, modes of interpersonal relationship, communication, purposeful motility, creativity, and self-integrative efforts, and all the finer phenomena subsumed in turn by these, such as concentration, judgment, concept formation, and verbal and motor learning. The four psychoanalytic emphases to be considered next reflect this psychoanalytic preoccupation with the ego.

I. The Test Situation and Relationship

The first of these emphases is on the value of analyzing the total interpersonal and social context in which clinical data are gathered.[2] This is in accord with the general scientific proposition that the conditions and techniques of investigation significantly influence the data obtained. In psychoanalysis, this means analyzing the fantasied as well as real aspects of the clinical situation and relationship, which in turn means analyzing the impact of transference and countertransference, among other factors, on the patient's behavior. The form, content, and quality of the patient's productions cannot be adequately comprehended otherwise. In the psychoanalytic situation the therapist has available to him his own as well as the patient's associations to, and reflections on, his behavior and the patient's. With these data he is in a relatively good position to make sense of the patient's course within and out-

[2] See, for example, the discussion by Gitelson (1952).

side the therapy hours. He does not regard transference and countertransference as unwelcome intrusions or forbidding obstacles. He regards them as processes which reflect the patient's illness and which are therefore valuable in understanding and treating the patient. But he also bears in mind the real relationship: what he and the patient are actually like, how they actually behave toward each other, and what their relative positions are in the treatment, all influence the course of treatment; there is more than irrational fantasy to be analyzed.

What has this psychoanalytic emphasis to do with testing? A great deal. It confronts the tester with the necessity of trying to understand as much as possible the interpersonal dynamics in the test situation. Otherwise, important meanings in the test data will be missed or misunderstood. Although in a different school of psychoanalytic thought than the Freudian, and although limited in his analysis to the patient's problems in dealing with authority, Schachtel (1945) has made an instructive attack on this problem. Concerning himself with the patient's distinctive reaction to the virtual absence of rules in the Rorschach situation, he shows how this reaction may be reflected in test attitudes, in various formal scores, and in the content, and how it expresses the patient's manner of handling authority problems in general.

There are, however, important determinants of the response process in the projective-test situation besides the lack of clear-cut rules—even in the Rorschach situation. While these cannot be detailed here, they can at least be quickly, though incompletely, surveyed. With regard to his professional role and situation, if we consider the tester first, there are demands, anxieties, resentments, and gratifications connected with the problems of professional relations and job security, and with problems of ability, training, and experience. Then there are personal aspects of the psychology of the tester to consider: his major adjustment problems, his preferred defenses and modes of interpersonal relationship, the impulses he fears most, the personal gratifications and se-

curities he seeks through testing and relationships with patients and colleagues, and the pattern of sensitivities and
blind spots that reflects his ways of solving his own conflicts.
These and other factors determine whether, to what extent,
and with which type of patient testers may be variously inhibited or assertive, seductive or remote, saintly or querulous,
overconscientious or lackadaisical in inquiry, and the like.
Test administration is not so standardized and cannot be so
standardized, except in textbooks, as to eliminate these variations among and within testers. These variations may be subtle, but they will be sensed and reacted to by patients, and
may influence the rate, variety, richness, adequacy, and possibly the content of responses, even though certain basic, enduring character trends of the patient become clear in any
case (Gibby, 1952; Sanders and Cleveland, 1953). These
variations among testers also tend to influence interpretation,
some testers, for example, being inclined to overemphasize
sexual conflict, others dependency conflict, and still others
normality.[3]

With respect to the immediate interaction between tester
and patient we must remember that the tester is a stranger
prying into deeply personal secrets. In more or less incompre-
hensible ways that smack of fortunetelling to the patient, he
will "divine deep significances" from seemingly silly, trivial,
or remote responses. Also, he is an agent of the therapist, who
in turn is likely to be regarded as an agent of the ambivalently
regarded family. The tester may then become someone to be
dealt with especially cautiously. On his part the tester may
respond variously to these prying, oracular, and substitute-
therapist aspects of his role.[4]

Focusing more on the patient, we often note that he tends
to regard his responses as extensions of himself and to relate
himself to the responses as he does to the tendencies or qualities within himself for which these responses may stand, such

[3] See in this regard the study by Hammer and Piotrowski (1953) of hostility
in the tester as it affects his interpretations.

[4] See also Klatskin (1952) on possible situational determinants of Rorschach
responses.

as hostility, dependency, and sensuality. Related to this is the way the patient tends to present himself to others. One patient may be an eager beaver, another unproductively self-critical, a third charming but sloppy and impulsive, and a fourth intent on giving out as little as possible owing to an unconsciously determined, orally conceived niggardliness in interpersonal relationships. A fifth patient may also give out little, but his principal reason may be fear of self-confrontation or fear of ego-alien but precariously repressed exhibitionistic tendencies.

It does not do justice to the variations in the behavior and responses of patients to describe them in simple, behavioral terms in the first paragraph of a test report and ignore them in the body of interpretations. Contemporary psychoanalytic theory would maintain that the test responses proper, as traditionally defined, cannot be adequately understood without considering them in the context of all the above-mentioned, and other, rationally and irrationally conceived aspects of the test situation and relationship.

Of course, the absence of systematically collected associations to test responses and the tester's limited familiarity with the patient's life history and current life circumstances restrict the amount of sound, clearly substantiated interpretation he can make of these aspects of test results. If, however, the tester attempts to integrate these interpersonal data with the implications of the formal and content aspects of the responses, and if he uses a battery of tests, he will often find his understanding of the patient deepened and the possibility of evolving a hierarchically organized picture of the patient's personality and illness increased.[5]

II.   LEVELS OF PSYCHIC FUNCTIONING

A second center of recent psychoanalytic interest is that of fluctuating levels of psychic functioning. This is a concept that has been emphasized particularly by Kris (1952) in his

[5] A fuller treatment of certain aspects of this topic appears in Chapter 4.

study of creativity. It is relevant here because almost without exception creative processes are crucially involved in the response to projective tests. Kris, taking his cue from Freud, speaks of "regression in the service of the ego," which refers to a temporary and oscillating movement in the direction of relatively primitive functioning for creative purposes. This subtle, controlled, adaptive primitivization of functioning allows archaic, normally unconscious and preconscious fantasies, modes of reasoning, memories, concepts, and images to come to consciousness in order that they may be subsequently molded, revised, reintegrated, and otherwise manipulated by critical, reality-oriented ego functions. This *progressive*, critical aspect of the creative process is what tends to distinguish genuine creativity from unsocialized daydreams and psychotic outpourings.

One needs only to stop and think about responding to the Rorschach test or Thematic Apperception Test to realize the importance of this creative "regression in the service of the ego" for the ability to respond at all productively and self-expressively. In the Rorschach situation, for example, images must become available to consciousness with a relative freedom that can come only by the relaxation of defensive barriers, the suspension of critical judgment, the blurring of the line between fantasy and external reality that characterize regressive or primitivized functioning; but, as in any creative work, subsequent externally oriented, analytic and synthetic, critical ego functions must be brought into play in order to work out responses that fit the inkblots or pictures and are well communicated and comprehensible to the tester. It is in these latter respects, for example, that schizophrenics typically fall down, and thereby betray their pathologically regressed or primitivized mode of functioning, despite fluctuations upward from their generally lowered level.

In projective tests these regressive and progressive processes often take place on the fringe of awareness, yet evidence for their existence may be obtained from introspective patients, from disruptions of the response process, and from abor-

tive and hypertrophied forms of these processes that characterize different types of pathology or normal functioning.
These regressive and progressive processes seem crucially involved in responding to the Thematic Apperception Test
(Holt, 1951) and Word Association Test (Schafer, 1945)
stimuli, as well as to the Rorschach inkblots.

There seem to be considerable individual variations in the
freedom with which patients can enter into this creative "regression in the service of the ego," in the areas in which they
can regress, in the extent to which they can regress, and in
their ability to recover from and productively use the fruits
of this regression. These variations may become crucial indices of the patient's degree and type of integration or pathology.[6]

III. Patterns of Defense

The third aspect of psychoanalytic thought to be considered
is the analysis of defenses. Since Anna Freud's (1936) book
on the mechanisms of defense, it has been more and more recognized that psychoanalytic explanation and treatment cannot be complete without an analysis of the types and particularly the layerings of defenses peculiar to the patient.[7]

When we consider the patient in the test situation we must
realize that his characteristic patterns of defense will almost
inevitably come to the fore. This will be partly because these
defensive patterns are prominent in all emotionally charged
situations, but also because this is a situation in which, as we
have seen, the patient is being mysteriously probed into and
in which he is therefore especially likely to be on guard. His
normal desire for privacy, his fear of confronting his own rejected tendencies in the test responses, and other motivations
will lead the patient to mobilize his characteristic defenses in
conspicuous ways.[8] He may then become especially repressive
in the Rorschach test and TAT, producing meager, essen-

[6] A fuller treatment of this topic will be found in Chapter 6.
[7] See, for example, the study of "moral masochism" by Brenman (1952).
[8] Compare Bellak (1950) on defensive indications in the TAT.

tially descriptive responses and "stories." Another patient may display noteworthy reaction formations against hostility by overconscientious application to the test stimuli and responses and by exaggerated compliance with the test instructions, real and fantasied; this will be his defensive way of proving his "goodness."

A patient's defensive structure is likely to become clear in the form and content of his responses, in the way he gives responses and relates himself to the tester, and in the variations in his responsiveness from test to test, since each test poses its peculiar challenges to defensive structure. It will also tend to be reflected in his pattern of intellectual assets and deficiencies as brought out by intelligence-test results particularly (Schafer, 1948), and in his general interests and sensitivities.

Finally, on the subject of defense, the patient's defensive mobilization during testing will tend to act as a major counterforce with respect to the creative regression previously considered. The interplay of the regressive and counter-regressive forces is often dramatic and instructive.

IV. Ego Identity

The fourth and last psychoanalytic emphasis to be mentioned is the concept of "ego identity" as elaborated by Erik Erikson (1950a) particularly.[9] This concept promises to extend our understanding of the synthetic function of the ego by pointing up and clarifying how complex configurations of drives, defenses, capacities, values, etc., may be organized around privately and usually unconsciously conceived social roles and self-images. The ego-identity concept helps us see how the interaction of culture, bodily experience, and infantile as well as later relationships provides themes around which to organize experience and action; it shows how what may be a pathological trend in one identity configuration may become an asset in the next, because the latter gives it a new meaning and value; the ego-identity concept also pro-

[9] See also Erikson's later work (1956).

vides a key for understanding how formal aspects of functioning may express the content of major fantasies about the self —how, for example, in one instance meticulousness may represent a living out of the identity of an aristocrat (the clean, impeccable one) and in another instance the identity of a slave (the conscientious, subservient one).

Turning specifically to projective-test results, in one case the dominant approach to the Rorschach inkblots may be artistic, while in the next it may be pseudomasculine, anti-esthetic, and anti-intellectual; in each case the place of affect and hence the significance of color responses will be somewhat different. To the "artist" a shaded CF may stand for a positively valued, creative, integrative experience of affect, while to the pseudomasculine patient it may stand for frightening, disorganizing, "feminine" affect. Also, at certain points in the response process, these dominant identity statements will be more prominent or better integrated than at others. The rise and fall of their prominence and integration will often mark areas of special adjustment difficulty or adaptive resources.

In addition, some figures in the Rorschach and TAT will be accepted and others rejected; this differential treatment of figures may reflect major rejected as well as accepted identity solutions—what the patient dares not become as well as the role to which he must cling or in which he may take pride. In one man's Rorschach test and TAT responses, the passive, virginal little girl may come forward as the preferred, secretly maintained, "good" identity and may be associated with esthetic sensitivity and cultural aspiration, while the sadistic, adult, heterosexual male figure may emerge as the rejected, "bad" identity and be associated with the patient's inability to consolidate his accomplishments and use his assets productively. In another case no identity may be treated favorably, and negative themes of ruin, decay, betrayal, and failure may predominate in the patient's imagery.

Projective-test interpretation oriented to ego-identity problems requires taking into account the context of age, sex, educational and familial status, and cultural background. As these vary, the identity themes and problems vary. But, in any case, identity solution or lack of solution appears to have a major bearing on the fate of various drives, defenses, abilities, etc. Defining identity problems in the test results may therefore brightly illuminate a total personality picture.

SUMMARY

In summary, in studying projective-test responses in the light of some outstanding, relatively new emphases in psychoanalytic theory, it seems fruitful to take into account what we can infer about the patient from (1) the test relationship and atmosphere, (2) the regressive and counterregressive movement in the creative aspect of the responses, (3) the defensive strategy reflected in the test relationship, the responses proper, and the pattern of past achievements and failures, and (4) the positive and negative, crystallized and diffuse ego-identity solutions and problems that may be at the heart of the patient's total approach and response to testing.

This psychoanalytic orientation to test results requires refined and thorough qualitative analysis—with all the serious risks such analysis at present entails. Ultimately, precisely defined and validated interpretive principles will have to be established. This paper is far more a prospectus for future, much needed research than a statement of completed study. At present, however, the conceptual spadework has barely begun that will turn up the variables and methods to be used in this promising scientific endeavor.[10]

---

[10] See also the more recent studies by Holt and Havel (1960), Prelinger (1958), and Prelinger, Zimet, Schafer, and Levin (1964).

3

PSYCHOLOGICAL-TEST EVALUATION OF PERSONALITY CHANGE DURING INTENSIVE PSYCHOTHERAPY

The intensive psychotherapist aims to help bring about personality change in his patient. His dedication to this goal is, however, matched by his difficulty in estimating precisely the depth of change effected by his therapy and in defining in detail the dynamic and structural modifications involved. The results of psychological tests administered before, during, and after psychotherapy can help him sharpen these estimates and definitions of change. This paper will outline and illustrate with case material a psychoanalytic approach to test results, demonstrating how this approach may organize and enrich test-retest comparisons and thereby contribute to penetrating analyses of personality change. Such an exposition would be incomplete and misleading, however, if it did not at once recognize existing clinical controversy and uncertainty concerning the effectiveness of various forms of psychotherapy, including classical psychoanalytic technique. Later I shall take up parallel interpretive and synthetic problems in handling test-retest comparisons.

In "Analysis Terminable and Interminable," Freud (1937) raised fundamental questions concerning the potential effectiveness of psychoanalysis as a form of therapy. Tak-

---

First published in *Psychiatry*, 18: 175-192, 1955. Reprinted by special permission of the William Alanson White Psychiatric Foundation, Inc., which holds its copyright.

ing a conservative position about the amount of change and the kind of change that it may bring about, he recorded his impression that psychoanalysis may often merely strengthen defenses rather than resolve basic conflict. He also emphasized that much of the change occurring may be quantitative rather than qualitative, implying by this distinction that moderate shifts in the balance of forces within the personality might be the basis on which apparently great therapeutic changes are brought about.[1] But, considering the many formidable obstacles in the way of achieving benefits from therapy, Freud acknowledged the significance of even this quantitative accomplishment. Other writers, without questioning the superior accomplishments of classical psychoanalytic technique as opposed to other psychotherapeutic approaches, have recorded similar or related views (e.g., M. Balint, 1950; Glover, 1931; Hoffer, 1950; Oberndorf, 1948; A. Reich, 1950; Rickman, 1950.)

The major challenges to the advantages and potential of classical psychoanalytic technique have come from Fromm-Reichmann (1950) and from Alexander and French (1946). In discussing certain modifications of psychoanalytic technique summarized under the heading "intensive psychotherapy," Fromm-Reichmann takes the position that intensive psychotherapy may not only parallel classical psychoanalysis in its effects, but may even be superior to it as a treatment method, even in cases judged suitable for classical technique. The same trend of thought seems to run through the discussions in Alexander and French's *Psychoanalytic Therapy*. It is not, however, simply a matter of controversy *within* psychoanalytic circles. As psychoanalytic influence has spread into psychiatry at large, such terms as modified psychoanalysis, psychoanalytic psychotherapy, and dynamic psychotherapy have become commonplace, and, as pointed out by a number of psychoanalytic writers (e.g., Eissler, 1950; Gill, 1954; Knight, 1952; Rangell, 1954), the results of these modified

[1] For an illuminating case study and theoretical discussion centering on such quantitative shifts, see Brenman (1952).

treatment approaches, while often impressive, have tended to be confused with those of psychoanalysis proper.

In an emphatic discussion Eissler (1950) has assailed the Chicago Psychoanalytic Institute for fostering such confusion. He contends that the traditional, thorough psychoanalytic treatment approach is the only truly rational therapy; that it alone is capable of bringing about genuine and enduring improvement in any aspect of functioning which is not gained at the expense of other aspects of functioning or of the personality as a whole. According to this view, any appearance of change for the better occurring in conjunction with forms of therapy other than psychoanalysis must be based principally upon suggestion, imitation, unwitting reinforcement of resistances, or transference phenomena—in short, upon magical, archaic, obscure interpersonal processes rather than upon rational, realistic, and clarified ones. The basic test of change, Eissler says, is whether it is a change in structure or merely a change in content. Change in structure pertains to basic modifications in the distribution of psychic energy, as a result of which, on the deepest levels as well as the most superficial, significant alterations occur in patterns of gratification and defense, modes of thought and fantasy, and attitude toward the self and others. The end result is ego mastery of major trends and appropriate generalization of the changed orientation. In contrast, change in content refers to change in superficial behavior and conscious thought content and feeling; it implies no modification and mastery of the patient's underlying instinctual, defensive, moral, imaginative, and attitudinal dispositions. Eissler gives as an example of change of content the spendthrift who becomes a miser, in no way altering his structuralized pathological attitude toward money. According to this conception of therapy, only classical technique can bring about structural change.

Gill (1954), taking a broader view of the problem, points out that there is a continuum of therapies. At one end of this continuum is classical psychoanalysis with its maximal cultivation and interpretation of the regressive transference neurosis; at the other end is supportive, nonexploratory, non-interpretive therapy in which the therapist discourages and ignores transference manifestations and is consistently active, directive, and reality oriented rather than, like the psychoanalyst, relatively passive, nondirective, and fantasy oriented. In Gill's view, intensive psychotherapy occupies a position between these two poles, combining supportive and uncovering techniques, employing activity and passivity on the therapist's part at different times, and dealing with transference and resistance without encouraging the full flowering of a regressive transference neurosis. Accordingly, intensive psychotherapy may achieve results of intermediate depth, breadth, and stability; while it seems more suitable as a treatment technique than analysis in certain types of cases, its results should not be confused with those brought about by full psychoanalysis. Gill further calls attention to the relative autonomy that disturbing conflicts may achieve from their deepest origins, and he suggests that intensive psychotherapy may resolve these derivative conflicts in what is a real though limited structural change even though the basic conflicts may not be resolved.

This brief survey of the effectiveness variously ascribed to different psychotherapeutic approaches is important for the present topic because any therapist's impressions of the personality changes he is observing are themselves open to at least some reinterpretation depending upon his critic's point of view. Consequently, what may in individual instances appear to be disagreement between the implications of test results and the therapist's judgment may be due to conceptual differences between therapist and tester leading to misunderstandings about the extent and nature of such change as has taken place. This sketch of the problem also makes plain the dangers of overoptimistic interpretation of *manifest* changes during therapy and within retests. It might also be mentioned that on the whole the psychoanalytic literature on this subject is characterized by relative neglect of the necessity for stating concrete criteria by which the depth and stability of personality change may be judged. Some papers on the termination of analysis attempt to state criteria of basic improvement, but for the most part they remain relatively general (M. Balint, 1950; Hoffer, 1950; A. Reich, 1950; Rickman, 1950).

LITERATURE ON THE TESTING OF PSYCHOTHERAPEUTIC EFFECTIVENESS

In recent years a number of research papers have appeared on test findings relevant to the assessment of therapeutic effectiveness (Carr, 1949; Haimowitz and Haimowitz, 1952; Hamlin, Berger, and Cummings, 1952; Muench, 1947; Piotrowski and Schreiber, 1952; M. Rioch, 1949; Watkins, 1949). All of these papers, however, are unsatisfactory in one or more fundamental respects. Some of them deal with the results of nondirective or client-centered therapy; working within the Rogerian orientation, they utilize shallow, behavioristic data and concepts that cannot be helpful in distinguishing change in structure from change in content or in estimating the depth and durability of change. Others, overlapping this first group, use such global, oversimplified categories in their comparisons as *improved* and *not improved,* or else, in a too-gross research design, they compare the results of prolonged, intensive, skillful psychotherapy with those of infrequent, intermittent, superficial psychotherapy. Some of the research designs and presentations of data seem to assume naïvely that all change for the better should proceed in the same direction and should culminate in the same general personality pattern. Many of these studies tend to take for granted the effectiveness of psychotherapy; they do not endeavor to draw distinctions between apparent improvement based on transference and genuine, self-sustaining improvement; they do not attempt to distinguish between insight that is highly intellectualized and insight that has a definite and enduring effect on emotional experience and patterns of interpersonal relationship; they do not explicitly recognize that there are various pathological starting points in the therapeutic situation and that the direction of change may differ considerably from one case to the next, moving, for example, from pathological impulsiveness to some capacity for control in one case and from pathological overcontrol to some tolerance for impulsiveness in the next.

Further, almost all of these test studies suffer from oversimplified statistical treatment of data. Their statistical analyses are based on the averages of single scores, in violation of one of the basic assumptions underlying projective testing—and any dynamic study of personality—namely, that each personality must be seen as a total configuration before it may be profitably compared with other personalities.[2] Isolated, minute fragments of personality cannot be meaningfully compared; a specific trend that is one man's strength may be the next man's weakness. Also, the rationale of the statistical trends discerned in these studies is almost always elaborated *ad hoc;* it ignores the absence of change in other scores that could just as well have been expected to change and did not, and changes in which scores could just as easily have been rationalized to indicate the benefits of psychotherapy. As a result of incompleteness and inadequacy in such respects as these, existing psychological-test research on the personality changes brought about by psychotherapy do not mirror familiar clinical reality.[3]

Clearly, in considering the effects of psychotherapy, the phenomena dealt with are intricate ones. They do not lend themselves to one-dimensional answers, and, in their meanings and implications, they derive from and ramify into all

[2] I have discussed this more fully in "Psychological Tests in Clinical Research" (Schafer, 1949).

[3] The two studies of greatest interest in this connection are those by Piotrowski and Schreiber (1952) and by Rioch (1949). Both reports deal with the results of intensive psychoanalytic psychotherapy and present provocative and apparently meaningful data. However, since the statistical evaluation of the quantitative findings in these two studies is either faulty or incomplete, it is unfortunately impossible to visualize their findings in detail or to estimate the representativeness and stability of the reported trends. There are also some interesting single case studies of psychological-test changes occurring during treatment, but these will not be reviewed here. See, for example, Fromm and Elonen (1951).

aspects of current theories concerning personality and psychopathology. The complexity of the problem must be emphasized because in many quarters psychological tests are thought of as neat instruments with a logic all their own that can reduce complex and obscure material to a tidy set of all-embracing and coherent formulations. Nothing could be further from the truth. Ultimately the interpretation of test findings rests on the tester's theory of personality and psychopathology. This frame of reference he acquires chiefly from the same clinical and theoretical sources as his therapist colleagues. Although he operates in a different context of data, the tester must deal with the very same complexity as the therapist and is beset by the very same doubts, questions, and need for fine but important distinctions. He may conceal this plight with an overlay of knowing test jargon or psychoanalytic clichés; he may elaborate his own variations on already-formulated theory in order to protect his preconceptions concerning psychopathology and his test interpretations; but *on his own* he cannot shed any more light on these murky phenomena of personality change than is provided by the entire body of clinical experience and theoretical understanding.

It has, however, been demonstrated repeatedly that projective tests represent a uniquely penetrating approach to the study of personality and psychopathology. There is therefore good reason to expect that studying personality *change* through test results can help in identifying, articulating, and understanding the effects of therapy. The theory and concepts used both in testing and in therapy should be the same, but the test data do seem to have certain advantages for clarifying and assessing psychological trends.

Test Analysis as a Measure of Psychological Change

Advantages of Projective Techniques

Psychological tests have some major advantages over the clinical interview or therapy situation in arriving at essential data for evaluating the dramatic, elusive, and baffling changes that occur during psychotherapy. The first advantage is their indirect approach to the patient's functioning. Indirectness characterizes the so-called projective tests, such as the Rorschach and the Thematic Apperception Test, and also general tests of intellectual organization and functioning, such as the Wechsler-Bellevue Intelligence Scale and tests of concept formation and word association. To some degree these tests represent ambiguous, relatively unstructured, and impersonal situations; they have no apparent autobiographical specificity; they appear to concentrate merely on "imagination," "reasoning," "perception," or on previously developed abilities, interests, and attainments. In these respects such tests are quite unlike the clinical interview or therapy situation, the content of which is ordinarily characterized by total and explicit autobiographical specificity. Their indirect, unstructured, and impersonal approach tends to facilitate the clear emergence of both the self-expressive and the defensive aspects of the patient's functioning (Rapaport, Gill, and Schafer, 1945-46; Rapaport, 1950b; Schafer, 1948, 1954).

The second advantage of clinical testing is its relative standardization as contrasted with the psychotherapeutic interview. Even though the nature of the interpersonal relationship between the tester and the patient may vary from one patient to the next, from one tester to the next, and sometimes even from one test to the next, in relative terms there is certainly a greater uniformity among test situations and relationships than among therapeutic situations and relationships. Central to this greater uniformity is the fact that the principal reality situation to which the patient is responding in the test is almost perfectly standardized; that is, all patients are presented with the same ten Rorschach cards, are asked the same Wechsler-Bellevue Intelligence Scale questions of information, vocabulary, and so on, and are shown the same Thematic Apperception Test pictures to tell stories about. This uniformity contrasts with the highly varied and variable reality situations which are discussed in the therapeutic interview and which evolve within the therapy and outside it during the treatment. The relative consistency of external challenging reality in the test situation becomes the basis on which relatively fine interpersonal comparisons can be made, and, with respect to retesting, the basis for relatively fine *intra*personal comparisons.

Of course, the intensive psychotherapist, like the psycho-analyst, uses the patient's relationship with him as a yardstick for measuring changes in the patient's psychic structure. The less active, directive, and judgmental the therapist has been, the more accurate this interpersonal yardstick will be. But, as is well-known, the patient inevitably grows familiar with the psychotherapist's personality and with his interpretive and supportive emphases. He gets to know his way around in the therapeutic relationship. The result is that the pathology he expresses through this relationship may become indistinct and elusive. And the therapist himself, growing extremely familiar with many of the patient's deviant trends and con-stantly making temporary allowances for them, may lose some of his sensitivity to their social implications and conse-quences. In contrast, the rules of the game in the testing situa-tion are less clear and the challenge of the test relationship is relatively fresh. Thus, in a microcosmic way, the retesting can achieve an essential replication of the original stress situation in which the patient was first tested.

The third advantage of testing is the fact that a *battery* of tests may be employed, each test posing different psychic problems for the patient. The problems pertain to mobiliza-tion of intellectual assets and past attainments; maintenance or relaxation of defenses; capacity for and style of creative regression in the service of the ego (Kris, 1952; Schafer, 1954);[4] withstanding frustration; the anxiety associated with free fantasy; and so on. A broad, even though spotty, survey may thus be made of total ego functioning in a series of standardized, relatively indirect, unstructured, and imper-sonal reality situations.[5] The retest comparative analysis is

[4] See also Chapter 6.
[5] Unfortunately, because of space limitations, the examples presented in this paper are drawn only from the Rorschach test. This does not imply that other tests are superfluous, for actually intelligence-test results seem peculiarly sen-

not likely, therefore, to be biased by dramatic but narrowly circumscribed changes.

In addition to their indirectness, standardization, and wider scope, the test data are advantageous for studying personality in general, and for ascertaining the effects of psychotherapy in particular, because of the several types of analysis to which they lend themselves. It is true that these types of analysis are applicable to therapy data too, but so far they have not been worked out in as much detail for therapy data as for test data, and they lack the wide acceptance already achieved by general principles of test analysis.

Specifically, four avenues of approach are open to the tester: (1) the formal scores and their patterns, (2) the content of the responses, (3) the type and degree of organization of thought, perception, and verbalization, and (4) the patient's behavior in the examination situation, both as regards his relationship to the tester and his relationship to his own responses. Ideally, implications drawn from all four sources of information should *converge* in the test analysis or else should complement each other in the sense of bringing out basic conflicts or antitheses in the personality.[6]

---

sitive to certain vital aspects of ego integration, and Thematic Apperception Test stories indispensably clarify key aspects of the self and conceptions of human relationships. On the clinical role of intelligence-test results, see Rapaport, Gill, and Schafer (1945-46) and Schafer (1948). On the TAT, see Chapter 7.

[6] Using this variety of data does mean, of course, that the tester attempts to deal with the total clinical situation in which he obtains his material. This is in accord with the best principles of analysis of any data, but it is open to the criticism that the distinction between the test situation and the therapy situation is broken down and the tester loses his valued objectivity, more or less duplicating what the therapist does and merely compounding the therapist's uncertainties. This criticism overlooks some of the previously described advantages of the testing situation, particularly its standardization and the variety of standardized problems presented. These factors allow a relatively greater clarity of comparison of even the most "clinical" aspects of the test situation— such as the nature of the patient's relationship to the tester—than is allowed by many therapeutic situations. The risks of error in test interpretation are greater in dealing with the total clinical situation, but the much greater opportunity to achieve precision clearly offsets any of the dangers involved. An additional major safeguard against reckless speculation or "wild analysis" on the tester's part is the principle of convergence or balance of inferences from the four different sources of information mentioned above.

Convergence of inference is evident in the following example. First, the patient's *score patterns* in the Rorschach test indicate pronounced perceptual emphasis on tiny details and on form in the inkblots, which in turn suggests rigidity and meticulousness. Second, the Rorschach test *content* pertains rather frequently to dirt, geometrically regular objects, and controlling mechanisms such as a governor on an engine, this content stating themes of cleanliness, order, and control. Third, ruminative, perfectionistic, overdetailed *thought processes and verbalizations* indicate ingrained pedantry. And fourth, *test behavior* is hyperconscientious and excessively self-critical with respect to accuracy and achievement, indicating strong reaction formations against hostility. In this instance, all avenues of analysis converge on the conclusion that the patient presents a severe compulsive character problem.

A complementary rather than convergent pattern is exemplified in the occurrence on the one hand of formal test scores and content that indicate intense pressure of impulses, particularly hostile impulses, and on the other hand patterns of thought, verbalization, and test behavior that indicate an overcompliant manner of coping with and concealing these impulses. Here a meaningful configuration of trends is established by using the multiple avenues of approach just described.

The Psychoanalytic Frame of Reference for Interpretation of Test Data

Thus far in the exposition of the analytic approach to test results, attention has been focused on some advantages to test data and on the sources of data within the total testing situation. It is also necessary to consider the general psychoanalytic frame of reference within which the meaning of test results may be developed. One basic model in psychoanalytic thought for analyzing behavior is that built around the reference points of *id, ego, superego,* and *external reality* (A. Freud, 1936). Actually, the *ego* reference point may be looked at as two reference points—namely, the *defensive ego,* those ego functions concerned with warding off impulses the expression of which would stimulate intolerable anxiety, and the *adaptive ego,* those ego functions concerned with testing reality; exercising judgment; concentrating, remembering, and anticipating; integrating impressions; coordinating and regulating the discharge of feeling and impulse; interacting realistically with other persons; and the like.

In studying test results, these same five reference points or major variables may be considered. As already described, the tester holds one of these variables relatively constant, namely, the external reality situation. In evaluating the effects of psychotherapy, this analytic model may be applied to the original test results and then reapplied on the occasion of re-testing.

At this point there are two sets of variables to work with simultaneously, the previously mentioned four avenues of approach (the scores, the content, the thought processes, and the test behavior) and now the five psychoanalytic reference points (impulse, superego, defensive ego, adaptive ego, and reality aspects of responses). The following example illustrates the coordination of these two sets of variables. In the patient's Rorschach test there is a strong emphasis on color responses without any form elements, including the responses "blood," "sky," and "ice cream." These so-called Pure Color responses indicate weak or minimal capacity to regulate, control, or defend against affect and impulse. At the same time, the test content is frequently violent, tumultuous, passionate, and acutely despairing; it includes people fighting, storm clouds, lightning, fire, and devastation. Thus, the content points to the same volatility as the emphasis on the unformed Pure Color response. Simultaneously, as regards thought organization, perception, and verbalization, the patient's responses are often formulated hastily and changed quickly or else broken off in the middle; some are fluid or arbitrary and only belatedly altered into conventionally acceptable and logical form. Finally, in test behavior and attitudes the patient is moody, facetious, negativistic, and generally overresponsive to the tester. In all respects this example contains convergent indications of impulse-dominated functioning and of weakness in the ego functions of defensive inhibition and adaptive delay and regulation.

APPLICATION OF INTERPRETIVE METHODS TO RETEST COMPARISONS

In the analysis of retest results, the following comparative variables are especially important: the area of change, the direction of change, the quantity of change, the quality of change, and, in the altered personality organization, the final balance of forces. With regard to the area of change, the test results may indicate, for example, changes in the goodness of judgment, the sharpness of reality testing, the intensity of guilt, the strength of defenses, and the freedom of impulse expression. With regard to the direction of change, the results may suggest that judgment is becoming better or worse, reality testing becoming more or less accurate, defenses becoming stronger or weaker, and the like.

The quantity of change and quality of change are the two vital problems that so deeply concerned Freud in his retrospective discussion of what psychoanalysis can and cannot accomplish, and they also bring to attention the problem raised by the psychoanalytic critics of psychotherapy who insist that effectiveness of forms of therapy other than classical analysis rests upon a primarily irrational basis. It will be worth while, therefore, to spend somewhat more time on the quantitative and qualitative aspects of change than on the others.

In considering quantity of change, it is obvious first of all that wherever a change has occurred and in whatever direction, it may be great, moderate, or small in extent. For example, the retest may show much stronger ego controls but little or no concurrent increase in self-awareness. Frequently, however, change in retest results seems to lag behind change observed in therapy. Often the test records of patients who seem to have improved significantly clinically do not differ strikingly from their pretherapy records; a small change in the total test pattern in the direction of better adjustment may be all that is evident. Offhand, one might think in such instances that the tests are not sufficiently sensitive to the constructive, adaptive, conflict-free aspects of the ego. It can be demonstrated, however, that if a well-rounded battery of tests is used, this battery will ordinarily be sensitive to major ego assets (Rapaport, Gill, and Schafer, 1945-46; Schafer, 1948). Thus, the fact that test changes tend to be matters of limited degree rather than of extensive kind might be viewed as consistent with Freud's conservative appraisal of the extent of change that psychotherapeutic methods—including analysis— can usually bring about. Of course, the ultimate answer to this question will have to come from systematic research in both therapy and testing, employing a wide variety of specific criteria of change.

In considering qualitative change or structural change, it is necessary first to re-emphasize a point that is well-known in psychoanalysis, though perhaps not so well-known or well remembered among nonanalytic practitioners of intensive psychotherapy—the fact that, on an irrational, unreliable, noninsightful basis, marked changes may take place in the face the patient turns to the world. Optimism may replace pathological pessimism, trust may replace mistrust, and determination may replace apathy. Yet all these changes may be on the basis of a so-called transference neurosis or resistance maneuver. It is also well-known that "magical" changes of this sort tend to occur most commonly in those areas where the therapist has been most active in providing cues concerning data on which he bases his confrontations, interpretations, and implicit or explicit recommendations. It is for this reason that the early dreams in analysis are regarded as the most genuine and informative. In discussing technical problems involved in analyzing dreams of seasoned patients, Freud (1911a) said, "All the knowledge acquired about dreams serves also to put the dream-constructing process on its guard." That is, as treatment progresses the patient learns to speak the language of the therapist even in his dreams, and he may resort to more and more defensive manipulation of dream content and associations.

To a great extent it is the *content* of what the patient talks about in his therapy that lends itself to this manipulation and distortion. This content includes the patient's desires, fears, resentments, values and hopes, past and present experiences with important persons in his life, and even his daydreams, dreams, moods, and symptomatic ups and downs. In addition, the patient's behavior and attitudes in the therapeutic relationship will usually be discussed to a significant extent, with the result that, according to his true and false conceptions of the therapist's demands, standards, and tolerances, the patient will become progressively more sophisticated about "what goes" and "what doesn't go" in the therapy and in daily life. Of course, ultimately this "insight" into the therapeutic relationship must also be analyzed.

Unlike the content of his verbal communications and his behavior and attitudes in the therapeutic relationship, the formal aspects of the patient's thought organization are less often singled out for *intensive* therapeutic discussion. For the therapist to insist on prolonged discussion of formal thought patterns in the treatment hours would tend to substitute an intellectualized, remote atmosphere for the air of emotional immediacy, directness, and concreteness ordinarily considered desirable in intensive psychotherapy.[7] To the extent that thought patterns are ignored in explicit discussion, the

[7] In some cases, such as those involving severe obsessional patterns or certain forms of schizophrenic thought disorder, it is therapeutically advisable or even necessary to analyze the defensive or symptomatic aspects of the deviant thinking. Even in these instances, however, the details of the thought patterns under analysis are not likely to be thoroughly mapped out and verbalized, nor will all instances of their occurrence be explicitly identified.

patient is likely to be relatively naïve and less on guard in this realm of analysis and less able to manipulate his self-expressions in an effectively resistant manner.

What are these formal thought patterns? They cannot be surveyed exhaustively here but they include the following: the degree of autistic distortion running through psychic functioning—irrespective of the content and locale of the autisms; the pervasive, defensively prescribed methods of organizing, articulating, and communicating emotional experiences; consistent selective emphases in perceiving and remembering; characteristic patterns in the organization of space, time, and motility; degree and style of humor; capacity for introspectiveness; and tolerance for free fantasy and self-confrontation.

It is not primarily the patient's relative naïveté, as in the circumstance mentioned above, that makes these thought patterns so informative and stable. Chiefly it is that such formal aspects of the organization of thought ordinarily have a long history, are highly overdetermined, and often seem to have achieved a significant degree of autonomy from the drives and conflicts out of which they evolved (Rapaport, 1951a, 1951b). This autonomy means that the processes appear to operate with relative independence of archaic drives, defenses, and conceptions of reality, to be sustained by energies of their own, and to be relatively fixed and recognizably individual. Thus, in addition to the fact that these formal patterns are not easily discernible in consciousness by the psychologically untrained patient, they are not easily altered. It would obviously require a major reorganization of the forces within the personality for them to change significantly. Unlike content and superficial behavior, these structuralized dispositions are not at the mercy of passing transference reactions and resistances. They are part of the grain of the ego and cannot be changed superficially—except by concealing histrionics; and, through the advantages of tests described earlier, such as indirectness of approach and standardization of stimulation, any false veneer can usually be rather easily penetrated. For

these reasons the vicissitudes of formal thought patterns may
be used as relatively reliable indices of structural change during psychotherapy.

Consider in this regard the example of the cold, narcissistic patient who begins trying to please his therapist—and also, of course, to thwart the analysis of his narcissism—by playing the part of a warm, affable, cooperative person. During
the retesting this patient may be conscientiously agreeable
and compliant in his relationship with the tester. He may
even preconsciously limit the content of his responses to
"warm" concepts such as flowers, landscapes, and handsome
decorative objects in the Rorschach test; and he may emphasize trust, empathy, and constructiveness among the characters in his Thematic Apperception Test stories. He will not
know, however, that in the Rorschach test there are highly
technical, formal indications of narcissism, such as relative
perceptual emphasis on weakly formed color responses; and,
by unwitting perceptual emphasis on these weakly formed
color responses, he may give the lie to his adaptive front. Even
his restriction of content to what is "good" and "attractive"
may backfire diagnostically, for there is evidence that this
content is what many narcissistic persons tend to overemphasize defensively in the tests—as in life. Thus, the defensive,
shallow nature of the patient's good will might be inferred
from the unusual one-sidedness of the content. Here is an instance, by the way, where the total personality picture
evolved by the tester is enriched by incorporating observation
of the patient's clinical behavior in the test situation without
letting it displace the more traditional and formalized aspects of the analysis.

This last example of one-sided content emphasis leads into
the fifth and last variable to be considered in retest comparison—the balance of forces in the psychological pattern as it
appears in the last set of test results. The notion of balance
implies that, in different patients, a change in the same area,
going in the same direction to the same degree, and having
the same quality—all as defined above—may have very differ-

ent significance. In one case the new development may be adequately offset by other aspects of the total personality, while in another case this may not be true. For instance, the development of increased conformist tendencies in a patient who was, to begin with, extremely rebellious and deviant in his social orientation and behavior is quite a different thing from an equal increase in conformist tendencies in a patient who initially leaned toward conformity and who finally could be said only to have consolidated his position in a lopsided manner, rather than to have balanced off one trend against the other.

Examples of Retest Analysis

The following concrete examples show how the various interpretive considerations outlined above are applied in retest analysis. The data used for comparative analysis are fragments of Rorschach test records. The discussion centers principally on distinguishing change in content from structural change.

(1) A young woman, an incipient schizophrenic, gave, during the first testing, the following response to Card IX: "Well, this looks like two frightened eyes looking out from rubble as if someone's been in a building that has been bombed and he's looking out to see if it's safe to come out—I get the picture of movement and violence in this: it seems like an atom-bomb cloud here." The patient explained during the inquiry that it looked like rubble "because it's disorganized, as if it's in the process of coming down or disintegrating." She explained the impression of violence by saying, "I usually think of wide-open eyes being associated with violence, and it looked like very solid material and yet it was not organized, so it must be in movement, and I get the feeling of it being vertical instead of horizontal, and coming down." In its content this is a grim and terrified response, and in its formal characteristics it is an autistic response. Its autistic features include the perceptually vague, physiognomic, and arbitrary aspects of its detail and its total organization, as well as the inferences about past events which the patient makes from these distorted impressions and upon which she even elaborates a little story. A weakened or lost distinction between reality and fantasy is implied. Both in con-

tent and in form this is a type of response not unusual in the records of schizophrenics.

After 13 months—a period during which a psychoanalyst carried this patient in intensive psychotherapy—the patient gave the following response to the same card, Card IX: "This looks like one huge fountain with all different colored lights on it and a person way up here looking out on it all and quite surprised that he's there and that it looks like this. I don't know why I'm fascinated with the colors today or why I don't like blue, but I like this better than the last picture [which had blue color in it]. I guess I like red and orange and green together [the colors of Card IX] but I can't see blue. In the color blue I get the sense of giving up, I think, and in the red and green I get a sense of some kind of contrast or difference, some kind of conflict but at the same time that difference makes it interesting and realistic."

In its manifest content, this is an optimistic image: it has connotations of prettiness, emotional security, and—in the discussion of the colors—a rejection of despair and a welcoming attitude toward awareness of conflict. In content, then, one might say that great improvement is evident. If, however, the formal aspects of this response are considered, essentially the same manifestations of thought disorder are seen that were previously evident. The forms and spatial relationships remain more or less arbitrary, the reasoning about the colors is somewhat illogical in addition to being highly intellectualized, and the impaired distinction between fantasy and reality is again suggested. Moreover, when the patient rejects the blue color because of its depressive, discouraged feel to her, she even provides a clue to excessive reliance on the mechanism of denial in her present functioning. Well-developed emotional security and optimism would have enabled her to use the colors genuinely in a well-defined response such as red apples, orange lobster claws, and green leaves below orange petals; instead she is limited to talking about the colors *qua* colors, or at best treating them as artificial or symbolic rather than real and intrinsic.

It is not implied by this example that the patient was unchanged or unimproved by her therapy. By the time of retesting she was manifesting significant improvement symptomatically, in her social adjustment, and in her intellectual understanding of her problems; other aspects of her test results indicated these changes for the better. Even the denial through change of content on Card IX suggests a surface increase in optimism and tranquillity, and, for a young schizophrenic, that in itself is considerable change. For the present discussion it is important to recognize that shifts occur in retest results in which, despite a hopeful change of content, there seems to be no underlying structural change, the autistic predisposition remaining virtually untouched. This phenomenon is well-known among therapists of schizophrenics.

An alternative explanation must be considered. A schizophrenic whose conscious awareness was initially flooded with material of a primary-process type might, subsequent to genuine, insightful improvement, continue to be able to think freely in the fashion of the primary process and continue to be inclined to think this way; however, he might be able to choose the time and extent of such regressive occurrences and thus might become to a great extent an active master rather than a passive victim of ego regression. The regressive "schizophrenic" thinking would then be in the service of the ego in the sense elaborated by Kris (1952). In the present case, however, the virtual absence in the second Rorschach record of nonautistic forms of response supports the assumption that ego mastery has not been attained and that the change here is primarily a change in content.

(2) A schizophrenic young man showed, after 22 months of intensive psychoanalytic psychotherapy, significantly more adaptive efforts and effective social behavior. The content of his Rorschach responses will be ignored in favor of a contrast between some of his Rorschach scores and some qualitative Rorschach material pertaining to thought disorder. This patient's first Rorschach record included five definitely formed color responses—the so-called Form-Color responses, which are interpreted as referring largely to striving toward good rapport with others, or, in other words, to adaptive efforts in interpersonal relationships. Two of this patient's five Form-Color responses were, however, poor in some respect. His second Rorschach record included nine Form-Color responses. This increase is great enough to warrant the inference that he was now making greater efforts to be socially adaptive. However, four of these nine responses were unsatisfactory in some respect,

and, in addition, more flagrant and more numerous instances of thought disorder appeared in the second Rorschach than in the first. For example, one expression of persisting thought disorder occurred on Card III in the retest: "These look like two men sort of standing around a cauldron as if they might be cannibals and these red spots look like monkeys hanging by their tails." So far, so good. "And these red things look like bleeding breasts as if they were cut off these two men—but actually I don't suppose they'd be men." When asked during the inquiry what made the upper red areas look like monkeys, the patient replied, "They fit in the general picture of jungle and cannibals." Again, so far, so good. "And they are red, which is not too inappropriate for the tropics..." In his *bleeding breasts* concept and particularly in his final reasoning about tropical color the patient ego-syntonically used schizophrenic mechanisms of thought.

In this case it appears necessary to conclude that, while greater adaptive efforts may be in process, not only are these efforts still frequently out of tune—as indicated by their poor average quality—but, if anything, the basic schizophrenic disorder is more pervasive. What is now seen may be a better adjusted or stabilized schizophrenic personality. Such stabilizing among schizophrenic patients, while not well understood, is also not unfamiliar to psychotherapists. If, in addition, the appearance in the retest of two Pure Color responses is noted—responses that tend to correlate with regressive, undifferentiated, and poorly controlled affective experience—there is further suggestion that spread and consolidation of the schizophrenic pathology is going on side by side with increased social conformity.[8]

Changes in Rorschach color responses of the sort described in this last case are common in the records of schizophrenics who show social improvement in the course of intensive therapy. Paralleling the clinical impression, one finds evidence in the retests of increased adaptiveness together with indications that much of the adaptiveness is shallow, forced, and out of tune. This color pattern indicates in itself the tenuousness of the social improvement—a tenuousness that must be expected

[8] See, however, the alternative conclusion suggested for example (1).

as long as the underlying autistic inclinations remain in force. In these instances it is possible that, on the strength of the therapeutic relationship, the patient is willing to invest more in his social existence but will not generalize to any significant extent from the security he has achieved with the therapist to the security that might be possible with "real people." One such socially improved schizophrenic increased from two Form-Color responses (one of which was unsatisfactory in some formal respect) to five Form-Color responses (four of which were unsatisfactory).

For a contrast, one may consider the following more encouraging case:

(3) A schizophrenic young woman was tested four times—the second time after 11 months of intensive therapy, the third time after 15 months, and the fourth time after three and a half years, during the last two years of which she had been treated as an office patient. In her first Rorschach record there were three Pure Color responses; in the second there was only one; and in the last two records there were none. Of the Color-Form responses (a response intermediate between the socialized Form-Color and the regressive Pure Color) there were four in the first record, five in the second record, and only two in the fourth. The frequency of Form-Color responses remained about the same throughout this period; however, the *proportion* of Form-Color responses as opposed to other color responses obviously increased over time. Thus, according to the Rorschach test, the result after three and a half years of therapy was a definite shift of weight in the direction of controlled adaptiveness and a virtual disappearance of exceptionally labile, primitive, and unmodulated affective and impulsive responsiveness. A major change is suggested in affective experience and pattern of control of impulse. Clinically, and elsewhere in the tests, the patient still showed significant emotional immaturity and instability, but a structural change could nevertheless be suspected. Accompanying these changes and supporting their structural implications was a virtual disappearance of autistic material in the later Rorschach records.

The color response is not the only one that is sensitive to change, nor, of course, is change restricted only to schizophrenics. In the case of a 36-year-old woman who was severely narcissistic with some borderline psychotic trends, change of a very different sort occurred in conjunction with a year of intensive psychotherapy. A fragment of her record will be discussed in detail to illustrate the typical interpretive infighting involved in working with retests.

(4) On Card I of the Rorschach test the patient originally saw first a bat, then a map, then, in the center, a dressmaking form, and finally a human figure from the waist down. In her second Rorschach record she saw a bat, islands, a rear view of a woman from the waist down, Ku Klux Klan headpieces, then, in the same area as the dressmaking form, "a menacing female figure, entirely—the hands, bosom, hips, but no feet," and finally, "a friendly Teddy bear." Of particular interest is the change of the dressmaking form into a menacing female figure. From a content point of view the shift of emphasis is from a safely inanimate object with narcissistically defensive decorative connotations to a threatening live figure with no concealing and beguiling narcissistic surface. It was a major accomplishment in the first year of this woman's treatment that some slight capacity to tolerate awareness of her own hostility had been restored. This Rorschach change of content appears to indicate the effects of the lifting or weakening of defense and of greater self-acceptance.

From a formal point of view it is noteworthy that the response changed in score from pure Form, a type of score indicating emphasis on intellectual control or inhibition, to Human Movement, a score suggesting, among other things, tolerance for conscious fantasy and self-confrontation (Hertzman and Pearce, 1947). This formal aspect of the response is one over which the patient could not have had conscious control. If she had simply been trying to appear "insightful," she could just as well have seen a threatening object or creature rather than a threatening person. There is reason therefore to infer a degree of structural change here as well as a change of content.[9] Her reference to KKK headpieces in her retest responses to Card I also suggests the increased freedom of awareness of hostility.

Up to this point the retest analysis is encouraging. However,

[9] For a contrast, one need only think back to the example of the first patient who, in her second Rorschach test, spoke about the welcome sense of conflict among the colors on Card IX but actually gave no substantial color response and left the impression that she was as autistic as before.

from another formal point of view, the sinister menacing female figure is a type of response that—*in Rorschach records*—suggests a readiness to externalize or project hostility rather than accept it as part of oneself. Even the KKK concept—*as a Rorschach response*—suggests special readiness to externalize hostility. Thus, while the patient may be functioning under a different set of dynamic and structural conditions and may be more conscious of and alert to hostile interaction in personal relationships, she may still be compelled to deal with her own hostile impulses in primarily defensive fashion, perhaps especially by projecting them. Even though she may be less superficially insensitive and unresponsive and have less of a Pollyanna façade (this was an actual clinical change), it seems that she has shifted her line of defense more than relinquished very much of her need for defense.

But some of the earlier optimism about these retest changes may be regained if her final response to this card is considered —the "friendly Teddy bear," for this image introduces *variety* of content and emotional tone into her response sequence. To review, by now she has seen a bat, islands, the lower part of a woman, KKK headpieces, a menacing woman, and a Teddy bear. Her impressions include neutral, hostile, and friendly themes, and she manifests no marked emotional lability or severe falling-off in quality of response. Such variety and stability give her responsiveness a range and balance which suggest that the sense of threat associated with the liberated hostile images is not deeply disruptive. Otherwise she might have been too anxious about the hostile images and too absorbed in them to have moved on freely to the "friendly Teddy bear" concept. Of course, one might still wonder in this case whether the friendly Teddy bear did not indicate an effort to wind up Card I with a cute and cuddly gesture in order to minimize or negate the two previous hostile images. The somewhat redundant and fabulized use of "friendly" does have an element of strain and artificiality in it. In short, this benign postscript to Card I might be nothing more than a persisting denial and narcissistic maneuver. This last doubt—and all of the earlier ones—cannot be resolved simply by studying the responses to Card I. The rest of the Rorschach test must be scrutinized along with the results of the battery of tests. As already indicated, ideally a battery of tests should be employed in every initial testing and in every retesting.

But even if the Teddy bear response reflects a defensive narcissistic maneuver, this patient's range of expressiveness is obviously considerably greater in the second Rorschach record. Possibly her security to confront disturbing matters may be so much greater that she no longer needs to be the equivalent in her life of a dressmaking form—a lifeless frame for adornment. Her emotional experience is probably texturally richer. For the time being, this fragment of the total retest comparison leaves the impression that, from a structural point of view, she is probably *in transition* though still highly resistant to insight and seriously disturbed in her relationship to herself and to others.

So far attention has been centered on changes of Rorschach content, scores, and thought patterns. The final example to be presented will illustrate a fourth major type of possible change—change of attitude and behavior toward the tester and one's self.

(5) The patient was an extremely infantile, demanding, phobic man of about 30, with borderline psychotic features. In his first approach to Card I of the Rorschach test, after a relatively long delay of 50 seconds and several shrugs and anxious laughs, he said, "I don't know. I don't know. Well, if there were a lot more things it could be a chest but that's about all. I don't know what it is." He was urged to take his time. "I don't know. I don't know what it is." He was urged to try a little longer. "Nothing. I just wouldn't know. I've never seen anything like that. I'm terribly sorry. Is it supposed to be something?" In inquiry, when asked what made it look like a chest, he replied, "I don't know. I don't know. It just looks like the abdomen. I don't know. My mind's on the chest. That's probably the reason." At this point he was asked whether he meant a chest or an abdomen and he replied, "I wouldn't know. Put down zero on that! I flunked that test! How could you write so much? I hope other cards are better than this!" During this response the patient burped in the tester's face with no sign of embarrassment or apology or effort to cover it.

His second Rorschach record was obtained after he had had approximately two years of intensive psychotherapy. Even though his basic character pathology had not been substantially altered, his superficial behavior had become considerably more adaptive and compliant. At this point he responded as follows to Card I after five seconds: "Two birds on each side of the top.

The whole thing looks like a bat. That's all." Asked if there was anything else it might look like, he replied, "Well, from here it looks like the diaphragm, a man's, without the head and without the legs." During inquiry he added that the man's figure looked as if it had a penis. Considering only his behavior and attitudes, there is an impressive change here in his decreased emphasis on inadequacy and immaturity, on an abjectly apologetic caricature of failure, and on violation of ordinary social propriety. There is at the same time considerably more impersonality and control, more freedom in the use of imagination, and more spontaneous taking of responsibility for being cooperative and productive.

As indicated by the patient's clinical follow-up, he was still capable of severe symptomatic and social regression, illustrating the untrustworthy nature of changes restricted mainly to superficial behavior in the test situation. It is the same as with changes restricted chiefly to test content. Yet it is not to be shrugged off that, from the tests, the patient could be said to be making somewhat successful efforts at the time of retesting to appear mature and responsible and to raise his anxiety tolerance, even if mainly as a submissive, ingratiating gesture to his therapist. Some patients fail even in such restricted efforts during retesting.

Generally, behavior and attitude changes in demandingness, anxiety and frustration tolerance, facetiousness, self-criticism, and resiliency under stress are important to observe in retests. They often point to noteworthy clinical change, whether it is a superficial and unreliable change in content or a deeper-going, enduring structural change. It can only be mentioned in passing that, from the patient's attitudes toward the test situation and toward his own test responses, it is frequently possible to decipher messages he wants to send his therapist concerning his progress in therapy or lack of progress, and, through analysis of these messages, it is even possible to surmise with some confidence major attitudes and expectations in the transference and resistance.

Assessment of Increased Ego Mastery

A detailed summary of the possible indices of increased ego mastery in the results of a battery of tests cannot be undertaken in this paper.[10] So many pathological baselines exist against which to measure increased mastery that a complete review of diagnostic testing would be required as a preface to such a summary. Consequently, only certain general orienting formulations will be presented.

Unlike psychoanalysis, intensive psychotherapy does not always have the goal of rendering pathogenic unconscious complexes available to conscious representation. This divergence from analysis is particularly evident in therapeutic work with so-called borderline cases and with schizophrenics. The reason is that these patients are frequently characterized to begin with by defensive weakness or failure and by a resulting state of consciousness in which they are too vulnerable to awareness of ordinarily unconscious material. In such instances, strengthening of defenses rather than their analysis may well be one of the major therapeutic goals—to be achieved, of course, in the light of psychoanalytic understanding and possibly with the help of some uncovering, clarification, and interpretation (Knight, 1953). When the therapeutic goal is rather to shrink the boundaries of conscious awareness than to expand them, the retest results need not reflect an increasingly rich and bold elaboration of emotionally charged, possibly even raw themes of conflict, desire, frustration, and the like. Rather, it is usually necessary in these initially inadequately defended cases to look for evidence in the retests of strengthened repressions, reaction formations and counterphobic emphases, improved accuracy of reality testing, increased ability to stave off intrusions of disruptive egocentric or autistic preoccupations, decreased emotional lability or inappropriateness, and improved capacity for control, concentration, and conformity with at least minimal demands of convention and social intercourse.

In types of cases better integrated than the borderline and

[10] Relevant background considerations of theory and interpretation may be found in a number of existing publications. See, for instance, Holt (1951, 1954), Rapaport, Gill, and Schafer (1945-46), Rapaport (1950b), and Schafer (1948, 1954). For suggestive research findings, see Piotrowski and Schreiber (1952), Rioch (1949), and Fromm and Elonen (1951).

schizophrenic ones, the therapist's uncovering and interpretive orientation may result in retest changes similar to those seen in the retests of analysands. There is likely to be increased richness and boldness of thematic material dealing with conflict, drives, and affects. This increase is likely to be particularly evident in the Rorschach test and Thematic Apperception Test—the tests that encourage fantasy and creative regression in the service of the ego. It must be assumed, however—and experience with retest results confirms this assumption—that ego mastery does not express itself in any of the following forms: (1) blank neutrality and banality; (2) Pollyannaish bliss; (3) a parade of psychopathology and suffering; (4) repeated declarations of improvement, insight, and tolerance of conflict; (5) dramatized emotional "emancipation"; (6) a dictionary of technical and theoretical psychoanalytic terms and "symbols." These are some of the pseudo-healthy emphases encountered in retest results; they usually express persisting resistances and extravagant transferences, and they usually involve intensified repressions, denials, intellectualizations, rebelliousness, mocking overcompliance, histrionics, and/or hostile identification with the therapist. It must also be assumed—and this assumption is again supported by experience—that in the setting of ego mastery there will be little or no severe emotional lability and impulsiveness associated with the test responses expressing normally unconscious, therapeutically uncovered content; nor will there be conspicuous secretiveness or persistent statements of one theme (such as "pleasurable orgasm").

Genuine ego mastery will be suggested by the following: (1) an adequately rich but not overwhelming representation in the projective-test content of the imagery of impulse, affect, anxiety, and conflict; (2) no severe impairment of the formal aspects of the responses; (3) appropriately cooperative behavior in the test relationship and situation.

(1) Increased richness of content should be evident if psychotherapeutic discussions have been at all meaningful and tolerable to the patient, except when, as in borderline cases,

the content was pathologically rich to begin with. This increased wealth of self-awareness and self-expression should not, however, invade the patient's functioning in impersonal, relatively well-structured problem situations such as those presented by an intelligence test. The absence of such invasion indicates that the regressive, creative self-expressions in the projective tests—as in therapy—are in the service of the ego, appearing temporarily and in appropriate situations and are not based on failure of the ego and invasion of all functioning by conflict. Also, the increased directness and forcefulness of content should be characterized by *variety* and *balance* of themes; some variety and balance should, for example, be evident in statements of mood (happy, neutral, sad), psychological emphasis ("deep" and conflictful, innocuous and conventional), operation of basic drives in interpersonal relationships (sex, dependency, hostility), and socialized inclinations (fun, responsibility, creativeness).

(2) As regards the formal adequacy of responses, the liberated ideas and feelings, however raw, archaic, or dreamlike they may be in content, should not appear frequently in forms that are perceptually arbitrary, logically indefensible, or verbally distorted. For example, in the Rorschach test inaccurately seen sex organs, poorly controlled color responses with hostile connotations, emotionally optimistic scenes which are confabulated, and "insightful" verbalizations which are peculiarly stilted, precious, or cryptic are all negative rather than positive signs of change; they suggest failure of the ego in coping with the expanded self-awareness. Similarly, in the Thematic Apperception Test the content of the stories may be highly charged emotionally but the stories should not be filled with perceptual distortions of the stimuli, obscurely rationalized elaborations of emotional reactions and relationships, arbitrary inferences from fragmentary details of the pictures, emotional and logical non sequiturs, fluidity of characterization, and disruption of verbalization. This distinction between formal adequacy and relative richness—even primitiveness—of content is the rock on which re-

test analysis is based. It enables the tester to differentiate genuine improvement from the effects of suggestion, imitation, compliance, acting out of autistic fantasies concerning the therapeutic relationship, and strengthening of resistances due to incomplete or inexact interpretation of the patient's problems.

(3) As regards appropriateness of behavior in the test relationship and situation, the expanded awareness of conflictful material should be accompanied by a capacity to express this awareness with at least moderately good emotional control and distance, this control and distance manifesting themselves in proper qualifying phrases if the material is fantastic, in some humor, in some spontaneous self-criticism that is not too harsh or relentless, and in no striking evidence of a desire to shock, dismay, thwart, dazzle, or otherwise manipulate the tester. Also, the patient should not be extremely perfectionistic or haphazard in his performance—that is, too "reformed" or too "emancipated." Here, however, as in all previous respects mentioned, a wide range of individual variability must be allowed by the retest analyzer in order to leave room for many different lines of resolution of problems. The history of the patients' problems, their present and possible future life contexts, and components of temperament, endowment, opportunity, and so on, all enter into the great variety of workable personality syntheses observed in clinical practice and in daily life.[11]

A Retest Report Exemplifying the End Result of Retest Analysis

The following retest report is presented to exemplify the end product of retest analysis based on the results of a battery of tests—the Wechsler-Bellevue Intelligence Scale, the Rorschach test, the Thematic Apperception Test, the Object Sorting test of conception formation, and a word association test.[12]

[11] For a fuller discussion of these criteria of ego mastery, see Schafer (1954, especially Chapter Six).
[12] For the rationale of this test battery, see Rapaport, Gill, and Schafer (1945-46) and Schafer (1948).

It describes the previously mentioned narcissistic woman who, in the Rorschach retest, saw the menacing female figure instead of a dressmaker's form. According to the therapist's report at the time of retesting, this patient had shown significant symptomatic and social improvement; she was less fearful, relied less on alcohol, had no more night terrors, was less given to transient conversion reactions, and socially was less inert, isolated, and rejecting of responsibility. She had, however, achieved only a little stable insight and only a little alteration of her pathological character traits.

The retest results indicate some degree of improvement in many areas of psychic functioning. Generally, these improvements include both decrease in the prominence of pathological tendencies and increase in emotional and imaginative freedom. The basic character picture remains much the same, however; it still seems necessary to regard this as a case of serious character disorder.

Specifically, the following improvements are suggested: somewhat greater self-acceptance and capacity for self-confrontation; somewhat less emphasis on need to maintain strict control; somewhat less reliance on narcissistic defenses; somewhat greater efforts to be socially adaptive even though these efforts are marked by tentativeness, caution, and strain; somewhat higher anxiety tolerance and less tendency to fall back on physical symptom formation in the face of stress; somewhat improved capacity to enjoy passive-receptive gratifications; somewhat greater freedom to be playful, relaxed, and humorous.

The increased adaptability implied in the above description seems to be associated with significantly less rigid defenses against hostile and rebellious impulses. Hostile and rebellious themes in the present Rorschach record are more conspicuous than they were originally. The implication of this change is not that the patient has become more hostile and rebellious than she was originally, but that she is better able to experience and express such tendencies now. On the other hand, the form and the intensity of some of these test responses dealing with hostility suggest that a great many problems have remained unresolved in this area. In particular, there are strong indications of projective handling of hostility and intensely disturbing castration fantasies concerning her own status and her approach to men.

As with the hostility and rebelliousness, phobic tendencies appear to have come more to the fore now, again presumably as the result of weakening of old defenses. The phobic trends do not appear to be overwhelming, however, and counterphobic resources are still evident. In addition, much of the patient's fearfulness seems concerned with what she herself might do along destructive lines.

The patient's tendency to fragment and isolate experience and to make little effort to survey and integrate details of her life is still striking. Tendencies toward autistic response are also still evident. Particularly when she felt under pressure for intellectual achievement, as in the intelligence test, her thinking sporadically became quite arbitrary and out of touch with the problems presented to her; she also became somewhat suspicious of being misled. At such moments her responses had a distinctly psychotic quality. The bulk of the test responses do not, however, break with reality. It is implied that the patient's autistic responses in daily life will be occasional and relatively short-lived.

In the Thematic Apperception Test, where the patient has to communicate her outlook on interpersonal relationships and one's place in the world, her stories remain mostly evasive, superficial, or moralistic. They suggest general superficiality in her conscious approach to problems. They provide no substantial evidence of her having achieved an integrated set of values or point of view in life. Some stories indicate greater capacity for and interest in intimacy with others than was true of her first set of stories, but other stories in the present record are quite cynical and callous; similarly, some of her present stories show a noteworthy degree of understanding and tolerance of human difficulty while others are implicitly highly intolerant; in the same inconsistent way the patient accepts dependency needs in the identification figure in some stories but emphasizes the need for absolute control and autonomy in others. These essentially antithetical stands taken by the patient in her stories appear to reflect a transitional position which includes both some tentative reaching out toward closeness and understanding, and some emotionally reactionary clinging to old narcissistic defenses and attempting to reinforce them. While she emphasizes her need for a feeling of permanence and for finding a man she can have faith in (which requires a good deal of attentiveness from him), she views any permanent emotional commitment, as in marriage, as leading only to dreary mediocrity, ill will, and lack of self-fulfillment.

INDICATIONS AND CONTRAINDICATIONS FOR
RETESTING

I would now like to discuss briefly the indications and con-traindications for retesting. Retesting may serve an impor-tant function when questions come up concerning major changes in therapeutic regime and milieu, such as hospitali-zation or its termination; the patient's returning to work or school after a period of decompensation, withdrawal, or in-activity; the tapering off or discontinuation of therapy; and the revision of the exploratory or supportive emphasis in the therapy. Retests may greatly help in the evaluation of change in borderline or fully schizophrenic cases where, because of the patient's persisting relative uncommunicativeness or need to present only his sickest side to the therapist, the therapist remains in poor touch with many positive aspects of the pa-tient's inner experience and external behavior. And, of course, retesting may always serve an important even though informal research function concerning psychopathology and psychotherapy.

The major contraindications to retesting are the following. First, retesting aimed specifically at circumventing the resist-ant patient's defenses in order to get at the content of con-flict and then to confront him with it. This is contraindicated in most cases because of its overvaluation of content discus-sion and its neglect of the necessity of either analyzing or ac-cepting the resistances and negative transference that stand in the way of direct communication of conflict and frank deal-ing with it. It is well-known that the discussion of content in the setting of intense resistiveness is typically therapeutically futile and might possibly even backfire because of its poor timing or its quality of psychological rape. Also contraindi-cated are retests when the therapeutic relationship is very fragile, as with a very paranoid patient. To such a patient, testing has too much the air about it of finding out things secretly and making him too vulnerable to emotional abuse. The pathologically mistrustful patient is therefore more than likely to respond to retesting with a disruptive increase in anxiety and increased distance and guardedness in the therapeutic relationship. Giving the patient the impression that major decisions will hinge on the outcome of the test results alone is also contraindicated. This impression is bound to warp the retest results themselves because it may stimulate intense anxiety in the patient and disruptive uncertainty about which way to slant his test responses.

Of course, to hinge major decisions on retest results alone represents a misuse of tests, since a test report cannot provide all the necessary information for any significant decision about life plans—whether these plans bear on hospitalization, form of therapy, or manipulation of the patient's environment. Testing and retesting must always remain *supplementary* examinations. They may significantly amend, extend, articulate, and confirm the formulation of the patient's problem elaborated in the course of intensive clinical interviews, but by themselves they cannot be used as the basis for a total dynamic, prognostic, and dispositional formulation.

4

TRANSFERENCE IN THE
PATIENT'S REACTION
TO THE TESTER

In the minds of those interested in psychoanalysis, recent research findings concerning the influence of the tester on the test results inevitably raise questions concerning the relevance of the concepts transference and countertransference to these findings. This discussion will deal only with the relevance of transference. The psychological analysis will concern only those elements of the test situation that seem to foster transference reactions and those that work against them.[1]

Transference in the psychoanalytic relationship will serve as the model for this analysis. The test situation held up for comparison to this model will be that of a patient taking the Rorschach test during an initial total psychiatric evaluation.

First published in the *Journal of Projective Techniques*, 20: 26-32, 1956.

[1] A fuller discussion of the psychology of the tester as well as of the patient being tested will be found in Schafer (1954, Chapter Two). Here it must at least be mentioned that the tester's countertransferences (his historically rooted neurotic reactions to patients' transferences), his ready-made transferences to patients as a group as well as to patients of different age, sex, cultural background, value orientation, and psychiatric syndrome, his way of coping with his own pathological trends, and the irrational elements of his responses to psychiatric colleagues, all constantly endanger the objectivity and roundedness of his test analyses and the effectiveness with which he communicates the results of these analyses. Intermingled with these problems, and fostering them, are the problems of maintaining self-esteem, professional security, and interprofessional rapport in the present historical circumstances of fluidity and controversy in theory and practice. Additionally, there are the inescapable problems created by variations among testers and psychiatrists in their talent, training, and experience.

I

To begin with, a few remarks about our model, the psycho-analytic treatment situation. In recent years psychoanalytic writers have become more interested in therapeutically po-tent factors inherent in the analytic situation itself. Among other variables, these writers have concerned themselves with the givens in the treatment situation that stimulate and en-hance transference manifestations, givens that ultimately help bring about the transference neurosis. "Transference neu-rosis" implies more than quantitatively intensified or extended transference reactions, that is, misunderstandings of the pres-ent in terms of the past. Transference distortions may intrude into all human experience; they are not restricted to the psy-choanalytic treatment situation. The concept "transference neurosis" refers specifically to a regressive alteration of psy-chic functioning within the psychoanalytic situation. By means of this alteration the analysand's emotional relation-ship to the analyst becomes so laden with expressions of path-ogenic, unconscious, infantile instinctual conflicts that his need for other neurotic expressions of these conflicts is greatly reduced. In time, the transference neurosis more or less ab-sorbs the energies of the "true" or original neurosis, although it is, of course, made of the very same stuff.

The question being asked in some recent psychoanalytic writings is this: What are the givens or constants in the analyt-ic situation itself that foster this intense, pervasive, regressive transference neurosis? This question bypasses, but does not minimize, the fundamental contributions made to the trans-ference by the persisting infantile conflicts pressing toward expression and repetition, by the actual unique interaction of a specific therapist personality and a specific patient per-sonality, and by the patient's misapprehensions concerning psychoanalysis based on his general impressions and on the manner of his referral for and his introduction to treatment.

Gill (1954) has stressed the following elements of the ana-lytic situation as "unremittingly accelerating and deepening the regressive transference":

... the [patient's] recumbency and inability to see the analyst who sits and may look, with the inevitable accompanying sense of being inferior; the frustration by silence and through other techniques; the awakening of strong needs without gratification; the absence of reality cues from the analyst; the general atmosphere of timelessness, with the relative disregard of symptoms and the taking of the whole personality as the relevant province of activity; free association, bringing into the field of consciousness the thoughts and feelings ordinarily excluded from the usual interpersonal relationship; the emphasis on fantasy; and last but not least the frequency of visits, which, metaphorically speaking, we may regard as the constant irritation necessary to keep open the wounds into the unconscious, and indeed as a general strong invitation to become dependent, to regress, and to feel safe enough to do so because there is time enough and stability and frequency.

From MacAlpine's (1950) somewhat earlier discussion of this subject we may abstract the following additional factors: the ego-regressive effect of curtailing the stimulating object world during the analytic sessions; the elements of fixed routine and discipline in the analysis which are reminiscent of infantile routine; diminished personal responsibility in the analytic sessions; and the full sympathetic attention of another being which leads to expectations in the patient of being loved, praised, indulged, controlled, guided, confided in, forgiven, or even punished—these expectations being followed by disillusionment, and then, in response to this frustration, by regression. The nature of the interpretations offered, aimed at bringing infantile residues to unequivocal expression, must be stressed too, of course.

While these considerations are not systematically coordinated and do not exhaust the complexities of the psychoanalytic situation, they make plain the type and range of variables relevant to a psychoanalytic study of clinical situations.

II

How do these considerations apply to the Rorschach test situation? Recent Rorschach research has emphasized the influence of specific personality trends, such as hostility and anx-

iety, on the test results. Accordingly, this instructive research falls in the domain of the study of transference readiness brought into the test situation: it does not clarify dynamic factors inherent in the test situation itself. The present discussion must therefore be based partly on varieties of observed test behavior, partly on clarifications during therapy
of reactions to testing, and partly on transposition from psychoanalytic discussions of comparable situations. It must be
stressed that we shall be concerned largely with the patient's
more or less latent, irrational, magical, dramatized conceptions of the test situation; we shall take for granted his realistic appreciation of the possible advantages to be gained from
taking the tests and his objective perception of the tester as
a disinterested professional consultant. In other words, we
shall be concerned with reactions following the lines of the so-
called primary-process modes of thought rather than the logical, realistic secondary process.

The following givens or constants seem to characterize the
psychological position of the patient taking the Rorschach test
during an initial psychiatric evaluation.

(1) A large element of free imagination, hence of fantasy,
is encouraged in the response process. On the strength of the
patient's wish to respond, and in order for him to be at all creative in responding, there then takes place some regression
in the patient's level of psychic functioning. To a limited,
more or less ego-regulated, but still significant extent this regression allows derivative representations of unconscious, rejected tendencies increased access to consciousness (cf. Kris,
1952).

(2) At the same time the patient is relieved of much of the
responsibility for the content of his responses, since with more
or less justification he can put considerable responsibility for
what he sees on the presence of rather fantastically rendered
test stimuli and on his obligation to deal with these stimuli
somehow. This opportunity to externalize responsibility and
to ward off superego anxiety further deepens the reaches of

consciousness and tends in subtle ways to infantilize the patient's emotional position.

(3) The test requires communication of intimate, even if not immediately revealing material without a basis in trust in the relationship with the tester. Where therapy may be patient and tactful in this respect, testing is abrupt and demanding. This rude psychological intrusion by a stranger (the tester) stimulates in the patient an anxious sense of violated privacy, emotional vulnerability, and defenselessness.

(4) Even though objectively the examination is not concerned with moral judgments, its evaluative nature stimulates fears of being harshly judged, shamed, and punished. One's worth as a person seems to be being weighed, and superego projections may flourish—especially when restrictions of response develop because of anxiety or limited assets. Patterns of behavior deriving from archaic authority problems may then be exaggerated. Schachtel's (1945) contribution to this point and to the following is most valuable.

(5) The absence of cues from the tester as to the desirability of this or that mode of response or content of response, together with the frustration of the patient's greater or lesser efforts to get the tester to structure the task thoroughly with rules, standards, or approval, fosters anxious uncertainty and feelings of abandonment or, as Baer (1950) has put it, in discussing the threatening effect of the meaninglessness of the inkblots, fear of "loss of objects." The patient's uncertain and isolated position will stimulate relevant and persisting infantile anxiety and will thereby increase his readiness to misperceive the tester regressively as an archaic parent figure.

(6) A significant loss of control occurs in this interpersonal relationship due to the tester's setting the basic conditions of test performance, such as the type and number of stimuli to be dealt with and the general task to perform. Diminished control in relationships and problem situations threatens the maintenance of one's accustomed modes of maintaining self-esteem, establishing defensive security, and achieving impulse

gratification. The patient's resulting sense of helplessness and vulnerability in this respect has its regression-stimulating aspect.

(7) The danger of premature self-awareness also hovers over the response process. This is because, consciously or preconsciously, the patient is attempting to interpret his responses as he goes along. The concurrent probing psychiatric evaluation during the initial work-up period, plus the patient's sense of desperation in his current life crisis, may well exaggerate the impact of these self-analytic efforts. These efforts may be crude, highly intellectualized, or incorrect. Together with the stimulated freedom of self-awareness and the absence of external restraining cues referred to above, the self-interpretive efforts expose the patient to disturbing conclusions about what is "wrong" with him.

(8) Last to be mentioned here is the general temptation existing in all clinical relationships to regress to archaic modes of interaction and mastery. The tester, as an extension or surrogate of the therapist, who in turn is a surrogate of the important familial figures, may be responded to and communicated with in the language of transference rather than reality. Not infrequently, transference messages are meant to be sent through the tester to the therapist.

As a result of these constants in the test situation, and others no doubt may be added to the list, a significant amount of intrapsychic and interpersonal temptation, frustration, and anxiety is stimulated. In consequence of these disruptive feelings, the tester may well take on looming qualities, such as those of an omniscient, omnipotent, controlling, judging, possibly loving and rewarding but possibly disapproving and punishing parent or sibling. The specific qualities ascribed to him will be determined largely by the historically rooted structural, dynamic, and economic configuration characterizing the patient at the time of testing. This same configuration will also determine a good part of how the patient then deals with the tester and his test.

These transference-colored reactions to the test and tester

are usually seen most clearly in the behavior of severe neurotics, borderline cases, and psychotics. Under these situational
pressures, such patients are poorly able to maintain tentative
trust, controlled and constructive self-criticism, reflectiveness,
concentration, humor, initiative, perseverance, cooperation,
productivity, resiliency in the face of difficulty, feelings of
conviction, and effective verbal communication—the signs of
higher-level ego organization. Disruption of these ego functions thus serves as an important indication of ego weakness.
In contrast, the manner in which many moderately well-in-
tegrated neurotics take the test is relatively nondisrupted,
impersonal, and opaque with respect to archaic reaction tendencies. The latter patients appear to be better able to respond
to certain counterregressive, transference-impeding, more
or less realistic givens in the test situation. The progressive
rather than regressive pressures must also be clarified if we
are to understand the setting in which projective test responses are formed. They include more than the patient's correct recognition of the tester as a disinterested consultant.

III

The counterregressive, transference-impeding constants
in the usual test situation appear to include the following:
(1) the reassurance against traumatization provided by the
obvious transiency and relative remoteness of the patient's
relationship with the tester; (2) the security in communication fostered by the virtual absence of explicit, direct communication by the patient of highly charged autobiographic
material; (3) the ego-mobilizing effect of the at least implicit
demand in the situation that the test responses be perceptually, logically, and verbally adequate; (4) the support provided
by the maintenance of face-to-face interaction, when the testing is carried out in this manner; (5) the unavailability of
the tester's interpretations of responses, so that explicit and
public self-confrontation is not enforced and sharpened within the test relationship as it is in therapy; (6) the presence of

a specific external stimulus and externally defined task requiring maintenance of at least ordinary perceptual vigilance.

These and other factors seem to limit the patient's freedom of fantasy and the extent of his creative ego-regression during the response process. They focus a good part of his attention on a piece of external reality; he is not simply or primarily pushed toward reveries, memories, and associations undirected by usual modes of conscious thought. Thereby the development of intense transference reactions is retarded and the formation of a full-blown transference neurosis is obviously precluded. These same considerations may be applied to the understanding of why projective-test responses cannot be treated as if they were dream material (Schafer, 1954, Chapter Three).

The upshot of these transference-inducing and transference-impeding, regressive and counterregressive pressures in the test situation seems to be the formation of a rudimentary, restricted, often inconspicuous but sometimes dramatic transference reaction to the tester. The relatively standardized nature of the test situation is crucial in this respect since it highlights even subtle manifestations of irrational, transference-colored behavior and attitudes. Such behavior and attitudes will be observed not only with respect to the tester and his situation but with respect to the test responses themselves, and they will be reflected in the vicissitudes of the response process. While by no means representing a full-blown transference neurosis, these rudimentary transference manifestations will inevitably express the patient's fundamental libidinal, hostile, defensive, moral, and adaptive reaction patterns. Dynamic continuities of this sort have been solidly established by psychoanalysis.

IV

What conclusions may we draw from considerations such as these? First of all, we should not set behavior and attitudes in the test situation apart from the test responses proper, either in our interpretations or in our test reports. Instead, we should interpret behavior and attitudes as crucial aspects of the response process. We should make sure, however, that the test scores and content and their sequence provide independent support for these interpretations, or at least that the scores and content form a meaningful configuration with what we take to be the implications of specific test behavior and attitudes. We must also be careful not to commit ourselves rashly to overspecific inferences concerning real figures and experiences in the patient's life. As testers, our legitimate objects of study are existing psychic structure and major dynamic trends operating in varying strength in the present. It is these structural, dynamic, and economic factors that are highlighted by the constants in the test situation. Thus, while we may often speak with confidence of a particular patient's distinctive readiness to form dependent, demanding, seductive, or sadistic relationships, or of his determined intensification of repressive, intellectualizing, or other defenses in reaction to stress, we may rarely justifiably conclude that these modes of relationship are limited to the real mother, father, or siblings, or that they were laid down by specific past interactions with them. Here we come up against subtle patterns of displacement, defensive regression, and layering that becloud the representation of actual past and present object relations. We may, of course, attempt to describe what the patient emphasizes in his current conceptions of significant figures out of his past.

A second conclusion to be drawn from the preceding analysis of the test situation is that our interpretations, which are, in a basic sense, predictions, should be restricted in scope in two respects. First, concerning the overt forms of expression of interpreted trends, these can be safely predicted only in situations that involve variables operating in the test situation too, such as the relative absence of rules, diminished control over external events, intimacy without a basis in trust, and others listed above. But even with respect to situations that match the Rorschach test in their stressful, regressive, transference-inducing aspects, the predictions of overt be-havior must remain tentative and general; in this way allow-ance is made for the selective, not entirely controllable im-pact of particular external personalities and circumstances. Our predictions are guided by character structure but limited by fate. As regards specifically anticipating the patient's re-actions to therapy and to his therapist, it must be remembered that the therapist's role is complex; its elements vary in prom-inence depending on the patient's problem, the therapist's personality and competence, the choice of therapeutic tech-nique, and the phase of the treatment. These elements of the therapist's role include his being interpretive, clarifying, ap-preciative, detached, encouraging, disciplining, educating, and possibly misleading, confusing, seductive, and punitive. To each of these elements the patient may respond for a time with a partial or total shift in his transference. So far as pos-sible, therefore, predictions from test results to transference phenomena during therapy, if they are made at all, should try to be specific about conditions facilitating or hampering these phenomena. Predictions simply in terms of "cure" or "suc-cess" grossly oversimplify clinical life.[2]

The second restriction of prediction to be respected fol-lows from the observation that many of the trends we interpret are latent and partial. The ultimate form of expression of these trends is determined largely by their place in the total personality, that is, in the individual's hierarchy of drives, de-fenses, controls, values, assets, and his past, present, and fore-seeable relationships and life opportunities. Without a thoroughly worked out picture of the patient's personality, the disposition of many partial and/or latent trends cannot be safely predicted.

Recognizing these two limitations of prediction based on Rorschach test findings leads to a fuller appreciation of the value of using a battery of tests. Through a battery of tests we observe the patient's ego at work in a variety of problem situations, and we observe this work not only in test scores and

[2] See Chapters 3 and 5.

content and their sequences but in reactions to the tester and the test situation. Having more than one tester see the patient may also enrich the behavioral and attitudinal findings. In these ways we may survey the extent, intensity, and variety of the patient's readiness to react regressively with particular types of transference. With the help of such a survey we may better assess the patient's adaptiveness, reality testing, anxiety tolerance, capacity for self-confrontation, and other major aspects of his ego strength.

Finally, the preceding analysis of the test situation indicates that we should not be alarmed or discouraged by recent research findings that the tester may influence the test results. The test situation is dynamic and not static; its dynamic nature helps to account for the fact that our instruments are so revealing of personality and pathology. In addition, experienced testers tend in practice to develop individual baselines as to how much or how little shading, color, form, or movement is to be considered unusual. Deliberately or unwittingly they adapt their rules of thumb to their individual styles of test administration and the usual reactions these elicit. So long as we keep our interpretations extensively rooted in all aspects of the test results, and so long as we formulate results with appropriate tentativeness and without overgeneralizing, we need not be excessively concerned with what are, after all, the limited distortions of single scores so far demonstrated by research. Freud's discoveries, and particularly the recent developments in his ego psychology, appear to provide the most searching and comprehensive means we have of understanding and capitalizing upon the total Rorschach situation.

5

ON THE PSYCHOANALYTIC
STUDY OF RETEST RESULTS

Psychoanalytic assessment of personality change brought about by therapy concerns itself with changes within the ego (intrasystemic changes), changes in the relation between the ego on the one hand and the id and superego on the other (intersystemic changes), and changes in the relation of the ego to reality. The ego is steadily in the center of attention, and we seek signs of increased ego strength. Of the numerous concepts describing preferred functions, aims, and characteristics of the strong or mature ego, I will consider here only some major ones, and these only in a brief and not systematically ordered fashion. I will also indicate some of the modes of analysis of retest results that appear to be useful in assessing ego change.

THE EGO

A strong ego may be characterized in part in the following fashion. Its function is largely active rather than passive. That is to say, it is neither helplessly compelled to discharge tensions emanating from the id, superego, and its own components, such as ego interests, nor is it compelled to maintain exhausting expenditures of its energies in countercathexis against these tensions. Instead, the ego freely and effectively uses its energies to control, defend against, modify, and discharge these tensions in accordance with current adaptive, reality-oriented pursuits (Rapaport, 1953b). In this mode

First published in the *Journal of Projective Techniques,* 22: 102-109, 1958.

of operation, secondary process typically predominates over primary process (Freud, 1900; Rapaport, 1951b), or, in related terms, the reality principle prevails over the pleasure principle (Freud, 1911b; Hartmann, 1956). This implies effective working of the ego's synthetic or organizing function (Hartmann, 1950; Nunberg, 1931; Prelinger, 1958) and relative autonomy of ego functions from instinctual drives (Hartmann, 1939; Rapaport, 1951a). Affects are tamed (Fenichel, 1941a; Freud, 1926; Rapaport, 1953a; Schur, 1953): they operate as signals within the ego; neither do they repeat traumatic situations nor are they conspicuous by their absence; they are varied and enter into complex reactions. At the same time, in so-called regressions in service of the ego, the primary-process modes of function are used by the ego to enhance creative and adaptive efforts of various sorts (Hartmann, 1939; Kris, 1952; Schafer, this volume, Chapter 6). For the most part, however, the predominant ego mechanisms are not archaic, overriding introjective and projective ones. Associated with this last factor (though instinctual and other factors are also crucial here), a clear distinction is maintained between self-representations and object representations (Federn, 1952; Jacobson, 1954).[1] And, finally, the strong ego deals directly and effectively with psychosocial problems peculiar to the current developmental phase in the life history of the person, be he five, 15, or 50 (Erikson, 1950a, 1950b).

A BRIEF RETEST COMPARISON

With these considerations in mind, let us study now, as an example, the response given to Card V of the Rorschach test by a 15-year-old boy with many years of psychiatric treatment and two other testings behind him: "It looks like a collision between three jackrabbits." In the inquiry he explained further: "The center one was sort of running along and one came from either side and ran into him, all mashing into one body." Further questioning brought out the form determi-

---

[1] See also Jacobson's more recent work (1964).

nant, and then the patient added: "I've seen them running along the prairie at night and it looks almost that color; they are often dark because it is at night. The shadows play tricks on your eyes." A year and a half later, he gave a more familiar version of this response to Card V: "Two rabbits that ran head on into each other." It is easy to say simply that in the second testing schizophrenic forms of thought disorder have disappeared from this response. But how would we characterize in more detail the implied changes within the ego? What hypotheses might we set up?

First, we might think of sharper differentiation between self-representation and object representation. Initially, the rabbits were "all mashing into one body"—a type of response strongly suggesting inner experience of losing the differentiation of these representations. Where his self ends and the other person begins is obscured. With the help of other data on this patient, it would not be too speculative to hypothesize further that on some level he relates himself to the center rabbit and his parents to the two side rabbits barging into him and as much losing themselves in him as he is lost in them.

Second, from the standpoint of activity versus passivity of the ego, in the first version of this response the suggested subjective experience is one of passively being invaded and losing boundaries; in the second, there is a sense of active conflict and engagement. In the second version there is also a suggestion of his having removed himself enough from the conflict and having kept enough distance from it to see the parents clashing: that is, he got himself out of the way and could now recognize external conflict. In addition, the immobilized destruction of the presumed identification figure in the first version implies helplessness of the ego before a destructive superego; in the second version we see directed, assertive action and, by implication, a degree of containment of the superego. In this detachment and objectification, as well as in the sense of active participation in both colliding and getting out of the way, the activity of the ego appears to be significantly enhanced.

Third, we might consider the response in the first record from the standpoint of its relatively direct representation of archaic fantasy in consciousness; this immediately suggests pathological weakness of defense. In the second record the form of the response is one not unusual in neurotic and apparently normal records, and I think particularly in the records of adolescents and young adults. Not only might we hypothesize, therefore, that defense is better established, but fourth, in terms of psychosocial level of development, we might emphasize a more vital and adaptive adolescent mode of experiencing and expressing conflict. Note, however, that in the content we still have only innocuous rabbits rather than the more frequently seen massive, powerful animals. Fifth, sixth, and seventh, we might stress three conceptually closely related changes toward relatively greater autonomy of ego function from drives and affects, ascendency of secondary process over primary process, and more adequate, less arbitrary synthetic functioning, all three contributing to improved reality testing.

Eighth, genetically, the level of the ego mechanisms implied in the first version, in contrast to the second, is primarily primitive, regressive, introjective. Ninth, the threat of affective experience within the self has presumably diminished in the second record; conflict can be faced, and in the process the self and its affects need not be annihilated. And, finally, recognizing that in both responses we deal with creative productions, we might say that a regression in the service of the ego for creative and adaptive purposes has taken place more clearly in the second response; initially the creative regression was much less in the service of the ego.

The same patient, in the first testing referred to, gave this response to the upper gray on Card X: "Two unknowns holding up the top of the picture here." When asked what he meant by "two unknowns," he replied, "It was sort of a pole, post; the little blots either seem to be leaning against it or holding it up. It reminded me of that part in a Marx Brothers' movie where a cop walks up to Groucho and says, 'Are you holding up the building?' and Groucho says, 'Yes'; the cop says, 'Keep moving on!' and Groucho does and the building falls down." The patient was then asked what he meant by "holding up the top of the picture." He replied, "It looks like they were holding up a post but you just don't go around holding up posts, so I thought they were holding up the picture." To this explanation he added the comment: "Weird logic!" When asked again about calling the figures "unknowns," he replied, "They don't hold the shape of any animal I know of but they were animals to me because they were holding up the posts. I don't know where to begin to explain it, either forwards or backwards." In the second testing he simply said, "Two little animals trying to hold up a post."

Now, in the initial version of this response we find striking impairment of synthetic functioning among other functions of the ego; we see this in the reference to the two unknowns, in the circularity of reasoning about their being animals, and in his subjective feeling of confusion and inability to pin down the causal sequence within the response.

In terms of developmental level of functioning, a very early and predominantly passive ego state is implied. In fact, it is more than likely that inquiry presupposed the patient's having been responding on a higher level of thought organization than was the case; his subsequent confusion strongly suggests that his response was initially global, syncretic, and passive in nature. He nevertheless actively tried to establish synthesis in his reasoning that you just don't go around holding up posts so the creatures must be holding up the picture, but this activity of the ego we may assume to have been enforced by a more basic passivity, which had created his difficulty to begin with and which then sustained it in enforced, arbitrary attempts at organization. It is nevertheless striking that he spontaneously added "Weird logic!" after this explanation, indicating some capacity to shift, rather abruptly, to a higher level of psychic functioning and to take some distance, although in the next verbalization, about why they are animals, he shifted right back to the more archaic level.

His association to Groucho Marx and the collapse of the
building has several points of interest, among which I shall
mention only the reference to an imminent sense of collapse
stimulated by the picture (a not unusual response to it), representing an archaic fear that probably triggered off his
forced synthetic efforts. The association has strong implications of feelings of ego passivity in that there is a little self
(and ego) holding up a huge, alien, and threatening structure and compelled to remain in this immobilized position
rather than being freely mobile with its energies. This "structure" refers perhaps to the rest of his personality and to that
with which his personality merges—his parents' personalities.
At the same time, of course, the anecdote suggestively communicates to the therapist, through the tester, that he respect
the patient's fragility and not, like the cop, push him along
too fast.

In the second version of the response the animals are simply
trying to hold up a post. The self-representation remains little and straining, or, in other words, not powerful or effective, just like the persisting rabbits on Card V, but for the
most part the regressive movement, the blurring of and es-
trangement from the self, and the arbitrarily synthesizing,
basically passive mode of ego function are only slightly indicated.

An examination of the score changes from the first to the
second testing supports these hypotheses—and that is all they
can be at this point: hypotheses. The number of responses
was almost the same in the two records: 20 and 24 respectively. However, the number of Human-Movement responses increased from two to six, the color responses increased from
two arbitrary Form-Color responses and one Color-Form response to four appropriate Form-Color responses and three
Color-Form responses. In the second testing, shading responses began to be adequately represented, the form level
increased from around 70% to around 90%, two fragmented, Do-type responses disappeared, and the extended

form percent which was close to 100% initially was now in a more optimal position around 90%.[2] All of these score changes point in the direction of more active ego function, better differentiation of the self from the outside world, increased autonomy of the ego for creative and adaptive tasks, improved stability of defense, enhanced capacity for creative regression in the service of the ego, significant vitalization and/or taming of affective experience (including anxiety). Altogether one might speak of a more consistently maintained, higher level of ego function and a significant decrease in adaptation-impairing, compulsory countercathectic expenditure of the ego's energies. That the patient was still severely ill was apparent clinically and from an examination of the results of the battery of tests readministered to him, but there was ample evidence in both respects that significant change within his ego in the direction of greater strength had taken place.

REGRESSION IN THE SERVICE OF THE EGO

I would like particularly to emphasize the concept of *regression in the service of the ego,* as discussed extensively by Kris (1952) in a variety of areas pertaining to creativity, and as discussed by Holt (1954), Bellak (1954), and myself (1954) in regard to responses to projective tests. I believe it may prove to be a most valuable concept for assessing personality change through projective-test results as well as therapy. Elsewhere I have tried to show that freedom for regression in the service of the ego involves a number of major components relevant to ego maturity and strength: I refer to absence of extreme severity and archaic operation of the superego, optimal flexibility of defenses, secure and clear affect signals, relatively well-defined self and identity with limited fear of losing identity and the boundaries and inner coherence of the self, a sound basis of trust in interpersonal relationships and in one's self, an adequate mastery of early traumata, and

[2] See Rapaport, Gill, and Schafer (1945-1946) for scoring criteria.

a feeling that one's being and productions occupy a meaning-ful place in some community and will continue to do so. Be-cause it appears that regression in the service of the ego is in-dispensable for imaginative, self-expressive responses to pro-jective tests, viewed here as creative tasks, the assessment of retest results in the light of freedom for such regression has implications for all of these ego factors. Such an assessment is also useful in identifying the patient's propaganda pro or con therapy and the therapist that stems from his current transference conflicts. This difficult and important distinction is one well worth considerable discussion by itself at another time.

ADAPTIVE AND DEFENSIVE SUCCESS AND FAILURE

Also in another place, under the heading of indications of adaptive and defensive success and failure, I have discussed six formal and attitudinal aspects of the Rorschach record pertinent to the problem of assessing the capacity for ego-reg-ulated regressive movement for the sake of creative adapta-tion (Schafer, 1954). These criteria are the emotional tone of the record, the achievement of specific and articulated form, the achievement of accurate form, moderation and bal-ance of thematic emphasis, integration of the formal, content, and emotional aspects of responses, and the absence of thought disorder. A seventh aspect we may classify as modera-tion and balance of score patterns, provided that we leave fairly wide limits for individual variation within the essential-ly normal range. I believe these same criteria may be applied, with appropriate modifications and translations, to the study of TAT material and to some extent to intelligence-test re-sults.[3]

[3] E.g., in intelligence test results, the achievement of articulated problem-solving attempts, accuracy of problem-solving methods and solutions, mainten-ance of appropriate and varied emotional tone, absence of extreme score de-viation on the subtests, absence of thought disorder. Thematic moderation and balance, and integration of the various response aspects, would not be easily defined for intelligence-test results.

While all these aspects are of equal importance, I would like to single out here the emotional tone of the record. This affective and attitudinal aspect is not ordinarily conceptualized as an essential part of the test responses, yet it is of the greatest diagnostic significance. It has major implications for strength and stability of ego controls and the maintenance of self boundaries, and thereby for the answers to questions concerning acuteness of pathological condition, need for hospitalization, and urgency of therapeutic intervention. To draw an extreme contrast, at one pole is the patient who sees in the Rorschach test two people embracing, concludes that they are having intercourse, grows angry and suspicious because the test is obviously getting at sex, slams the card down, paces the office, and refuses to respond further to that card or to the test as a whole; and at the other pole is the patient who sees the same two persons embracing, leaves the response at that level of content development, responds to it with some mild pleasure or interest or surprise, and then continues giving responses more or less as usual. The attitudinal and affective factor must not, however, be given more weight than the other factors.

Attention to these seven formal and attitudinal aspects of the record plays a vital part in retest analysis. In retests, we see a great variety of content newly emphasized, re-emphasized, or even further emphasized. This content ordinarily suggests many pathological tensions. If we apply these seven factors as a frame of reference, however, we are in a position to estimate how modified and how workable an ego structure of a particular sort is, that is, how well structured and active the ego now is to contend with these tensions. Each patient after therapy will still show distinctive balances of emphasis on the various pregenital drive components, distinctive foci and diffusion trends in identity formation, distinctive goals and ideal images, and the like. The seven criteria may be applied irrespective of specific contents.

METHODOLOGICAL REMARKS

In the last section of this discussion I will consider some general and some specific methodological problems involved in using retests in a research project to assess personality change.

First of all, independent judges must be used to establish reliability of interpretation. Second, blind analysis of the test protocols is required to avoid contaminated interpretations. By "blind" I mean the judge should be ignorant of the clinical history and of the nature and course of therapy. The patient's age, sex, and socioeconomic, religious, educational, occupational, and familial background should, however, be known.

Third, while certain gains in objectivity would accrue from the judge's not knowing which set of test records was the first and which the second, this scientific precaution would also unduly obscure significant trends in the data. I refer to the importance of recognizing phases of change in the course of therapy. Not all patients will be considered to have fully completed their therapy at the time of retesting. They may consequently be retested during a transitional phase. Repeated retests often show such sequences as proceeding from impulsiveness through inhibition to relative flexibility of controls and defenses; from inhibition through impulsiveness to relative flexibility; from apathy through wild autism to improved, active reality testing; from hypomania through depression to more stabilized affect; and so on. As phases in a sequence, the intermediate states mentioned might be viewed as significant changes toward more adequate ego functioning, while considered by themselves or in random order these intermediate states might be viewed too narrowly and therefore misleadingly.

I include here the recommendation that the patient be compared with himself, and not only compared or averaged with other persons before therapy and then after therapy. An increase or decrease in the incidence of Color-Form responses, for example, will have different significance depending on its initial quantity and its context of M, F+%, R, etc. The appearance of oral content or an increase of it may signify a noteworthy liberation within the person or a noteworthy regression, again depending in part on the original and subsequent matrices. Autistic trends may continue to appear in the record of a borderline or fully schizophrenic patient on retesting even though the formal scores and the behavioral and emotional aspects of the records indicate that the patient's ego has matured and stabilized to a significant degree. The rationale of this finding, I believe, has yet to be worked out.

Also relevant to this point are the transitional forms of test response, such as implicit or blocked M's and FC's in the Rorschach test. While not scored, they indicate waxing or waning ego resources. Noteworthy too here are forced and artificial responses such as movement or color impressions without conceptual substance or TAT stories that bear down hard on empathic understanding or unashamedly elaborate pathology or are ever so frankly autobiographical. Whether transitional or forced, all these retest patterns may be best interpreted if we know the point from which the patient started. Again, we must compare the patient with himself and should know the serial order of the test protocols. Incidentally, it is so likely these days that patients are on tranquilizers during the first testing and off them during the second, that care must be taken to try to control for this factor.

Fourth, in addition to emphasizing the important implications of direction of change within the same patient's protocols, I would also emphasize a quantitative factor, namely, that significant ego changes are often indicated only in relatively small score changes or thematic changes. If test protocols are subjected only to interindividual comparisons, the scope of these changes may be underestimated. A fresh look at our scale of change is necessary. For example, the appearance in a second Rorschach record of certain hitherto absent determinants, such as color or human movement, even if those determinants are used only once or twice, may indicate the be-

ginning of a major revolution in that patient's psychic econ-
omy. In contrast, an increase of one or two, where to begin
with there were six or eight movements or colors, means very
little. Likewise, the disappearance of one M— or one contamination is far more significant than a decrease from four of
these to three. A logarithmlike function might best describe
these relations.

Fifth, the research unit should be interpretations and not
scores or theme counts. Only then may we continue to work
in context, which is to say, work with clinical data clinically.
Scores, content, sequence, attitudes, behavior, and style of
verbalization must all feed into the interpretations. Any one
of these by itself is not a reliable, specific, and hierarchically
localized indicator. Moreover, the interpretations should deal
with specific personality characteristics and should conceptualize the direction of change and estimate the quantity of
change on a gross scale. Retest interpretations should not initially be couched in such global terms as "improved," "unimproved," or "worse," for these are second-order inferences
based on a synthesis of inferred changes and are subject to
many as yet scientifically unfounded conceptions of what is
better than what.

Sixth, any attempt to establish the part played by therapy
in observed changes must include control groups of either
comparable patients who have not been treated or comparable patients treated by other techniques. In the retest records of young patients, for example, we may find changes
that reflect developmental advances occurring relatively independent of therapy. In the retest records of patients who
initially had suffered acute decompensations of relatively adequate adjustments, we may find changes that reflect spontaneous "sealing-over" processes and not therapeutic intervention. Where hospitalization or some other drastic change
in life circumstances accompanies the beginning and contin-
uation of therapy, the retests may reflect changes due primarily to these major modifications of the patient's social field of
forces.

Seventh, it is important to assess changes in the patient's attempts at relatively pure secondary-process functioning, as brought out by intelligence tests particularly. Significant leads will be found regarding the steady availability of relatively free ego energy and the autonomy of ego function from conflict. A well-ordered set of Wechsler Adult Intelligence Scale retest results counts a great deal when the initial scores, verbalizations, and modes of problem solving were disordered.

Eighth, I will mention the value of regarding practice effects in retests as possibly significant indicators of personality change. Severely ill patients especially are by no means likely to show clear-cut practice effects. Often the second testing shows an astonishing lack of such effect. Shock reactions in the repeat Rorschach test and TAT may persist. Shock may even appear for the first time in the retesting, reflecting further encroachment of illness, therapeutic weakening of denials, repressions, and isolations, or emergence from a relatively affectless schizophrenic state. Similarly, insight into Arithmetic, Object Assembly, and similar items in the Wechsler may appear in some retests but may be lost in others.

Ninth and last, though obvious, the quality of data and judges can hardly be overemphasized. Good formal design will be of little help when inexperienced psychiatric residents and graduate students are relatively independently gathering the therapeutic and test data and processing them. The empirical study of personality changes demands a high order of conceptual and clinical sophistication if it is to contribute, as it should, to our theories of therapy, psychopathology, and personality development.

6

REGRESSION IN THE SERVICE OF THE EGO: THE RELEVANCE OF A PSYCHOANALYTIC CONCEPT FOR PERSONALITY ASSESSMENT

The psychoanalytic concept *regression* is by now well-known in clinical psychology and personality theory. Freud (1900) initially introduced and elaborated it to help account for dream phenomena, but later extended and revised its application to help account for neurotic and psychotic psychopathology and the disruption of infantile and adolescent development. By and large this usage of the concept has remained dominant. For this reason the mental mechanism *regression* almost inevitably carries conflictful or ominous implications in our minds. The same is true for the other mental mechanisms, such as projection, denial, and intellectualization. In recent decades, however, as the psychoanalytic theory of the ego has developed, more attention has been paid to how mental mechanisms also may serve adaptive ends. Even regression has begun to be viewed in this light; the result has been the introduction by Ernst Kris (1952) of the concept *regression in the service of the ego*. It is on this specific development in psychoanalytic thought that I will concentrate in this discussion. I will explore the value of this concept in personality-assessment research, or what has been called "the assessment of human motives."

It must be recognized first that the assessment of human

First published in *Assessment of Human Motives*, ed. G. Lindzey. New York: Holt, Rinehart and Winston, 1958, pp. 119-148. Reprinted here with the kind permission of the publishers.

motives requires simultaneous assessment of the psychic structures which form, channel, and obstruct motives. Some of these structures, such as well-established defenses, are themselves motives if considered from a certain point of view, while others, such as well-established abstract concepts and patterns of motor coordination, have less motivational character. In either situation, however, a structure may be said to be characterized by the following five features: (1) a slow rate of change; (2) relative autonomy of a primary or secondary nature from instinctual drives;[1] (3) a high degree of automatization as one manifestation of this relative autonomy—that is, structures take on a tool or means character and are not primarily determined in their course by current conflict or adaptive demands on the organism; rather, current internal and external pressures ordinarily merely trigger the action of these structures; (4) being created not entirely by the person but being acquired by him in part through learning from and identifying with the family and larger community; these experiences steadily transmit to and sustain in the developing person traditional structures of experience and action with adaptive (survival) value; (5) being steadily and preferentially available and not being created anew on each occasion of stimulation. Psychic structures are therefore economical as regards energy expenditure in functioning. Concepts and skills, too, are structures in all the aspects defined above, and

[1] In recent years psychoanalytic writers have emphasized that the ego must not be thought of as developing out of the id in the course of development; rather, id and ego develop simultaneously out of an originally undifferentiated matrix and they mutually influence and define each other (Hartmann, Kris, and Lowenstein, 1946). Rudiments of ego function and structure, such as learning ability, exist from the beginning, if only as potentialities; the sensory apparatus and sensory and discharge thresholds are also given ego rudiments. Ego functions are not necessarily outgrowths of conflict. In other words, some ego processes have primary autonomy, in contrast to structures which are derived from conflict, which have more or less secondary autonomy. The latter have attained relative independence from conflict during development and become institutions in their own right, and function without being specifically attached to particular drives or conflicts. Many character traits, values, and sublimations are examples of personality characteristics with relative secondary autonomy.

there can be no question of their economic value in behavioral functioning. For assessment purposes, as for therapeutic purposes, we must therefore understand how psychic structures develop and what the rules of their operation are. The same motive operating under different structural conditions is experienced differently by the subject and has different manifestations and different consequences. The concept *regression in the service of the ego* therefore merits discussion in this connection because it clarifies the rules by which psychic structures operate.

One might come to the relevance of *regression in the service of the ego* for personality assessment in a second way. The assessment of human motives requires that we bring to bear the considerations concerning biological and social adaptation first formulated comprehensively within the framework of psychoanalytic theory by Hartmann (1939) and presented in somewhat different terms by Erikson (1950a). These formulations emphasize in one respect the study of how motives fit in with, are modified by, and modify organism-environment relations. We cannot understand motives simply from the point of view of instinctual drives, intrapsychic conflict, and maturation. In fact, we cannot fully understand drives, conflict, and maturation without a simultaneous consideration of the adaptive problems and supports of the organism in its environment, and the mechanisms available to it in meeting these problems. Here again *regression in the service of the ego* enters, now as an important adaptive process. In the psychoanalytic literature, *regression in the service of the ego* has been applied in more or less detail to develop our understanding of wit and humor, artistic creativity and the audience's response to it, productive fantasy and imaginative processes, problem solving, sleeping and dreaming, capacity for orgastic experience, ego-building identifications, motherliness, empathy, intimacy and love, and the therapeutic process, including the hypnotic process and hypnotic state. A concept of such wide and central applicability to human adaptation merits the fullest possible consideration in a discussion devoted to problems of assessment.

A third way of introducing the relevance of this concept—a more immediate and circumscribed way—is to recognize that assessment of motives usually includes the use of projective techniques, and that in understanding the processes whereby these techniques are projective, that is, self-revealing in depth, *regression in the service of the ego* appears to occupy an important place. This place has previously been discussed by Holt (1954), Bellak (1954), and me (1954).

In what follows I plan, first, to offer a general definition of this concept, with illustrations; second, with special reference to art and the comic, to describe the reversal of this regressive process and its culmination in progressive phases in which the products of the regressive movement are elaborated and synthesized; third, to outline conditions that foster and hamper this process; fourth, to consider problems of individual variation; fifth, to sketch, with the help of illustrative test material, the application of this concept to the understanding of responses to several widely used psychological tests and to the understanding of the process of interpreting these responses; and sixth, to mention some implications of the entire discussion for personality-assessment research. In all, this presentation will amount to no more than a preliminary synthesis and illustration of concepts.[2] Such a synthesis is the only basis for formulating the new and more penetrating hypotheses which we need to integrate personality research with psychoanalytic theory. My formulations, above and below, draw heavily on the work of Kris (1952), Hartmann (1939, 1950), Rapaport (1950a, 1951a, 1951b, 1951c, 1953a, 1953b, 1957), and Erikson (1950a, 1950b, 1956), and, of course, Freud (1900, 1905, 1907, 1915, 1921, 1923).

[2] I will not attempt here a systematic metapsychological presentation of the concept, that is, one which defines its dynamic, economic, and structural referents (and also, following a discussion of metapsychological analysis by Rapaport and Gill [1959], its genetic and adaptive referents). These three—or five—metapsychological points of view are, however, represented in many details of my discussion.

REGRESSION IN THE SERVICE OF THE EGO: DEFINITIONS

Regression in the service of the ego is a partial, temporary, controlled lowering of the level of psychic functioning to promote adaptation. It promotes adaptation by maintaining, restoring, or improving inner balance and organization, interpersonal relations, and work. It is a process which increases the person's access to preconscious and unconscious contents, without a thoroughgoing sexualization or aggressivization of major ego functions, and therefore without disruptive anxiety and guilt. In other words, the primary and secondary (relative) autonomy of higher ego functions is not impaired; the encroachment of id tendencies is circumscribed. The process implies central controlling functions in the ego which may suspend some other functions, such as defensive functions and logical functions, and may emphasize genetically primitive mechanisms, such as projection and introjection.

A second definition is immediately called for, that of *level of psychic functioning*. For this definition we must consider the distinction introduced by Freud between the primary process and the secondary process. The primary process, which is genetically and formally the more primitive, operates with unneutralized drive energies, and its regulative principle is tension reduction (the pleasure principle); it strives toward immediate discharge of energy accumulations by a direct route and through the mechanisms of displacement, condensation, substitute formation, and symbolization. The secondary process operates by the principle of least effort; its energies are relatively neutralized, i.e., relatively bound in motives and structures of a highly socialized nature, and freely available for whichever ego activities of the moment may require energic support; it is oriented toward objective reality; it follows the safest course toward the sought-for object in reality, using delays of impulse, detours, and experimental action in thought, until the suitable object and modes of action have been found.

The contrast between primary process and secondary process may be detailed further. *Thinking*, under the domination of the primary process, tends to be unreflective, timeless, and concrete; under the domination of the secondary process, thinking is reflective, shows time perspective, and uses abstract concepts corresponding to reality relations. Concerning *memory* in particular, domination by the primary process means that available memories are organized around the imperative drive or drives, while other memories, not relevant to immediate drive pressures, are unavailable; the contrast to this is the conceptual and reality-oriented organization of memories and their free availability, depending on the needs of the real—external as well as internal—situation. Concerning *perception*, the contrast is one of drive selectivity and organization, disregard of total external context, and diffuse, physiognomic, and animistic formal characteristics on the primary side, and, on the secondary side, adaptive selectivity and organization, boundness by objective context, and articulated, stable formal characteristics. From the standpoint of *affects*, primary process involves diffuse, unmodulated affects and affect storms limited in their variability, while secondary process involves articulated, varied, and subtly blended affects. From the standpoint of *motility*, primary-process domination implies rapid spilling over into action and participation, and often grossness of action (as in convulsive laughter), while secondary-process domination implies restrained and modulated motility (as in the smile or the free laugh). Looked at from the standpoint of the *self*, primary-process functioning tends to eliminate the boundaries and inner coherence of the self so that what is thought and what is real are confused, the wish is equivalent to the deed, fantasies are events, and past ego states are present, contradictory selves; secondary-process functioning maintains the boundaries and coherence of the self in these respects. From the standpoint of *defense*, the contrast is one of weakness (consciousness overwhelmed by normally unconscious impulses, affects, and fantasies) versus strength. From the standpoint of the *ego ideal*, the contrast is one of megalomanic, unattainable, infantile conceptions versus conceptions relatively more regulated by reality testing or realistic considerations of the possible rather than the exalted. From the standpoint of the *superego,* the contrast is one of archaic severity versus closeness to the ego. From the standpoint of the *ego as a whole,* the contrast is one of passivity versus activity, respectively, discharge of impulse occurring relatively independently of the ego, or the ego being unable to modify the damming up of impulses by its counter-cathectic energy distributions, versus impulses being discharged by means of the ego's controlling and executive apparatuses or being merely postponed in their discharge by controlling and defensive ego functions (Rapaport, 1953b).

In psychoanalytic discussions the contrasts listed above have often been presented in terms of id versus ego or the system Unconscious versus the systems Preconscious and Conscious. They have been stressed in the study of such phenomena as dreams; extreme fatigue; states of emotional excitement; schizophrenia; altered states of consciousness such as fugues, amnesias, intoxications, and deliria; preliterate cultures; and the behavior of the infant and young child. Werner (1948) has discussed many of these contrasts from a related point of view, and Piaget's (1928, 1929, 1930, 1932) studies are particularly relevant. Obviously, the contrasts drawn represent ideal polar positions. Any specific behavior must be assessed in terms of its relative position with respect to these poles or in terms of the particular admixture of primary and secondary processes in it. There are all degrees of transition.

To return to *regression in the service of the ego,* it refers, then, to the ego's permitting relatively free play to the primary process in order to accomplish its adaptive tasks. The ego detours through regression toward adaptation. It is warranted to speak here of *regression* in so far as primary process or its close derivatives, normally warded off, are allowed a place in conscious experience; and it is warranted to speak of the process being *in the service of the ego* in so far as the regression serves ego interests (such as being creative or empathic), is relatively easily reversible, and is amenable to productive working over by the ego in terms of its adaptive pursuits.

CREATION OF ART AND THE COMIC

Taking as his starting points comments by Freud on daydreams and creative writing (1907), and on wit in its relation to the unconscious (1905), Kris has discussed at some length the operation of regression in the service of the ego in artistic creativity and in wit and humor. In the so-called inspirational phase of creativity, the artist is more or less immersed in relatively archaic content and archaic, less stable modes of experience. That is to say, ego structures concerned with organized speech, perception, and movement which operate relatively automatically in higher stages of organization may lose their automatized quality and decompose, as it were, into simpler, cruder, and by now strange or startling elements. In the process of deautomatization the raw components of sensory, verbal, and motoric experience may be partially rediscovered. The wit or joke maker may undergo similar changes in moving regressively toward nonsense in word, metaphor, or gesture.[3]

With regard to art and the comic, however, observation makes it obvious that a subsequent or alternating progressive or elaborational phase is crucial to an adequate end result, which is to say that the regressive process is reversed and the yield of the regressive process is subjected to critical scrutiny, selection, and synthesis. In the end, the regressive yield is shaped into a conceptually and affectively ordered statement or communication that effectively integrates both the experience and intent of the artist or wit and the stringencies of the current reality to which he offers his product. The artist who has first withdrawn into working with introjects, fantasy, and immature modes of experience, now returns to a real and mature relation with others, his audience. In his work he repro-

---

[3] In some instances, as in orgastic discharge, the controlled regression involves yielding to biological automatisms; these are not to be confused with psychic automatizations within the ego.

jects these introjects with a new and enhanced reality. The successful work of art and the joke are adapted to current situations and to tradition, from both of which they derive many of their forms and materials. In part, the contrast between the phase of inspiration and elaboration is that between individualized self-searching and self-expression on the one hand, and craft and tradition on the other. With regard to the joke, a similar process is evident in the necessity of introducing sense into nonsense, as Freud long ago pointed out, thereby eliciting an approving response from others, and appeasing the ego's demand for rationality and the superego's demand for moral restraint.

PSYCHOLOGICAL DETERMINANTS OF REGRESSION IN THE SERVICE OF THE EGO

What are some of the major conditions favoring and hampering artistic and comic regression in the service of the ego? The factors to be mentioned are not sharply distinguished from one another. To a great extent they represent somewhat different points of view applied to the same observations. It will be advantageous, however, to mention these factors separately because of their individual connections to a variety of psychoanalytic concepts.

The hampering conditions appear to center chiefly around the unconscious significances of this regressive process. Psychoanalytic study, according to Kris's summary, shows the process to have such prominent unconscious meanings as passivity, sinful and defiant transgression, and magically potent destructiveness toward authority and whatever persons and things are involved, be they external or internalized, real or fantasied. Kris's extensive discussions of society's image of the artist through history, of the artist's image of himself as artist, and of the meanings of schizophrenic art, develop these unconscious meanings clearly. The artist in one form or another has been traditionally linked to the divine on the one hand (e.g., Plato's "divine madness") and on the other to the devil and to rebellion against the divine. These links were literal and explicit in ancient times and are implicit in the Bohemian and crackpot stereotype of the artist in current times. These divine and devilish fantasies the artist shares with his audience and in so doing often provides behavioral support for them.

Image magic and word magic, historically and genetically related to ritual and effigy, are also involved in unconscious fantasy about creating. In image and word magic, such as we observe in children's play and fantasy, the intent is to transform the world and not to create an internal experience in the mind of a specific sort. Thus, not only does the artist engage in forbidden investigation and exhibitions in his work; he omnipotently controls, manipulates, and destroys by rendition, simplification, distortion, or transformation—by taking over the object, making it his own, and attaining independence from it. The experience of inspiration itself appears to be fantasied as one of passive, feminine receptiveness, both with respect to the father (divine inspiration of old) and the nursing mother (in the blissful feelings of tension reduction, of being filled with supplies from without). Bergler (1944, 1945) has emphasized the attempt to establish psychic autarchy in this process; unconsciously, carrying out the process within oneself means rejecting and destroying the hated mother. Levey (1939, 1940) and Sharpe (1935) have stressed the reparative aspects of the process—its protecting or restoring the mother and the infantile union with her. The artist's reprojection of the object with enhanced reality in his artistic product serves the reparative function.

In addition, creative fantasy derives not only from childhood play but in large measure from early masturbatory fantasy, with its closeness to action and discharge. In its more neutralized aspects fantasy includes the interposing of organizing and delaying factors in the mental experience. These organizing and delaying factors, together with the representation of relatively socialized tendencies in the motivational hierarchy, are aspects of neutralization (delibidinization and deaggressivization) of the energies involved in creative fantasy as opposed to asocial daydreaming or too starkly self-revealing "creative" outpourings. Thus, if relatively unneutralized, creative fantasy may also revive or express conflict over masturbation.

Therefore, even though in the service of the ego, that is, fulfilling an adaptive task, the regressive process in creativity may be heavily burdened by conflict in so far as anxiety and guilt attach to passivity, femininity, masturbation, destructiveness, maternal rejection, and other tabooed impulses and acts. In fact, the artist, like the wit, has been shown to be dependent on the favorable response of his audience to alleviate his guilt, even if that audience is not the public at large but one or two selected figures in reality or fantasy. The artist's very emphasis on inspiration appears to alleviate anxiety and guilt by externalizing responsibility for the process and its results: there is an outside source who is responsible—the divine, the devil, the muse, opium, alcohol, nature, etc.

On its part, the audience derives gratification through similar regressive and progressive processes within itself. To a significant extent, the audience relies on the artist or joke maker as an external source of responsibility for its pleasure while unconsciously identifying with him. As in the artist, there occurs an intermingling of active and passive ego function.

In brief, it may be said that the variety of dangers involved emanate from the very motives and fantasies that empower creative work. The dangers are reductions of the ego's relative autonomy from the id, disturbances of the complex balance between active and passive ego function, and the ego's greater vulnerability to superego condemnation. The preceding discussion has focused on the creative process in the artist and wit; a similar treatment of the phenomena of empathy, intimacy, love, therapeutic involvement, etc., is, of course, necessary and appears to be feasible.

Conditions favoring *regression in the service of the ego* are numerous. Six *overlapping* factors will be mentioned. These factors obviously relate to existing definitions of ego strength (Fenichel, 1938) and neutralization of libidinal or aggressive energies (Erikson, 1956; Hartmann, 1939, 1950; Kris, 1952; Rapaport, 1951b, 1957), and to discussions of factors fostering healthy personality development and maturity (Erikson, 1950a, 1950b; Olden, 1953; Sullivan, 1947).

First, there is required the presence of *a well-developed set of affect signals*. The person must be relatively secure in his sense of being in touch with his feelings. Here the schizophrenic and the rigid obsessive are hampered. Freud (1926) has described how the ego depends on anxiety signals in order to regulate its defensive and adaptive expenditures of its energy. Actually, we depend on a variety of affect signals all the time. As for *regression in the service of the ego,* when the regressive process threatens to get out of hand, that is, when it comes too close to drives, affects, and fantasies not assimilable in consciousness, appropriate signals will trigger the search for defensive disguise of content or reversal of the entire process. Confidence in these signals makes it safe to regress.

A second condition is *a secure sense of self,* and, more broadly, a well-established ego identity. The considerations of Erikson (1956) and Federn (1952) are particularly relevant here. Moving closer to primary-process domination of functioning means not only that the boundary between id and ego suffers. In orgastic experience and in freedom to sleep and dream, this phenomenon—or capacity—is particularly evident. Anxiety over potential loss of self is central to what is often termed instinctual threat or superego threat. Where there is a secure sense of self and a stable identity, one may tolerate momentary blurring or loss of their boundaries and coherence. Where this security is weak or absent, one must ridgidly maintain self-boundaries and organization and a self-definition of a particular sort for fear of having nothing otherwise. The schizophrenic's fear of intimacy conspicuously involves a fear of disintegrating, exploding, being totally engulfed, or otherwise losing an already tenuous and fluid self-boundary and inner organization.

A third factor facilitating controlled creative regression is a *relative mastery of early traumata*. With this mastery, the person may feel free to have subjective experiences which imply in certain respects how it was once to have been a child and to have felt feminine, receptive, helpless, omnipotent, and generally fluid in internal state and object relations. In fact, relative mastery of early traumata implies that the crises and crucial experiences of early development have not been sealed off from the development of the total personality but have been given a place in it and have undergone progressive transformations and working through. This is the sense of Sullivan's (1947) discussion of healthy development, as it is of Erikson's (1950b). Olden's (1953) discussion of factors hindering and facilitating adult empathy with children stresses the same point.

A fourth factor is relative *moderateness* rather than archaic severity *of superego pressures* and, in close correlation with this, relative flexibility rather than rigidity or fluidity of defenses and controls. Under favorable conditions of this sort, one may "let go," increase inner awareness, and *play* intrapsychically without severe anxiety and guilt and with some degree of pleasure. The limiting and distorting effects of guilt on self-awareness and self-experimentation may reach extreme lengths, of course.

A fifth factor is a *history of adequate trust and mutuality in interpersonal relations,* particularly in the early mother-child relation. Erikson's, Sullivan's, and Olden's discussions, among others, are again relevant. The yield of the regressive process may ultimately be communicated in some form and used in the service of promoting a relation to others (audience, intimates, children, therapist, patients); at the same time it will be internally scrutinized and judged by the ego and superego, on both of which the mother has left a basic imprint. In both respects, a background of adequate trust will support the feeling that what is produced will be empathically and tolerantly acknowledged rather than responded to with panic, withdrawal, or arbitrary punishment. And this feeling will make it safe and pleasurable to regress temporarily.

The sixth and last factor to be mentioned here is the meaningfulness to the larger community of this process that culminates in *self-awareness and personal and effective communication to others*. The need for such cultural meaningfulness has been noted by Kris in his discussion of art and much emphasized by Erikson in his discussion of the ego-identity crisis in adolescence. That is to say, following Erikson, what one has been, is, and aspires to be must be valued by at least a segment of the larger community so that one may become a certain somebody with a sense of wholeness and may preserve this wholeness to advance one's social adaptation and impact. The alternatives are dissociation, ego restriction, or negative identity (becoming all that one is not supposed to be or is most feared by the family and larger community). These alternatives represent various forms of passive ego function predominating over active ego function.

The reader will see that if the preceding propositions concerning favorable conditions were to be put in negative form they would constitute a list of hampering conditions (e.g., poorly developed affect signals, weak sense of self, or weak ego identity, etc.). This list may be added to, though it overlaps, the earlier-discussed factors potentially hampering controlled ego regression (e.g., magical meanings, masturbatory activity, shameful passivity and femininity, etc.)

The evidence does not clearly support the idea that creative artists or scientists operate under mostly facilitating conditions. It may well be that some regressive adaptations, such as those involved in direct interpersonal relations (empathy, intimacy, orgasm, therapeutic understanding, and communication), are more dependent on the facilitating conditions discussed than are others, such as artistic, scientific, and comic creativity. And this may be why the list of facilitating conditions is so much more closely tied to conceptions of healthy development and mature personality than they are to observations of gifted artists, comics, and scientists. The key question would here be, "Regression for what?" The further investigation of these suggested differences would be a valuable study in ego psychology, and it would bear on the aptness of applying the concept *regression in the service of the ego* to creative processes in general.

INDIVIDUAL VARIATION

Individual variation has not been ignored in the discussions referred to. Concerning *regression in the service of the ego* in artists, Kris (1952) emphasizes that in actuality we encounter all degrees of transition between ego strength and weakness in this process. The continuum from normal to schizophrenic creative efforts is steadily recognized. Affect signals vary in strength and controllability; anxiety and guilt may get out of hand; the sense of self may be dangerously impaired; early unassimilated traumata may be revived; severe superego and defensive countermeasures may be imposed; and severe disruption of the sense of mutuality and communication with more immediate and more remote members of the community may result. Also varying is the effectiveness of the phase of elaboration in achieving synthesis and communication. Further, we observe variability in the directness of drive representation in awareness, in specific dynamic areas being more accessible than others, in preference for acting out instead of remembering, or for regressing ideationally more in formal respects than in content respects. In this last connection, we seem to encounter formal primitivization without obvious drive representation in certain experiences of problem solving in the sciences and mathematics. Finally, individuals appear to vary in their typical level of psychic functioning: some, like borderline schizophrenics, steadily operate closer to the primary process or at least tend to fluctuate with great amplitude between the primary and secondary poles; others, like compulsives, cling rigidly and ego-restrictively to rationality and full control at all times.

We may add that variation in the typical level of psychic functioning appears to depend significantly on the ego identity of the person and what it and its community will support. For example, being an artist, a therapist, or a comic supports more controlled ego regression in certain respects than do other identities. Even within one identity the capacity for controlled ego regression varies from one time to another. We may also add that the degree to which the regressive process is voluntary and controlled varies. A regression originally precariously in the service of the ego may go too far and culminate in pathological regression, and only subsequently may the ego show resiliency and impress the regressive experience into its service. There is even reason to believe that art and wit are often used to recover from or stave off pathological regressive experiences involving large segments of the personality, and that organizational stringencies in work and in the particular medium involved help restore internal organization.

IMPLICATIONS FOR TEST ANALYSIS

Thus far we have defined *regression in the service of the ego,* especially with reference to the primary and secondary processes, we have sketched its place in the creation of art and the comic, and noted the importance of subsequent or alternating elaborative phases, and we have considered psychological conditions that foster and hamper controlled ego regression as well as aspects of individual variation in controlled and uncontrolled regressive experience. What now is the pertinence of these psychoanalytic observations and inferences for the use of tests in personality assessment? First, in using psychological tests we should assess the range and security of *regression in the service of the ego* in each individual. To do this we need a battery of tests, tests varying in their degree of structure and demands for secondary-process functioning. Projective tests like the Thematic Apperception Test and especially the Rorschach test, being relatively unstructured and personalized, appear to require more regression in the service

of the ego, more access to and use of the primary process, than
a test like an intelligence test. In these projective tests we require the subject to create something—an image or a fantasy.
We give him materials or a medium in which to work, but he
is in many respects put in the position of the creative artist
and must find within himself forms of experience and contents
to elaborate a response. To have free access to a wide range of
forms and contents, *regression in the service of the ego* is required; specifically, an enlargement of awareness, a degree of
blurring of the distinction between inner and outer, a relaxation of defense, an entrusting of ideas to preconscious and
unconscious elaboration, and other processes described above.
Otherwise responses will be limited to description, or, what
is not far from description, banalities. In the latter case we
observe severe restriction of the ego and little capacity to regress for adaptive purposes. The test instructions and stimuli
appear to afford the subject a considerable relief from anxiety
and guilt by giving him an opportunity to externalize responsibility for many aspects of his responses. Remember that the
artist and joke maker need audience response, tradition, and
inspirational experience to help them with the same problem.

We observe, moreover, that in the development of responses
to projective tests, progressive, elaborational phases are steadily evident. The end result—the response or story—is not normally dreamlike but more or less attuned to the reality of the
stimulus and testing situation. We hear from the subject a
comprehensible and relevant communciation about a creation
that "fits in," in terms of stimulus and situation. We find in the
subject's verbalization and affective tone established self-
awareness and self-boundaries, distance from participation,
and curious, interested, playful, and humorous expression.
When the regression goes too far and escapes the ego's service, we find fluid, overexpansive, insufficiently worked-out,
archaic material, and overparticipation. When the subject
does not re-establish the boundary between inner and outer,
he may become agitated, hostile, elated, depressed, or severe-

ly withdrawn. He lives out his responses. These phenomena we frequently observe in psychotics and some borderline psychotics.

Actually, subjects vary over a continuum in their capacity for creative regression during testing, and they vary in the typical level of functioning from which they must regress to create responses. Also, they vary in regard to the areas in which they are free to regress and in their capacity to regain distance and to elaborate and synthesize reality-attuned responses. Defensive requirements, as Bergler (1944, 1945) has pointed out with regard to the artist, may determine which forms and contents of experience are accessible, because revealing one area of depth may be possible only if it helps to conceal a more disturbing area. Thus, sexual contents may cover hostility or vice versa, passive receptive forms of experience may cover phallic-intrusive forms or vice versa, etc. To illustrate some of the above considerations, I will first present and discuss some illustrative test responses which show regression to image magic and other forms of functioning dominated by the primary process, that is, responses in which regression is not primarily in the service of higher ego functions.

Let us consider first the case of Mr. F.—19 years old, single, Jewish, with a history of violent paranoid schizophrenic manifestations for the past year and of at least transient schizophrenic manifestations for more than three years. On Card II of the Rorschach test (administered by a young woman) he responds as follows: "This looks like a, two little rabbits. These are rabbits, these black spots here, they could be bears, yeah. The red stuff shouldn't be here! It shouldn't be here! It shouldn't be here! It should be out of it!" Patient is agitated. He puts his head down on the desk. Examiner asks if there is anything else. "Nothing else." He mutters something about bleeding but does not look at card. In the inquiry he is first asked what makes them look like bears; he responds: "They are black and they are shaped like it. You know, cubs. Did you ever see cubs? I saw cubs in the Smoky Mountains National Park. I fed them. It was a lot of fun!" Patient's manner is now pleased and animated. He is then asked what he had in mind about the "red stuff": "It could be blood but I don't want it there!" Patient is again agitated. He is asked if he thought of the blood in relation to the bears or separately: "Where else could it be from but the bears! Here is the front, the face, the ears, the tails, and the paws. It looks as if they had cut their feet and it's bleeding [lower red area]. But that stuff up here [upper red]: I don't know what that is from. What could that be? I don't know. They must have cut their feet and have a nosebleed. Are you engaged?"

There is in this response sequence abundant and obvious evidence of regression to archaic modes of reasoning, image magic, participation, and loss of self-boundary (the distinction between inner and outer or between thought and percept). In addition, the disorder of verbalization evident in his redundancy indicates perceptual and/or conceptual fluidity. His reasoning about the nosebleed is based on the upper red area having a position near—though above—the nose; he follows here a primitive, concrete mode of reasoning rather than a conceptual one. He deals with the picture that he visualizes as if it were a reality situation with ominous implications, and he pronounces a verdict: the red should not be there. His intent is to transform reality and he is not having or communicating an internal experience of the mind. His earlier animation in talking about the cubs had already suggested proneness to lose distance, concreteness, and readiness for participation; while more moderate and more pleasant, that elaboration still had pathological regressive implications. His putting his head down on the desk and his later forwardness with female tester are further indications of impaired capacity for delay: affects rapidly spill over into acting.

On Rorschach Card IV one of his responses develops as follows: "This thing here [lower middle]: you want to know what this is? A person's windpipe." Asked in inquiry what made it look like that, he says: "Well, I remember seeing something like that before. You know, a chicken, a chicken's neck. I watched them murder—er—kill chickens once. They wrang the neck and chopped it off. I was sick that day, not from that, though; that didn't bother me." Again asked what made it look like a windpipe specifically: "Well, I have seen a picture of a windpipe. So, if it is real, it is a chicken's neck, but if it is a picture, which this is, it is a windpipe." Of particular significance here is his incomplete separation of what is real and what is imagined. By the end of the inquiry he has to play it both ways: there is a contamination between a concrete association and a current perception.

On Card 6 BM of the TAT, the card showing an elderly woman with her back turned to a young man, he gives this story: "Here is this guy; here is his mother. Are you ready? It is too bad you didn't know shorthand. He's just got fired again and his mother, he told his mother that and she is feeling kind of—she doesn't know what to do. He is a nice-looking guy though. He just can't hold on to a job. He is a nice guy though. He had a pretty tough break. You know what happens after that? [The patient stands and looks out window.] He doesn't let things worry him! He says, The hell with them! He doesn't care what people think! Maybe he will find himself some day! [Returns to desk at request of tester but stands at her side.] He gets away from his mother [covers his mouth with his hands] and then he will be okay. Why should I care about that guy in the picture? I have enough of my own problems! [Patient is very angry. Tester asks patient to be seated.] Am I making you nervous? Come on, you don't have to do so much writing!"

And on Card 7 BM, the card showing the heads of an elderly man and a young man, he gives this story: "[Nervous laugh.] Holy cow! Look at this character! [Nervous laugh.] Holy cow! [Nervous laugh.] I have seen this before too. Here we have a father and son, a father-son relationship here, and the son feels rather gloomy and discouraged. The old man—he has been through the mill and he is supposed to be helping the son out. He tells him not to worry but the son will have to learn for himself. He is much of a character, this guy. [Who is?] The son. This guy looks sad. Most people when they are gloomy don't look like that. He is a jerk! [Patient is angry.] This guy doesn't get anywhere! It is tough luck but he doesn't get anywhere! Two stupid characters if I ever saw them! Taking life too seriously! They should be like me: Not a worry in the world! [etc.]" The primary-process characteristics described in connection with his Rorschach responses clearly reappear here, though now in forms determined by the nature of the TAT situation. Again, the patient is not having an internal experience in the mind but is living out a real event and pronouncing verdicts, struggling after the fact to achieve distance but failing, and falling back on obviously unconvincing and inappropriate denials. Note particularly his defunct reality testing in reasoning that the young man in the second story is a jerk because he does not look the way the patient projectively decided he felt, that is, gloomy.

Consider now excerpts from the Rorschach record of a 55-year-old man, married, with several children, in acute turmoil over an infatuation with a young woman, and diagnostically in a hypomanic and paranoid state. He instantaneously responds to the first Rorschach card: "That is a pelvis. That is a pelvis to me. So you can see I am sexy-oriented [laughs] or am I?" His first reaction to Card II: "Well, my instant reaction is that this is another pelvis but they played around with this one and this has something new. Here is the female vulva, here [lower red]. These red things here are kidneys [upper red]. The open area has no meaning to me other than to make this ridiculous remark: Why the hell did they take the uterus out and left a hole right through her body? Now I see something else. There seem to be a couple of, I am going to call them Teddy bears. You cut off the body below the shoulders. The forepaws, like this, hanging down [demonstrates]. The two red spots have no meaning at all in this connection. They have unusually long snouts to kiss with. This is fun! I am beginning to see something myself already [that is, significance in his responses]." The patient is now gay and animated.

On Card V: "This is a bat. It also looks like a peculiar kind of moth. Some of these things suggest an island. I can't tell you why unless it is the isolation this picture gives me.... This picture has rather low interest to me." He is asked to explain the reference to isolation: "There was loneliness to that picture. I wonder if that is related to the indication that that is a picture of a bat. That in turn goes back to the story of Fledermaus and the description of the bat: nocturnal and lonely, the despised nonbat, nonmouse and doesn't belong with either. A biological hermaphrodite—not in the sexual sense—a hybrid? I don't quite like that picture. That I think is the reason for my rejection of it and my low interest. It has emotional connotations for me. I don't like it." On Card VI, after first seeing a pelt stretched out to dry and wondering why they hadn't cut off the testicles that he sees at the bottom of the card, and next seeing the head of a turtle at the top, he says: "Here is a pair of hands (lower projections on side). I want to take hold of them. Once I did I wouldn't know what to do with them. I just want to take hold of them [demonstrates]." He goes on to see a reptile which also suggests to him the foreskin of a penis; a fancy woman's stole; and then, at the bottom, a pair of buttocks: "Now I begin to see the reason for not cutting the testicles off. ... I am beginning to get a little headache." In explaining this last inference, he contaminates the skin and buttocks responses: "Because I see this as buttocks, it is natural to, a person could be squatting to defecate and naturally you would see testicles hanging down."

On Card VII he sees two men explaining something to each other and pointing in opposite directions, each trying to convince the other of his point of view, and their relation is good: "They are in rapport with each other. They don't, either one, want to offend the other. There is a kindliness about this picture, concern for each other's feelings." In inquiry the patient points out the response in the upper two thirds of the card and adds: "Someone has neglected to show their feet or else they are very tiny. There is some defiance of the law of gravity but I am not interested in that because the emotional content of that picture is high and the headache is gone again. It was just a light one." He is then asked what indicates their rapport: "Their concern with each other. They are two good friends." He is again asked what indicates that: "By pure chance that picture shows feeling in the eyes. Why did I see it I can't tell you but I see that clearly. There is a bond of affection between these two men and I am conscious I am hiding something when I say that: they look like men but one of them is a woman. That is all I can give." And on Card VIII he sees the two popular animals clinging to rock structure in which there is an evergreen tree and surmises they are climbing up a cliff; during the inquiry he says, "The animals for no good reason all seem to be chameleons." Asked what makes them look like that: "Chameleons are changeable; they change their color. [What about that?] Because I am changeable! [I don't follow you.] Because I have just led myself into a trap, that's all! [The patient is visibly irritated.] I walked right into that! To go one step further—so I am climbing, trying to get some place, I am a chameleon, changeable, indecisive. I'll go a step further: I betray people after having won their affection. You got a lot out of that one, Doc!" Patient is quite agitated now.

Throughout these responses we see obvious image magic, participation, confusing reality and fantasy. For instance: "They look like men but one of them is a woman." The responses are projected pathologically and are taken as omens or magical signs of what he is—sometimes favorable signs and sometimes unfavorable, as in his being changeable. The trap he walks into is a trap defined by loss of self-boundaries and by failure of defenses, particularly of the defense of denial through which he attempts to make himself sexually potent, *en rapport,* strong, and independent. His regressive confusion also reaches one of its climaxes when he wants to take hold of the pair of hands on Card VI, evidently having a total experience, affectively and motorically, of wanting to hang on. The rapid coming and going of his headache in association with his denials through image magic further indicate archaic body participation in the response process.

Extreme responses of this sort are not rare in clinical testing. Sometimes they even turn up in the test records of supposedly normal or only moderately neurotic subjects. There is every reason to expect them to turn up in any large-scale assessment program. Moderate and transitional forms of primary-process encroachment are even more frequently observed and can be taken as partial indications of instability of psychic structure, that is, of the extent to which either the ego's use of the primary process tends to slip over into being overwhelmed by it, or the ego is busily staving off pathological regressions. Transitional forms of response will be cited from the record of a young psychiatrist. He was not without significant adjustment problems but capable of effective work and interpersonal rapport. On Card IV: "I see a very cruel, menacing-looking figure here. The head [upper middle]: It's even got a moustache and a big nose, narrow and slanting—not slanting—slitlike eyes, eyebrows arched, and wrinkles in the forehead. These are sort of hands [upper side projections], very skinny hands, out in a rather menacing, grabbing position and he is standing erect here; here are his feet and legs [lower side projections] and maybe this is a cape that is hanging down [lower middle]; it looks like it is hanging in front rather than behind. I don't know how these fit in." Asked what makes it look menacing: "The arms, and the eyes slanted, and the eyebrows went down. . . . It seemed to be looking right at me and the arms were out as if it could be used for grappling." There is some blurring of self-boundaries here, particularly in the reference to the figure "looking right at me." But apart from that—and that emerges only late in the inquiry—one is struck by the response's relatively detached though interested treatment, its progressive articulation, its built-in self-criticism in terms of details that do not fit in well. The ego remains to a great extent active, and we see overt manifestations of the elaborative and synthetic phase of the creative response process. It is in some ways a struggle for the subject and in at least one way a not entirely successful struggle, but still a far cry from the responses of the first two subjects.

On Card VI: "Again I get the same first response, of this being some sort of an animal flying along but it sure doesn't look much like it [whole blot]. Let's see what else. Oh! This looks like a tank [side detail, seen sideways]. Here are the treads. This [a projection] is hard to fit in: this seems like a cannon they carry on a tank, pointing backwards and they have a blanket over it like it is not in actual combat, in mothballs, so to speak, and the different colors of shading make it so that it is camouflaged. Hm: Here are two people standing side by side with their faces turned out this way and arms held out [each half of blot, held upside down]. It is sort of a dainty pose as if they were doing some dance like the minuet and the foot were daintily pointed out here, although they are rather large, ragged-looking people to be doing something like that. The fact that they are almost joined together except for the white line suggest some sort of anomaly like Siamese twins, and here is a little horn on their heads. This thing down here [usual upper projection], to put it all together, could be two people doing the same thing but on a weathervane, mounted on a post and these people turn the way the wind blows. Again, this, just by itself, could be a sort of flying animal, feelers, and wings and head [upper detail]. I thought at first it had just gone through something and made a hole and all of this [rest of card] was the debris that was falling off. The animal itself seems to have survived pretty well." Asked what makes it look like debris: "I could see the animal and couldn't figure out what the rest of it would be and it seemed to be flying fast so I thought maybe it had just gone through something, like through a wall or something."

Again, some blurring of the self-boundaries is not eliminated in the final response formulation, some of his quick initial impressions tending to dominate his subsequent efforts to synthesize. Even so, throughout he obviously attempts to articulate, relate, synthesize, note discrepancies from realistic conformations. Maintenance of interest, distance, and capacity for self-criticism is not impaired. One may conjecture a number of significant dynamic problems from the few responses cited from this record—problems concerning self-esteem, passive-compliant defense against hostile impulse, fear of damage, etc. And in some respects one sees that somewhat fluid forms of experience are not unusual in his psychic functioning. At the same time one sees an active, inventive, self-observant ego steadily at work. By implication, higher ego functions are fairly stably established; they are not overwhelmed in the response process and do not give way to image magic, participation, emotional chaos, or archaic projections and introjections.

It would be a mistake, however, to limit our attention to projective tests only. An intelligence test indispensably helps assess the extent to which secondary-process functioning may be maintained in its own right. Because they are relatively structured, impersonal, and consistent with conventional logical requirements and techniques, intelligence-test items invite or demand of the person that he respond in an entirely nonregressive manner. Assessment of individually administered and verbatim recorded intelligence-test results, such as those of the Wechsler Adult Intelligence Scale, including assessment of the distribution of subtest scores, clarifies to what extent there is something partial, temporary, and controlled about the regressive aspects of the projective-test responses. Of course, we can and do carry out such assessment on the basis of the projective-test responses themselves. We rely, for example, on the Rorschach scores: the *form level,* with its indication of adequacy of reality testing; the use of *color* and *shading* and the control of them through *form,* with their indications of cognitive regulation and articulation of affective experience; the *human-movement* response, with its indication of freedom of fantasy, interpersonal awareness, and other imaginative, personalized, and organized ideation; etc. And we also observe the test's qualitative aspects, such as differentiation and synthesis within content and form, and optimal emotional distance from response, in order to assess the relative power of the secondary process. In other words, the secondary process is not crowded out of the projective tests. The progressive, elaborational, synthetic phase of creative work is called for as much, if not more, in a projective test as in a free act of creation.

But because projective tests plumb deep, they sometimes dramatize the less stable stages or levels of personality organization. They may obscure adaptive potential. This is a well-known diagnostic difficulty in clinical work. It crops up in training too; for it is a cliché that students learning to use the Rorschach test and giving it to friends or fellow students seem to be surrounded by schizophrenics. There are many factors that appear to account for these usually misleading results. But whatever the explanation, these findings indicate the importance of using tests calling for more structured and stable forms of secondary-process response. My experience with a variety of more or less normal subjects, such as applicants for secretarial positions, state policemen, college students, pregnant women, and applicants for psychiatric residencies, has repeatedly confirmed the impression that a relatively efficient, well-organized intelligence-test performance must be given considerable weight in assessing adaptive potential. Clinically, this finding is often of great value in distinguishing between incipient and fully psychotic conditions. It is when primary-process expressions intrude into the intelligence test that we are almost certainly dealing with a full psychosis. Psychosis is indicated when, from a formal point of view, the intelligence-test responses become fluid, concrete, and disrupted in their communicative aspects, and when, from a content point of view, they express more and more material that is drive relevant rather than reality relevant. Thus, when a reasonably intelligent patient says that a fly and a tree are alike in being inarticulate or in that they can both be destroyed, when cryptic references to venereal disease intrude into the answer to the question *Why does the state require people to get a license in order to be married?*, and when a patient defines *obstruct* as a detour because an obstruction need not prevent you from getting where you are going if you can make a detour, we see primary processes intrude where they do not belong. We see pathological regression of the ego (pervasive, uncontrolled, enduring) to a more primitive level of function—in other words, structural pathology.

Many of these considerations also apply to the assessment of subjects through interviews and in therapeutic situations. It is, for example, a steady preoccupation of the psychoanalyst to assess the balance of primary and secondary processes and shifting levels of organization in the patient. Loewald (1960) has recently discussed important theoretical aspects of this assessment. One of the points he stresses is the regression in the service of the ego required of the analyst to comprehend the level from which the patient is communicating and hence to comprehend and respond effectively to the communications. He extends significantly the emphasis placed by Fenichel (1941b) on the requirement that the analyst oscillate between an experiencing and an observing (conceptualizing) position. Of course, Freud recognized very early that the free play of the analyst's unconscious and preconscious processes was indispensable for his effective interventions. There is every reason to transpose this view to the analysis of test results. In developing the possible implications of content, and coordinating these; in experiencing the subject's style of verbalization as conveying information concerning drives, affects, controls, aspirations, and assets; in being able to comprehend both the more realistic and articulated aspects of responses and their more archaic referents; in all these operations, the test interpreter must be able to move freely over his own range of levels of organization. And in the end he must do a piece of synthetic and elaborational work in which he sifts, interrelates, and weights the implications of his experience of the material. Unless his assessing is piecemeal and carefully prescribed by a manual, that is, unless he is

working atomistically for specific research purposes, the as-
sessor of human motives is called upon to do a creative piece
of work, like the therapist and like the artist.

Implied in all these observations and considerations is that
we do the object of our study, whether a patient or a subject
being assessed, an injustice if we are too dazzled by content,
by dynamics, by motives, and do not pay close attention to
formal aspects of functioning and their structural and economic implications.

IMPLICATIONS FOR PERSONALITY
ASSESSMENT RESEARCH

I have already mentioned the importance of including as
crucial variables intraindividual and interindividual differences in capacity for regression in the service of the ego. These
differences include specific conditions favoring and hampering such regression, the dynamic areas and extent of regression, and the style and quality of ultimate syntheses. I have
also indicated a way of thinking about test results in personality assessment, and I have pointed to the advantages particular tests offer personality assessment. I do not imply that existing and popular psychological tests, such as the Rorschach,
TAT, and Wechsler Adult Intelligence Scale, are the ideal
tools for assessment—although I and many others have come
to value them highly for this purpose. Rather, it is the problems these techniques pose to the subject being assessed that
are of interest, for assessment must include these problems
if it is to be penetrating. Subjects should be required to create,
synthesize, and communicate something, be it in a play con-
struction, a joke, a plan for group action, a painting, a TAT
story, or a self-interpretation of that story—or many of these.
Subjects should be required to function under a variety of
conditions other than those usually obtaining in their normal
waking state, such as internal states of sleepiness, tipsiness,
or high affect, and external conditions of varying degrees of
ambiguity. Also, subjects should be observed developing

identifications, intimacy, and empathy with others in a variety of group situations. To a significant extent these inner and outer conditions can be experimentally manipulated. A particularly valuable way to enrich the study of such regressive and creative processes in the assessed subjects is to have at least some of them undergo psychoanalysis. When one considers the usual scope of assessment programs in time and expense, this does not seem an extravagant proposal. The psychoanalytic findings in individual subjects should help answer many crucial questions in the interpretation of assessment data, or, if not that, they will certainly raise crucial questions which might otherwise pass unnoticed.

By intention I have slighted questionnaires. I recognize that skillfully constructed questionnaires contribute to assessment research. I believe, however, that all too often assessment suffers because it excessively emphasizes questionnaire results. Questionnaires are obviously tempting: many subjects may be quickly studied, and the results lend themselves so nicely to quantitative treatment. Research workers often hasten to have numbers to report in order to be "objective," although in so doing they often slight their subjects and their own resources. They hastily restrict themselves to what is conscious, readily available, and easily verbalized. Admittedly, it is not so easy to objectify and quantify creativity, humor, variations in states of consciousness, and varieties of conscious experience. Extensive phenomenological investigations must come first. Reliability checks and quantitative comparisons should be carried out only in due time. Holt's (1956) ongoing research, in which he is objectively assessing primary-process manifestations in Rorschach responses, represents a significant methodological advance in this regard.[4] While we may usually look down on the conception of scientific rigor in the writings of many psychiatrists and psychoanalysts, we must respect many for their patience, integrity, and courage in the face of bewildering complexity and ambiguity while they go on mapping out horizontal and vertical psychic ter-

[4] See Holt and Havel (1960).

ritories. They take the individual very seriously. Mass correlations of questionnaire results seem wasteful by comparison, even though they may appease scientific conscience by offering concrete results soon. The impatient scientist may invite his audience of colleagues to identify with him and approve his product—correlations—in order to lighten his burden of guilt at not having been creative. There is a risk of greater guilt in taking one's time, studying subjects intensively even if it limits the size of samples, looking into complex and elusive problems, and trespassing established boundaries of method and subject matter, but one then stands a better chance of assessing central factors and creating something memorable.

7

HOW WAS THIS STORY TOLD?

I

In a superior poem, content and form interpenetrate; they mutually define each other. In analyzing such a poem, any attempt to consider its *what* separately from its *how* artificially fragments a unitary statement and can therefore achieve only limited success. A paraphrase of the poem's ostensible content eliminates essential aspects of its sense, some of which lies in its musicality. A TAT story has this in common with poetry: we cannot grasp its full import if we consider only its content, its narrative detail. A story's meaning is definable only after scrutinizing the particular manner in which it has been told. A crucial question then is, *How was this story told?* To answer, we undertake a kind of psychological literary criticism, seeking in the choice of language, imagery, and sequence of development, as well as in the narrative detail, cues about the storyteller's inner experience of his creative effort and his creation. We listen especially for ambiguities, that is, multiple connotations, especially those not consciously intended, and for disruptions of the story-telling orientation, such as may become evident in hastening to a conclusion, abruptly altering a story's mood, becoming preoccupied with verbalization, or shifting the focus of attention from fantasy to the relationship to the tester.

In thus defining the subject's inner experience, we conceptualize significant components of his ego functioning *vis-à-vis* forces emanating from or representing the id, the superego,

First published in the *Journal of Projective Techniques,* 22:181-210, 1958.

objective reality, and the problems of organization within the ego itself. That is to say, we isolate such factors as modes, contents, and degrees of impulse gratification; foci, archaic elements, and intensities of moral imperatives; defense maneuvers; definiteness of self-boundaries; and adaptive resources in the form of wit, imagination, forcefulness, synthesizing power, and strength, variety, and flexibility of commitments to oneself and to others.

In the following I will discuss a number of TAT protocols from this point of view, letting the useful concepts and criteria emerge in concrete contexts. I will not undertake an exhaustive and systematic treatment of the analysis of *content as verbalized* within the confines of this paper. My examples will indicate the kind of analysis referred to in my opening remarks. My effort will be to show that in making his invaluable contribution to psychodiagnostic technique, Henry Murray has given us not only a thematic apperception test but a thematic communication test as well.

II

The sequence of cards in the protocols to follow is that routinely used by me in clinical work: 1, 5, 15, 14, A (old man on shoulders of old man, from original TAT series), 10, B (Picasso's *La Vie* from original TAT series), 13 MF, and then, for males, 6 BM, 7 BM, 4, 20, 12 M, and, for females, 12 F, 3 GF, 2, 8 GF, and 12 M. Card 12 M is included for both sexes because it frequently elicits significant fantasies concerning the therapeutic situation. The test instructions request that plots of stories be made up which will include "what's happening, what led up to it, the outcome, and the thoughts and feelings of the characters."

Case 1

A 52-year-old married man, childless, with an incomplete college education, had been working for many years in Hollywood as a film-story editor. His parents had been professional persons; his father had died when patient was 10, and his mother had died a few years prior to testing. He has one younger sister, also a professional person. The patient has a long history of heavy drinking, exacerbated since his mother's death.

The patient's initial TAT communication was a mock shudder during the test instructions. A question is immediately raised: Is this a man afraid of his fantasy life, that is, of allowing himself ego-regressive freedom of feeling and fantasy, and does he defend himself by mechanisms of facetiousness, histrionics, and minimization?

> Card 1.   Now from this I'm supposed to tell you what? [Instructions repeated.] He has just finished practicing and . . . and he is sitting there reflecting . . . over his violin . . . on a score which he's just tackled. Is that enough? [Make up more of a story.] . . . [How does he feel?] . . . I should say he feels a little . . . hmmm, disturbed, no, not disturbed: well, we'll [mumbles something], we'll say a little disturbed by the fact that he hadn't brought off, what will we say, the Scarlatti exercise to his satisfaction. He is a sensitive, thoughtful child who, like myself, needs a haircut. You can leave that out if you wish. Okay, that takes care of Buster. Oh, you put everything down [noticing verbatim recording].

(1) His opening question concerning the instructions may be expressing (a) an attention disturbance associated with anxiety, (b) impaired memory efficiency associated with his chronic alcoholism, (c) stalling tactics to gain time to compose himself before plunging in, (d) dramatization of the test's absurdity—a defense by counterattack, (e) reluctance to meet this demand on him, or (f) some combination of these factors. (2) After his initial effort to avoid an expressive story is blocked by the tester's prompting, he introduces the theme of failure and fall of self-esteem, but minimizes and is tempted to avoid even so moderate a description of affect as "disturbed." The approach is one of avoidance, denial, and restriction of the daydreaming component of story creation, implemented by detachment, and emphasis on conscious control and free choice, as revealed in such expressions as "I

should say" and "what will we say." (3) The boy cannot bring off the Scarlatti exercise: it is unusual to have a piece of music specified on this card—Scarlatti exercise even has a certain elegance—so that it is more than likely the patient also wants it known at once that he is a man of culture and refinement. From the standpoint of tolerance of fantasy, he seems too much focused on his relationship to the tester and too little on the boy and his problem. (4) His adding "like myself he needs a haircut" suggests (a) identification with the boy and expression of low self-esteem and feelings of helplessness through the boy's unkempt, unlooked-after aspect, and (b) a disclaimer of the earlier "sensitive, thoughtful" characterization of the boy through flippancy and taking even further distance from freewheeling fantasy. (5) Toward the end of this story he watchfully notes that his side remarks are being recorded, but, still striving toward detachment, he says his words can be left out *if the tester wishes,* that is, nonchalantly, it is all the same to him. (6) There is a final disclaimer of involvement or identification through condescension toward the boy—"Buster"—and implicit reassertion of his acute awareness that he is making up this story.

Card 5. Oh, they are not related then? A housewife, somewhere in her middle 30's or early 40's, appears questioningly and rather apprehensively through a door leading to a living room. She is alone in the house and having heard the doorbell ring she is wondering who the caller may be.... She knows there is no expected deliveries or tradesmen who might be calling and it is an hour before her husband is due to return from his office. Any more? [Who is at the door?] I don't know. You want that too? ... Her fears are allayed when she steps into the room and finds that the doorbell ringers are a pair of Girl Scouts delivering cookies for their annual drive.

(1) Apprehension is groundless, he insists: Girl Scouts are as innocuous as can be. In the first story he spent his time pooh-poohing discouragement, sensitivity, and aspirations; in this story he does the same to fear. (2) He introduces an unusual oral theme—delivery of cookies. The emphasis in

this may be as much on the extortion of supplies from the identification figure as on passive receptiveness, for it is a situation in which one must shell out to very good little girls for not so very good little cookies. Note in this regard that twice he emphasizes the tester's demands: "Any more?" and "You want that too?" (3) Note too that the child figure he introduces is feminine, alerting us to the possibility that feminine identification components will be conspicuous in the protocol and, therefore, in the patient's personality.

> *Card 15.* This might be an early 19th-century gentleman, possibly a Parisienne [*sic*] or a German mourning... at the tomb of a friend. Let's make him a Frenchman and say that he was killed in a duel, the friend. Let's make him a Frenchman and say the friend was killed in a duel—not over a mistress but because he said that Alexandre Dumas was a lousy wrtier. . . . Though the mourner doesn't necessarily share this literary opinion, he will miss his friend, who was a stimulating conversationalist and good company. Okay?

(1) Further attempts are made to document his being a man of culture (19th-century gentleman, Parisienne or German, Dumas, conversationalist). (2) "Let's make him a Frenchman and say that he was. . ." is twice repeated and follows right on the heels of "mourning": feeling is again squelched by verbalizations emphasizing control. The polishing of his verbalization by reorganizing the sentence about the friend being killed in a duel, that is, his concern with the literary quality of the verbalization tending to overshadow the fantasy content itself, further suggests striving toward detachment. In the remainder of the story, human involvement is several times minimized: first, the duel was not over a woman but over a literary opinion; second, there is his very cool way of saying, "While the mourner doesn't necessarily share this literary opinion. . ."; third, "friend" is immediately defined in a special way as a "stimulating conversationalist and good company," that is, someone who is a source of supply of ideas and fun but not a partner in intimacy. (3) The identification figure is in something of a passive relationship to this friend,

and "Parisienne" suggests a feminine conception of the identification figure (recall his Girl Scouts on Card 5). (4) The
theme of the story is that of being punished for attacking the
qualifications of a man of stature and this may well refer to
one part of the patient's oedipal conflicts and his attempt to
defend against them: the identification figure remains alive
as a passive and feminine person. But the patient's playing
it so cool throughout, it may be hypothesized, quite possibly
reflects a combined defense against (a) the ultimately self-
destructive oedipal heresy, and (b) his passive, feminine
trend which would make for sentimentality, feelings of dependency, and intense homosexually tinged involvement. Apparently striving to be neither masculine nor feminine in his
implicit self-definition, the patient is a condescending but
cautiously controlled and detached commentator.

> *Card 14.* I can't judge from that. Is he—this is a question
> —whether the young man is looking through a window on the
> outdoors or whether he is about to step into another room?
> [Another room?] This window could be part of another room.
> [Where is he now?] Could be one of several things. I have free-
> dom of choice? [Whatever you like.] He might be a burglar
> gaining access to a house ... although this seems improbable.
> ... [Just make it up.] Alright, I was just trying to decide. . . .
> Let's say he is a factory worker who has to be on the job at 8
> o'clock, that it is a wintry morning, that he is taking a deep
> breath of fresh air, preparatory to closing the window, starting
> his day—comma window comma starting his day's activities and
> waking his wife who is asleep in the adjoining bed. . . . He
> might be any number of persons. He might even be a citizen of
> Budapest who has been arrested by the police and is coming
> into daylight after a long period of solitary confinement. May-
> be he is just a fresh-air fiend. [What happens to the citizen of
> Budapest?] Let's say the citizen of Budapest is going on to trial,
> is going to be tried before a People's Court for anticommunist
> activity and that his chances don't look too good.

(1) The patient now plays up knowledgeability regarding
world affairs but the dismal theme makes him uncomfortable
and he returns flippantly to an earlier, ostensibly unemotional
theme—"fresh-air fiend." (2) In dictating punctuation he

introduces another stylistic feature common to those who want to emphasize their detachment from their story, i.e., their inner world. (3) Apparently there are three themes—burglary, fresh air, and revolution—yet they are closely related: the burglar figure is one who steals supplies; the fresh-air fiend is taking a deep breath, the emphasis being in one respect on excessive intake of refreshing supplies; and the counterrevolutionary has been through a long period of solitary confinement, the emphasis falling on (stimulus) deprivation as well as punishment. There is an accumulating oral emphasis (cookies, conversation, theft, intake, and deprivation). (4) As regards the punishment, it is associated with revolt against authority as it was in the previous story (criticism of Dumas). As noted, he is disturbed by the theme of aggression and counteraggression late in the story, and this feeling probably contributed to his dropping the burglar theme early in the story. (5) His initial difficulty in perceiving the situation, particularly his somewhat peculiar notion of going from room to room through a window, suggests some impairment of perceptual and conceptual organizing functions, which in turn suggests that the patient's chronic alcoholism may already have resulted in some psychological deficit.

Card A (old man on shoulders of old man). Let's see. Here are a couple of ... here are a couple of muffadilloes—that is a show-business term you won't understand: men with beards. Here are a couple of muffadilloes, presumably Hindus, certainly Asiatics, presumably Hindus, and most certainly, most certainly from some race of Asiatics: let's put it that way. It looks as if the younger man in the foreground were going to be mugged by the patriarch. They might be a couple of holy men but I don't know what quarrel between them would lead to such an outburst of physical violence. . . . I suppose that if you wanted to interpret this from the Christian point of view . . . the lower figure could be Christ—at least he has the Christus look—and the elder man one of his prophets. [The Christus look?] C-h-r-i-s-t-u-s. [What is that?] The appearance of Christ. Let's see, how does that go? . . . How did that go? Could you read that back? [Just go on.] Just the sentence structure: I am used to dictating. [Patient getting upset over loss of continuity; tester reads last sentence.] My Biblical knowledge is so sketchy that I wouldn't want to speculate as to what might be bringing about this apparent show of impending physical violence.

(1) The previous suggestions of possible psychological deficit are reinforced by his sterile reworking of the sentence about Hindus and Asiatics. Here he goes beyond detached sanding and polishing of his verbalizations; his remarks have the quality of something having gotten jammed in the works. Later he loses his train of thought and becomes increasingly upset when the tester will not rush in to his rescue: a strong suggestion is present of an anxious sense of fluidity of thought. He immediately rationalizes his difficulty in terms of his being used to giving dictation, thereby also adding to his status—which in a way he had already done by introducing the term *muffadillo*. (2) The later disruption of continuity of thought followed two events: (a) the tester's interruption, which irritated him (note his spelling *Christus*), and (b) his direct dealing with a destructive theme on a picture highly charged with hostility. The sequence hostility-disruption supports the inference drawn from the previous stories that directly confronting hostility disrupts his functioning seriously. Most likely we are dealing here with the combined effect of some psychological deficit and particular vulnerability to anxiety concerning aggressive interaction between men. The striving for status evident throughout his stories may be exacerbated by his unsure control of his faculties. The same may be true for his emphasis on controlled and detached verbalization, appearing in this story in such forms as "let's see," "let's put it that way," "I suppose that if you wanted to interpret this from the Christian point of view," etc. (3) In introducing the term *muffadillo* he begins to establish that beyond being a man of culture and of political awareness, he is a man of show biz; "Buster" on Card 1 and "lousy" on Card 15 are relevant here. Suggested by now is a proclivity toward transient, insubstantial identifications of the sort commonly encountered in highly narcissistic persons. (4) Paternal destruction of the identification figure is again introduced as a theme (see Cards 15

and 14). But this time the theme appears in a religious context, pointing thereby to inner guilt and not just fear of external authority. The patient's casual, callous, cynical statements may therefore reflect defense against recognition of guilt as well as of masculine assertiveness, feminine emotionality and fear, passive hungry yearnings, and possibly impaired mental capacity. From a characterological point of view his style of defense—facetiousness, condescension, transient identification, status seeking, nonchalance—is steadily narcissistic.

> *Card 10.* [Before card is presented, tester urges patient to make up complete stories by himself. Patient protests, referring to previous story, "I made one up: I said it might be a couple of holy men."] A Czech husband is comforting his wife. [Czech?] They look Czechoslovakian or possibly German—over the death of their son, little Jan—J-a-n—who has been drowned while swimming in a nearby river. While both parents are grief-stricken, there is some consolation in the fact that they have two other sons who will grow up and fight the Italians in World War I. Will you settle for that?

(1) Again he introduces the theme of death of the son figure. (2) The death—by immersion in water, by suffocation or taking in noxious substance—has oral-destructive connotations. (3) His sardonic ending minimizes the parental affection and grief and suggests that all the sons get killed off. (4) His concluding remark—"Will you settle for that?"—underscores the demands made on him, his ostensible compliance, but also his trying to get by with just enough and no more.

> *Card B.* (Picasso's *La Vie*). I can't figure from what part of the world these people come.... [Make up a story.] With the murals in the background it might be, indicate that they were Aztec.... [What is happening?] They seem Aztec although the faces of the young man and woman look European. Anyway, the girl wants, the girl wants to marry the boy, and her mother, holding her youngest child, is disapproving. If the girl keeps running around in the nude like that, maybe she will have to marry the boy after all.

(1) This story contains further cultural references, and (2)

another sardonic ending. (3) The girl is the obvious identification figure (see the introduction of little girls on Card 5
and the *Parisienne* distortion on Card 15). The assertive potential of the male figure is ignored. (4) The theme is passive
and masochistically colored: sexual self-victimization through
enticement of others.

    Card 13 MF. This looks like something the tabloids would
play up. . . . The mistress of a middle-aged man becomes too
importunate wanting him to leave his wife for her. Finally
goaded into frenzy, he murders, the man murders the mistress.
He succumbs to remorse as he turns away from the bed where
his love lies dead. Boyzo! Novels of 500 pages have been written
leading up to this situation and we don't have time to go into
it here. [Outcome?] The man will try to get away but eventually
be apprehended and placed on trial for his life. I will leave it
to the jury to decide the ultimate outcome. [What do you
think?] . . .I'll give you 3 to 1 that he fries.

(1) Verbalizations indicating his continued striving toward
detachment include his references to the tabloids, his excla-
mation "Boyzo," his reference to novels and his not having the
time to go into it to that extent, his leaving it to the jury to
decide, and his laying odds on the punishment. (2) The
theme of the mistress's demands being responded to with intense anger and violence, though minimized by his verbalizations, suggests that he views sexuality as a matter of demands,
as dangerous—a suggestion already noted in the ending of the
previous story—and as immoral. (3) The self-derogatory implication in his introducing a tabloid type of theme or giving
a theme a tabloid type of treatment or label must not be over-
looked: it suggests a view of his impulse life that combines
elements of sordidness, sensationalism, and disgust. (4) His
interesting switch from the pronoun *he* to "the man" in the
midst of the story suggests a momentary unclarity in his own
mind about who was doing what to whom and may reflect
fluidity of thinking. (5) In his concluding remarks he uses
an oral metaphor—"fries"—reminiscent of introducing cookies on Card 5 and death by drowning on Card 10 (see also
Cards 6 BM, 4, and 12, below).

Card 6 BM. Phillip Rittenhouse the Third, a member of an old Philadelphia family . . . a member of an old Philadelphia Quaker family—you'd better change Rittenhouse to Atkins— has been telling his mother . . . [patient interrupts to light a cigarette] . . . Phillip Rittenhouse the Third—oh, I changed it to Atkins—let's see, that was Phillip Rittenhouse the Third, a member of an old Main-line Philadelphia family—I said you'd better change that to Atkins—has been telling his mother that he is in love with Flora La Vere, a dancer in a Philadelphia night spot. The mother hasn't taken kindly to this morsel of news and turns away from her son while he looks perturbed and bewildered. The dowager threatens to cut off his share of the fortune if he persists in this folly. Looking into the future, his romance with the dancer eventually fades, he marries a nice Main-line girl, now lives in Ardmore and even plays cricket at the Merion—Me-r-i-o-n—Cricket Club. If you want another story, this could be, this could almost be a scene from *Long Day's Journey into the Night,* but the late Mr. O'Neill wrote that one better than I can synopsize it.

(1) Fluidity and bogging down of thought is strikingly evident in his floundering introduction of names. Note too that he distorts the name of the play he refers to—an event particularly ominous in view of its being related to his occupation. (2) He introduces another oral metaphor: "morsel of news." (3) The patient's use of names, sarcasm, and knowledgeable references to high society continues to indicate his efforts to defend himself through detachment and through striving for status. (4) The social-status content introduces still another identification fragment to be added to those discussed in connection with Card A (the two old men). (5) The major theme may be summarized as that of a passive, dependent, and receptive son submitting to a depriving, antisexual mother and renouncing his rebellious, sexual strivings (see also Cards B, 13 MF, and 4, below.) Note in this regard how he defers to Mr. O'Neill. (6) The alternative, implicit theme introduced by the reference to *Long Day's Journey into Night* is highly significant: it refers to a family in which the mother is a drug addict and the father and two sons alcoholic, a family in which the mother is unable to hear or to respond as a moth-

er for she still lives in the dreams of her youth, and in which the principal son is strongly identified with her, emotionally closer to her, and threatened with death by "consumption," a threat greatly increased by his father's destructive greed. This pattern of family relationships touches on some of the principal aspects of the patient's problems thus far tentatively defined: maternal deprivation, the father's destructiveness toward his son, the intense ambivalent attachment to the mother figure combined with an identification with the female role, oral preoccupation, and the doom that hangs over one. It is commonly found in the TAT stories of persons with a strong oral orientation (for example, addicts, manic-depressives, and passive personalities) that death by disease is likely to take the form of consumption or cancer, i.e., something eating away one's insides; similarly, death by murder, suicide, or accident, is likely to be by poison, drowning, strangulation, or starvation, i.e., intake or supplies being cut off.

> *Card 7 BM.* The boy is a respectable member of a middle-class Brooklyn family, has fallen among evil companions and got himself mixed up, got himself involved—don't say mixed up—in a holdup. His patient, understanding father is appearing with him in court and trying to offer a bit of paternal advice. The boy, both remorseful and defiant, is listening to papa but it is too late. He is sent to a prison term for his participation in the robbery. For further details, see page three.

(1) Again, stealing of supplies (see Card 14). (2) Again, punishment of the identification figure by the authorities. (3) Again, sarcasm and detachment concerning human involvement and morality. (4) Again, self-derogation by labeling his story a tabloid story—"see page three."

> *Card 4.* Joe Doakes is a factory worker who had the good fortune to marry a pretty wife. Joe is on the night shift and despite the fact that her husband is a handsome guy, the woman is lonely and has been playing around with another man. Hearing about this, Joe is about—hearing of this—not hearing of this—Joe is about to go out after the lover and his wife is attempting to restrain him. I am happy to say that he does [is re-

strained]. Joe gets transferred to the day shift and the domestic life of the Doakes family is again rosy. You can find this kind of thing related in the confession-type cheap magazines.

(1) Further self-derogation through cheapening the story. However, by now so many tabloid themes are accumulating that a broad streak of ego-alien sentimentality is powerfully suggested. (2) Further emphasis on detachment, through using names and underscoring his roles as storyteller, as in "I am happy to say." (3) There is a passive implication in saying that Joe had the good fortune to marry her: it is as if it must have been by luck and circumstance rather than through masculine assertiveness. This inference is supported by the storyteller's relief that the wife talks Joe out of fighting with another man. We have seen abundant evidence of how frightening a fight would be to him.

> *Card 20.* This might seem to call for the O. Henry touch. O. Henry? Yeah, O. Henry. It was a raw snowy night in Manhattan and a vagrant is standing in Gramercy Park leaning against a post. A vagrant is leaning against a post in Gramercy Park across from the Players' Club, across from the Players' Club, across from the Players'. It is a Pipe Night, Pipe Night at the club. [Pipe Night?] Pipe Night, capital P and capital N. And across the street the vagrant sees warm light and hears the vocal evidence of good fellowship. In pairs and in groups the members of the Players' drift out into the night. They get into taxis or in their own cars and pay no attention to the bum across the street—the man across the street, instead of bum—to the man across the street. He is too proud to shuffle over and beg and he finally turns his steps eastward toward Third Avenue. He would like a bottle of vino but he hasn't got the price. Eventually he heads for the Salvation Army where at least he can get some hot food and a bed for the night. By this time the snow has become heavier and, comma, crossing the Bowery, he is hit by a car driven by Isidore Appleman, a Brooklyn manufacturer of ladies ready-to-wear. It isn't Appleman's fault. He is released and the police carry off another unnamed drifter to the morgue.

(1) O. Henry and dictating punctuation further underscore the detached storyteller's position. (2) The identification

figure is alcoholic, is in a passive-receptive and yearning position, is envious of those with supplies, is feeling lonely and
deprived, and in a final act of self-abasement seeks oral supplies and physical comfort from the Salvation Army—only to
be killed by a man while so doing. (3) In picking out a name,
the patient chooses *Appleman*—a name with a distinct oral
connotation—and then adds a feminine connotation by having him a manufacturer of women's clothing.

> *Card 12 M.* Marian Miller is a nice girl and a very popular
> one. She has few problems in life and one of them is that she
> can't stop smoking. She tried every way to give up cigarettes
> but in vain. Finally a friend suggests a hypnotist. She is hypno-
> tized and the cure lasts for four months. Finally Marian gets
> a job in the movies which is—she gets a job in Hollywood—
> which is nerve-wracking and before long she is smoking again.
> She should have gone back for booster shots but she never has.
> This one is easy because it's what happened to my wife.

(1) The feminine identification appears again in his making
the reclining figure a girl. (2) The oral emphasis reappears
in the problem's being one of uncontrollable craving to smoke.
(3) The girl's relapse is rationalized as due to external stress
and there is skepticism about the possibility of help being
effective for more than a brief period. (4) The method of
cure, doubtful though it may be, requires suppression rather
than resolution, and requires submitting passively to a man
in a feminine position rather than active interchange or independent renunciation.

I will not attempt to summarize all possible aspects of this
patient's TAT material, but will review some of its highlights. We may say that the content (the themes) indicates
intense fear of destructive, authoritarian punishment for the
aggressive, sexual, and oral aspects of oedipal strivings, and
fear of being cut off from maternal supplies, of which he feels
very much in need. These fears appear to be associated with
inclinations to regress to a feminine, compliant, passive-receptive, helpless, and inadequate role in which his goal is the
seeking out of oral supplies, often in a self-abasing way (food,

air, smoking, drinking, conversation, handouts). This seeking is carried out ambivalently, apprehensively, and pessimistically, with wounded pride and flimsy efforts to restore a feeling of status and self-esteem.

In the style or form of his thoughts, his verbalizations, and his visual organization, he indicates that he attempts to cope with these fears in the following manner: (1) By a detached, cynical, worldly manner, through which he attempts to exercise great control and to be above any intense feeling—a maneuver by which he appears to be then neither masculine nor feminine but only uncommitted; the type of stories he introduces, the labels he gives them, and his strenuous avoidance of sentimentality combine to indicate that he is probably contending with intense sentimentality with feminine and passive aspects. Fear of affect (anxiety, guilt, depression, sentimentality) is generally pronounced. (2) By multiple, shifting, insubstantial identifications, in which he is a man of culture, one of the cognoscenti of the entertainment industry, politically aware, socially and economically elite, and a first-rate low-brow as well as high-brow. In addition, his choices of metaphor and imagery tend to underscore the markedly oral orientation evident in the content, while his bogging down in verbal mix-ups, his occasional fluidity of thought, and his perceptual and conceptual problems of organization suggest some degree of psychological deficit associated with his prolonged and excessive drinking. In this last respect, his evident striving for control, detachment, and superiority may be exacerbated to help defend himself against awareness of impairment.

The next few groups of stories, each selected from a full TAT protocol, take off from three of the striking aspects of the protocol just reviewed, namely, oral emphasis, fluidity of thought, and rigid striving toward detachment.

Case 2

To illustrate accumulation of oral context and imagery in another pathological context, I will present a few stories told by a 25-year-old depressive woman who had made a recent suicide attempt. Of course, the stories also point to other aspects of her pathological state, dynamics, and character structure than those referring to oral trends.

Card 1. The little boy is looking at the violin. He broke one of the strings and he is wondering if he can fix it. . . . His family hadn't wanted to buy him the violin but a teacher, a school teacher, persuaded them to and they told him he had to take very good care of it or they would punish him and get rid of the violin. He is very worried because he doesn't know how to fix it. . . . He won't be able to fix it and they will get rid of the violin and punish him by making him go to bed right after dinner.

Card 5. This woman is taking a last look at her living room. She has invited her husband's boss for dinner and she is not ready, I mean she is not dressed but the room is ready, and she is worried that the room isn't neat enough because her husband always says she is messy, and she is wondering if she will have enough time to go upstairs and change before the people come. Although she is very worried about it, she does have time to go upstairs and change and it is a very successful party. Her husband gets a raise and everything turns out all right.

Card B (Picasso's *La Vie*). These are three, four models in an art studio. The woman with the child is posing for a portrait of the Madonna and Child, and the young man and girl are lovers and they are posing for Adam and Eve. And the young man is asking the woman with the child if he can pose first, they can pose first, because they have a lunch date with an artist and the fee may mean enough money so they can get married. And the woman at first doesn't want to say yes because she wants to get finished and fix her husband's dinner, I mean lunch, but then she remembers how nice people were to her when she was engaged so she says yes. And the two of them pose and have dinner with the dealer, I mean artist, and they get the contract and they can get married.

Card 12 F. The old woman is a witch and the girl has come to her for a love potion and she is giving her a formula. But the man that the girl is going to marry has taken away the old lady's farm because he wants to run a railroad through it, so the old lady gives the girl poison instead of a love potion, and she is smiling to herself thinking the man is going to get his just deserts. And she is so angry at the man, although she realizes the girl will probably be tried for murder, she doesn't care. And the girl is standing there wondering if the potion will work and hoping it will, and deciding to herself she'll—she is having the man to dinner that night—she will put it in his after-dinner coffee. . . . So she puts it in what she thinks is his after-dinner coffee and it turns out to be her own and she drinks it and dies. So the man is accused of murder and is convicted and hung and the old woman is very happy.

The same patient, after eight months of intensive psycho-therapy in a hospital, during which time her depression had diminished considerably, and a premorbid narcissistic mode of functioning had been relatively recompensated, told this new version of this last story.

Card 12 F (retest). This is a young woman and her grand-mother and the young woman was waiting for her sweetheart, who is in the next room talking to her father, who has come to ask his permission, the father's permission, to marry the daugh-ter. So the old grandmother is eagerly giving the young girl ad-vice as to the care and feeding of husbands. [What are the girl's thoughts and feelings?] She is probably thinking the woman is talking a lot of nonsense. [Outcome?] They get married.

Note that the themes of magical oral control and of oral de-struction have now dropped out. At the last moment, how-ever, the care and feeding of husbands is introduced—a much more highly socialized emphasis on orality in the heterosexual relationship than in the previous version. It is noteworthy that the girl rejects the advice, suggesting rejection of a nurturant role.

Case 3

In the protocol of a 50-year-old woman with a history of Benzedrine and barbiturate addiction, oral emphasis is again apparent and also fluidity of thinking similar to that shown by Case 1. Only a few of her stories will be presented.

Card 5. What if it doesn't suggest much of anything to you? Well, it is obviously a woman opening a door. That's obviously a clique if there ever was one. [Clique?] C-l-i-c-h-e, if that's how you pronounce it; I guess not. She expects to find somebody there. She and her long-dead lover used to meet in this room. He has been dead many years, but she had become—let's see, where was I now? [Last sentence repeated.] She had a vivid imagination and she thought at times that she could see him there. That is why only half the room is showing. [Why?] We are taking this like a script for a television screen. The other half of the room is a shimmering substance that could be the lover. But in this case she never saw him again. Something had occurred in her outside life that made her realize she was living in a world of ghosts. She was walking along the street one day. A kitten came up to her, and, although she never liked cats, she felt sorry for the little creature and took it home with her and became interested in it and interested enough in it that she finally ended, became more and more interested in people and children and animals and worked at that. [Explain about seeing lover?] She used to think she saw him there but not any more. [More about the kitten?] She saw it on the street one day and felt sorry for it, etc. I think the kitten—well, she sees the kitten in the other half of the picture, to join the two together. [The two halves?] The other half, not shown: the TV screen dissolves and shows the other half of the room. [Thoughts and feeling?] She is really looking for the kitten and yet half, in a way, remembering her dead lover.

The initial problem of organization in thinking becomes apparent in the concrete interpretation that only half of the room is being shown, followed by her farfetched way of handling this by introducing the notion of this being half of a TV screen. There may even be some significance in her introducing the notion of a shimmering representation of a figure: possibly perceptual disturbance has been part of the patient's recent experience. Later, during the inquiry, thinking becomes quite fluid: is she looking for the kitten or for her dead lover? The patient again attempts to rationalize this discrepancy in a forced literary manner.

Card 15. Well it is obviously a scene in the graveyard. I don't suppose I could plagiarize to the extent of saying that is Dracula rising from his grave? [Anything you want.] Well, it does remind me of the story of Dracula. One of my childhood favorites. That is, Dracula was a werewolf and vampire, yeah, I don't know whether the things are synonymous or not. [Story?] Well, werewolves and vampires rise from their graves at night and go to suck human blood and this is just one of Dracula's nocturnal expeditions. [Led up and outcome?] I think some people can become werewolves and I think Dracula was one by birth. Finally they drove a stake through his heart. That is the only way to destroy werewolves. [Thinking and feeling?] I think if Dracula is the hero, they are apparently unmitigated evil. Some of their victims weren't always but I think Dracula is. [Thinking and feeling?] I don't really know. I don't know whether the author ever told you exactly what he was thinking. You are supposed to read his nature from his actions.

The irrelevancy in response to inquiry indicates fluid thought. The oral theme is dramatically introduced.

Card 14. Well, this is a boy looking out of a window, oh, say, from the seventh story of an old tenement house. You'd better put Paris before tenement. He is looking up at the stars at night and wondering what he'll—in this particular picture, he is wondering what he'll make with the rest of his life. I said the seventh story, didn't I? That was a mistake. [Mistake?] Well, I was going to have him finish up as François Villon but I don't think they made seven-story houses then, so I don't think I can go on with this one. It would be nice to finish this up by just tipping an ink bottle over it [nervous laugh]. Well, it is just a brief, fleeting glance: it is somebody you meet at a moment in their life when they have several different ways to turn, and they don't know just how their life will turn out.

Note the patient's needing help to pick up the train of her thought, and note particularly the concreteness of conceptual thinking and the associated inability to shift when she finds that she has two irreconcilable thoughts in mind—the seven-story building and François Villon. This fragmentation of thinking with a concretistic foundation very strongly suggests organically based psychological deficit, whether it be of a toxic and transient nature or of a structural and enduring nature. Similar problems develop in the following story; perceptual distortion is also apparent.

Card B (Picasso's *La Vie*). Well, if that—well, no. . . . Well, this is a drawing from an artist's studio. Obviously, I think he is trying to paint in the manner of Gauguin. The thing is, I can't figure out whether the figures are supposed to be alive.

Well, they wouldn't have wax figures in an artist's studio but I don't see what else.... The two characters could represent Adam and Eve and the other one the Virgin Mary but that doesn't make any story. I am afraid this story is going to have to be unfinished. [Anything it suggests?] No, I'm afraid it doesn't. [Artist's studio?] Well, the picture, but the three characters seem to be several different styles, but in violent contrast to each other and I can't quite make it out. One style is fairly realistic and then the others give off into more abstract points. [Which ones?] [Patient explains that the foreground figures are realistic and the figures in the background pictures on the wall, while "not really abstract, aren't quite delineated; they are roughed in a little more."]

Card 13 MF. We have here a picture of someone who has just ... just died and she's died of consumption and, well, it reminds me of the last scene of *La Traviata.* Let's see, that's also Camille, isn't it, too? Well, we might as well take the story. Camille was a Paris prostitute and she—I guess I'd better stick to Alfredo and Violetta—I don't know the name of Camille's lover—Alfredo or not. Well, they meet and fall in love with each other and are actually living on Violetta's money. She had quite a bit. When Germont, Alfredo's father, comes and pleads with Violetta to give Alfredo up, she does so and makes Alfredo think that she's taken another lover. And Alfredo believes her. But in this scene, she is dying of consumption and Alfredo comes back in her life but it is too late. She dies in his arms and he rises and puts his arm across his eyes. And I think that is the end of the....

Here we have death by consumption (see also discussion of Card 6 BM in Case 1, above). And on Card 3 GF, not reproduced here, a girl is led to moral ruin, despite a rigid moral upbringing, after bad company influences her to drink and to smoke marijuana.

Case 4

Further to illustrate stylistic devices indicating striving toward detachment, similar to those in the stories told by Case 1, I will present one story blandly told by a 17-year-old boy with a history of delinquency and with developing psychopathic characteristics. All his stories have the same style, and many the same basic theme.

Card 5. [Patient smiles.] She sees something. . . . Walking into her living room one day, Mrs. Rebecca Obagar-phuniak—O-b-a-g-a-r-p-h-u-n-i-a-k—found the body of her husband on the floor. She stood in the doorway for one minute petrified with amazement, in a cold sweat of apprehension and indecision. . . . She could tell Percy was dead by the large, spreading crimson stain on his fresh-pressed white shirt. Running to his side after one minute, she knelt beside him and felt his heartbeat—make that: felt *for* his heartbeat. There was none. Feeling his pulse she found there was none either. Getting a grip on herself she dialed the operator on the phone with shaking fingers and asked for the police. The law made the scene roughly two and one half minutes after she dropped the receiver. After a few questions, mostly concerning her blood-stained hands, they drove her down to the station where she was questioned some more. At all times she stoutly maintained her innocence but because of her bloody hands, and a meat cleaver found in a corner of the room, known to belong in her house, with her husband's fresh blood on it, she was disbelieved. Pointing back to a long period of good behavior, she at no time admitted to the slaying of her husband and did not assume the manner of a guilty person in any way. At this point the woman is still in jail. Her trial has not come up yet and it may be a while before it does—wipe that out: these things take time. She has seen no one and she is being held incommunicado against the time of her trial. Eventually it is possible she will once again go up the streets of her city as a free woman but the way that people are kept incarcerated for little or no reason in certain places, this is doubtful. However good her behavior may have been prior to her husband's slaying, the fact is he is dead; her blood is er—his blood is on her hands, was, and, according to the law, facts are facts, comma, Ma'am [in the voice of Sgt. Friday of *Dragnet* fame].

This patient had been hospitalized in connection with pending legal charges of theft against him. He was consciously opposed to being hospitalized. The content of this story is simply that a woman discovers her husband has been murdered, is suspected of the crime, and is still awaiting trial with an uncertain outcome. Striking in the storytelling is the steady absorption in literary device, in getting the right phrase, in specifying punctuation. This bland approach, which increases the story's length without enriching its content, is in the style of a detective, a district attorney, a judge, or a criminal examining the evidence. Note the legal and semilegal phraseology. The abuse by arbitrary social authority, the protest of innocence, the knowledgeability about circumstantial evidence, all are entirely in keeping with the manner with which the story is told—shrewd, detached, counteraccusing, and somewhat facetious.

Case 5

The following complete set of stories, told by a 16-year-old boy, also with a history of delinquency and evidence of developing psychopathic characteristics, repeatedly illustrates the use of the mechanism of externalization of responsibility. In this case, in several places the striving toward bland detachment fails and the patient manifests some anxiety or at least tenseness.

> *Card 1.* Start here or before that, with the picture? [Any way you think the story should go.] There is a little boy here and he is looking at his violin and he knows he is supposed to practice but doesn't want to. The kids outside are yelling for him to come out and play. [What will happen?] . . . . He will probably go out and play. [Thoughts and feelings?] Well, when he is out playing I suppose he feels, not guilty, he doesn't feel guilty; he is just afraid he is going to get caught. [By whom?] His mother, of course, but he didn't think about that until he got outside.

Ordinarily, the boy being forced to practice hears kids playing outside and longs to be with them: motivation is represented internally and in his going out he ordinarily does so with some awareness of his disobedience. In this story the pull is from the outside because the kids are yelling for him; moreover the boy does not think about the consequences until after he acts. The patient even points out that the identification figure does not feel guilty but only afraid of consequences from external authority. This does not imply that there may not be a severe superego problem—in fact, we may well suspect an instance of negation in his pointed exclusion of guilt feelings—but it does illustrate his efforts to deal with temptations and punishments through externalization.

Card 5. This look like his mother [the boy in Card 1]. Yeah, his mother hears nothing and goes in to see why he isn't practicing and when she opens the door and looks in, she sees that he isn't there and gets peeved because he disobeyed her. That's all. [More about the outcome?] Well, she will probably go outside where he is playing, get a good firm grip on one ear and pull him back inside. Now you know what my frustrations are like.

Card 15. Say! Morbid . . . . [A hard one?] It's hard to make a story about this. He looks shook up. He probably lost somebody very close to him and so he is going to the resting place to pray, I guess [melodramatic overtones in patient's voice puts all this in quotes somehow]. [What will happen?] Nothing earth-shaking, I suppose. He will probably go home just as sad as he came. [Whom did he lose?] His wife might have died or. . . .

Card 14. This is amazing! [Why?] Just what comes into my mind. The first thing I thought of was a kid leaving home, scrutinizing the window to see how he is going to get out or something. [Story?] He might have had an argument with one of his family or something like that and . . . he will probably decide for himself that his parents are unjust and unfair to him. He'll decide to take off and leave home [patient breathing hard].

The theme is again external abuse, and the solution is by action—physical withdrawal. But note his anxious breathing: the crust is not that hard yet.

Card A (old man on shoulders of old man) . . . . [A hard one?] There's two people there, aren't they? There's two heads anyway. It reminds me of the story of where the man carried the people across the river on his back. [Story?] I don't remember the name of it. It's an old fable. What do you call them? [Can you think of the story?] I can't make much out of that except that one it reminds me of, but it isn't my own. [Maybe you could take off from that one.] I can't remember exactly how it goes. Some people were trapped someplace, a river was overflowing and flooding, and this guy carried them over on his back. It looks too grotesque for that, though. That's about all.

He emphasizes external hazards and not the ordinarily elaborated conflict of purpose.

Card 10. Obviously, whoever they are or whatever they are doing, they seem to be in love. Maybe this guy had to go someplace, away for a while and he is saying good-bye. [What will happen?] I guess she will wait for him and he'll come back. [What was going on before?] I don't know. They were in love and they were probably courting and all that sort of jazz. They probably spent a lot of time together and he was unexpectedly called away someplace—the service or something like that.

Unexpected outside pressures are frequently introduced in the stories of persons inclined to externalize motivations and responsibilities. This approach becomes evident here when he introduces the man's being called into the service unexpectedly: the event is possible, but this is not the common way of introducing the theme of departure for military service in TAT stories.

Card B (Picasso's *La Vie*) . . . . Are these pictures on the wall or is that something . . . ? [What do you see?] I'm going to disregard them . . . . I don't know what this is. It doesn't look like a normal situation to me. [What does it look like?] I don't know. Mostly, I judge by the expression on their faces or something [that is, in previous stories]. . . . It's hard to tell. [Expressions?] They're expressionless. [Does it suggest any story?] Sadness, maybe. They look like mother and daughter a little bit. You never can tell though. [Any story?] No, I can't think of anything.

It is infrequent for these characters to be called expressionless. Doing so is often a reflection of marked reliance on the mechanism of denial; however, the same disruption may reflect, as it probably does in this case, externalization of responsibility for his inability to respond to the picture with conscious feelings.

Card 13 MF . . . . I can't tell by what kind of expression he has. . . . I can put myself in the same place but I can't ever recall being in the same position. [Same place?] That's what you do when you read a book or see a movie or something. It might possibly have been somebody he hated very much and wanted to kill: it might be his wife, it might be a girl friend. [Anything else about the situation? What happened before? And what will happen?] If it's his girl friend, I'd hate to be in his position. I thought at first it might be his sister or his mother. They sleep in the same room or something like that and he's getting ready to go to bed. I think of that because my sister goes trotting around the house all the time with nothing on. I say she shouldn't. She says it is all in the family: my mother's influence. The reason I mentioned the girl friend was because my mother has accused me of some pretty horrible things, myself and my girl friend.

Notice again that temptation is external—the bedroom situation, the provocative sister—and that the difficulty in making up a story is externalized—the uncertainty of the expression on the man's face. Even the accusation of sexual guilt— so commonly internally experienced in stories to this picture —is implicitly externalized.

Card 6 BM. That's easy. Her son, the lady's son was just killed in action overseas and this guy was sent by the War Department to bring the bad news. So she is gazing out the window with tears in her eyes, trying not to believe what he said. He is real fidgety about telling her. He doesn't like to bring bad news and that sort of stuff. That I get from watching TV.

The source of the material is external, as in the previous story, and the relationship between the two is insubstantial: something has happened to somebody else.

Card 7 BM. He [lower figure] looks mad and he [upper figure] looks satisfied, so he must be an instigator [upper figure]; like he is getting the guy all hopped up and mad at somebody.... He will get him so mad that he will want to do something but he doesn't know what to do and this guy here will tell him what to do, and whatever it is, it will suit his own ends [upper figure's]. [What might it be?] Possibly another person that this guy doesn't like. He is using him as a tool to do something he couldn't do himself, to accomplish his own ends.

This is a prime example of externalization of responsibility for anger, destructiveness, and self-seeking. While it is likely that this and other stories point to actual external "instigators," i.e., parental provocations, the relentless and dramatic externalizations in these stories indicate that by now we are observing an automatically operating mechanism.

Card 4 .... He looks mad about something, like he is going to do something foolish and she is trying to stop him. That is about the size of it. [What might he be going to do? How does he feel?] I think he is probably, what is probably on his mind is to hurt some person in some way and she wants to stop him for his own good before he does.

Card 20. Well, it looks like somebody taking a walk in the park. Maybe he was sitting at home and got tired of doing nothing and wanted some fresh air and went out for a walk. [What will happen?] Well, if he's got something on his mind, he will probably—must have been something on his mind to make him get up and take a walk—so he'll probably get a chance to think it out and then go back.

It is probably closely related to his steady externalization of motivation that when the identification figure is on his own he is bored, inactive, and doubts even his ability to think over something unless it is closely tied to acting—in this instance, taking a walk.

Card 12 M. This fellow is going to wake this guy up or something. I think they are probably planning to go someplace, or like Tom Sawyer or Huck Finn getting up in the middle of the night to go fishing or to their cave or something. [Where will they go?] Fishing or out behind the old proverbial barn to have a smoke or something. Sorry I wasn't in a more imaginative mood [noticing that test is over].

Reviewing the entire protocol one must be struck by the artful as well as sometimes fumbling or arbitrary avoidance of "antisocial" content: Card A, ordinarily seen as a hostile attack, is a scene of rescue; on Card B the usual conflict between the figures and the disapproval of the robed woman are eliminated; Card 13 MF is treated as just a scene of getting ready for bed; Card 12 M, with the help of perceptual distortion, is reduced to boyish adventure or slight misdemeanor; even Card 4 is "innocently" dealt with in terms of the angry man doing something "foolish"; etc. Either the protagonists are virtuous or inactive, or their impulsive behavior is disowned by the verbalization employed. This approach to the TAT is characteristic of patients with developing or well-developed psychopathic characteristics. They take the test as if it were a lie-detector test and try to give all the "right" (i.e., innocent) answers. Of course, other indications in this test, such as reliance on externalization, and the results of other tests in the battery, must be consonant with this diagnostic inference of psychopathic trends before these trends may be emphasized in a test report. Sometimes, reaction formations in an obsessive setting, projections in a paranoid setting, or denials in a hypomanic setting may also lead to such "whitewash" stories, but then the other aspects of the tests will usually indicate the different mechanisms and different diagnostic contexts involved.

III

The preceding sets of stories were drawn primarily from character-disordered contexts. The question, *How was this story told?*, will now be applied to a group of schizophrenic and borderline-schizophrenic TAT protocols. Not only will its diagnostic usefulness be further illustrated, but certain central aspects of the pathology of schizophrenia will be highlighted by it.

Case 6

The first protocol is that of a single, 32-year-old woman who had suffered an acute schizophrenic break.

    Card 1. How long should it be? [As long as you like.] Thinking, he looks a little bit like Yehudi Menuhin, is looking wistfully at the violin, perhaps a Stradivarius, hoping that he could play it as well as Yehudi Menuhin. I am wondering whether it was table or a piece of cloth [under the violin]. [What will happen?] He looks a little stubborn: eventually he will play it even if he only makes a sound, even if afterwards he throws it on the ground. I hope he doesn't do that.

Striking in this story, and in almost every one of her stories to follow, is the lack of synthesis and the lack of striving after synthesis in the story detail. The synthetic or organizing function of the patient's ego appears extremely inert or debilitated. She shifts rapidly as one fantasy fragment, impulse, or affect after another moves to the fore. Contaminatory thinking is evident when the resemblance to Menuhin reappears in the boy's aspiration. Perceptual distortion is also evident. The story's end involves temporal disorientation, in that the future is brought in as a determinant of the present: he will play it even if afterwards he throws it on the ground. Her mix-up of tense—"I am wondering whether it was table"—implies the same disorientation. Past, present, and future fuse. Also evident in the ending is inability to retain a sufficient degree of the storytelling orientation, that is, a clear line between fantasy and reality: when she says, "I hope he does not do that," it is as if she were regarding a real situation with herself as a passive observer. The previously discussed narcissistic and delinquent patients underscored too much their storytelling position, while this patient enters into the scene as a passive, emotionally vulnerable spectator.

Card 5. Well, it looks sort of like the woman heard a noise and looks apprehensive and coming to the door heard someone she didn't want in her house. Actually it is the music or radio, so actually it is not the person she fears, or perhaps she both fears and hopes. [Who would that be?] It could be perhaps her children wrecking the house; or perhaps her husband and dinner isn't ready. [What will happen?] It will be just an ordinary occurrence and nothing to be apprehensive about, as she appears—as I appear to be sometimes.

Card 15. Rather dismal. A block cut. It looks sort of like Scrooge. I don't know who he is mourning. He is carrying on rather too strong. If people are dead, they are dead! No sense carrying on like that! Eventually he will go home. [Led up?] Gee, I don't know. A lot of things. I don't know really. [Anything.] He looks awfully grotesque: perhaps he has murdered someone and is feeling guilty and responsible for all the other people under the gravestones.

Note the conceptually and emotionally fluid spread of guilt to all the dead, and the pathological loss of distance when she agitatedly editorializes that he should not carry on like that.

> *Card 14.* It looks sort of in a dark room, longing to escape to see someone he loves. He looks lonely. He looks fairly relaxed and will get to where he wants to go or will continue to look at the stars until he gets there—not the stars.... [What led up?] It's, he's, maybe he can't see the person he wants to see until morning and, or never again and feels sorry for himself.

In addition to the continued absence of synthetic effort and the fluid shifts of affect, the poignant statement that he will continue to look at the stars until he gets there has that quality of poetic allusiveness that, in the TAT, is characteristic of schizophrenic lapses in logical communication: it leaves too much to be filled in or too much unexplained. That we can fill in for her, by words or by empathic feel, does not mitigate the diagnostic implication. One of the commonest errors I have observed in test interpretation—and in interview interpretation too—is to discount schizophrenic lapses in communication because we know or think we know what the patient means to say. We should not have to extend ourselves at all to grasp the surface meaning of a verbalization.

> *Card A* (old man on shoulders of old man). Rather grotesque. He looks as though he is scratching his head but he is probably trying to wake him. Like mythical images, trees, lightning, like Salvador Dali. Eventually the man will wake up and will do what the other man wants him to do.

Another instance of schizophrenic thinking and verbalization in the TAT is saying that the picture looks one way but it is probably another way. The point implicitly made thereby is that the senses are deceptive. In another respect, the point is lack of commitment to testing or recognizing the real environment; this is one aspect of the ego's loss of autonomy from drive pressures. In the present instance, the drive-dominated fantasy takes precedence over the initial venture at reality testing, and no attempts are made to rationalize or synthesize the result.

Card 10. I've seen this one before. It looks like two people saying good-bye, mother and son. She is resigned to it. Neither are very anxious. Everything works out well.

Note the impoverishment of affect, something already indicated when, on Card 14, she abruptly introduced the "relaxed" description of the young man.

Card B (Picasso's *La Vie*). Very proportional too. This woman has a baby. She thinks it is her baby. Perhaps it is theirs. She is holding the baby and they think she is going to take the baby but she just wants to hold the baby. [Outcome?] She may keep the baby if she feels the two young people can't handle it and they will have to accept this. [How do they feel?] Resentful. [What led up?] I don't know. Perhaps she thought they weren't taking proper care or perhaps they were dreaming of a child, like Adam and Eve, and she is saying, "You are too young."

Note how the baby floats around: the older woman thinks it is her baby, then perhaps it is the baby of the young couple, then it is the baby of the young couple but the older woman is taking it away, and finally it is just a dream of the young couple. The problems stated are uncertainty about what is real and what is fantasy, and what is one's own and what is someone else's. In both instances, the self-boundary appears grossly impaired. This is another version of the loss of the line between fantasy and reality, implied earlier in the patient's losing distance in her "stories" to Cards 1, 15, and A.

Card 13 MF. This woman looks like she is near death and the man is terribly regretful and sad and is going to leave her be. Whatever he's done, that is their business! Eventually it will work out. I don't think she is dead. [What led up?] Well, possibly they were in love, were lovers. Possibly he came into her room and she wasn't feeling very well. If it is her husband, he will be back; it's only nature. [Feelings?] She is a little disgusted with him or the situation. If it is his wife, they will work it out.

Card 12 F. This old woman is wondering about something. The girl is thinking her own thoughts and not communicating to her because the older one looks like a witch. The young woman is thinking, "Please leave my thoughts alone, and later on I will tell you, you old witch!"

In the absence of any attempts to rationalize this story in terms of myth or fairy tale, in the emphatic tone attached to the statement of the young woman's thoughts, and in other aspects of the story's inadequate verbal communication, there is the strong implication that she believes her ideas are being influenced, her thought controlled (note the ending on Card A, above); in addition, the presence of hallucinations is strongly suggested. Also, the experience of fluidity of self-boundaries is restated in a new form: one's thoughts merge with the thoughts of others. The patient seems to feel that if she could restore some sense of the boundaries of her self (in particular, of her thoughts) she could resume communication—a statement which has much to do with the anxiety, uncommunicativeness, and negative reaction to probing therapeutic intervention that many schizophrenics manifest during psychotherapy.

> *Card 3 GF.* That looks sort of like me when I was dragged in here. She was given bad news. Her face is leaning on her right hand. I imagine she will find a way out of her trouble because she looks fairly agile, fairly young; she'll manage. [What led up?] I don't know. [Make it up.] Someone told her she can't have something she wants or needs or possibly can't ever have this thing. But she will either find something or someone else or will go lie down.

Of special note in this story is the treatment of the body self: "Her face is leaning on her right hand" suggests a fragmentation of the body self for, by implication, the face possesses motivation of its own and there is no inner unified self which directs that one will lean one's face here or there. In this same connection the patient reasons that the girl will find a way out of her trouble because she looks fairly agile and young: here a physical fragment (and a forced one at that, unusual for this picture) becomes the basis of an attempted personal reintegration and adaptation. Also of note, because it is so common in the protocols of severely schizophrenic patients, is the emotional *non sequitur* at the end, the action out of emotional context: "or will go lie down."

    Card 2. This is a man doing a job plowing the fields. It looks like sunset, close to the end of the day. The girl has books. Maybe it is her husband... or boy friend and the woman is the mother. The mother looks like she might be pregnant—not that it is my business! She wishes that her son would go in and the girl put her books down and leave her to enjoy the sunset in peace.

On 13 MF the patient had alluded to sexual intimacy by saying emphatically "that is their business"; she makes a similar statement here. The implied thought is that she is prying into someone else's sexual life rather than (a) creating a story, and (b) having her own sexual life pried into by the tester. She thereby indicates loss of the storytelling orientation and of self-boundaries; in addition, the disruption strongly suggests sexual delusions.

    Card 18 GF. First she looked as if she were trying to strangle this person, I don't know whether a man or a woman. Trying to comfort this person. Perhaps this person is dead. I can't really tell. If the person is dead or dying she will be able to bear up to it. She looks a fairly strong character. [Led up?] Oh, perhaps the person just had a heart attack or fell downstairs. It may be a woman. She is afraid that the person is dying or dead already. Like my mother felt when I was first brought in here, that my mind was completely shot, which it isn't!

    Card 12 M. At first it looked as though he was trying to hypnotize this boy or has hypnotized this boy and is going to have him do whatever he wants him to do. He looks sort of like Svengali. [What will he have him do?] Oh, walk in his sleep; perhaps go water the flowers because he is tired.

In the story to Card A she had already introduced the theme of submitting to another's will; on Card 12 F she had introduced the theme of thought control; the theme is introduced here for a third time: it is all the more likely now that delusions of influence are present.

    In summary of these selected aspects of the patient's stories (the stories obviously lend themselves to a much fuller treatment), what emerges is not only the suggestion of delusional thinking and hallucinatory experience, centering around ideas of influence and sexual matters, but, in terms of mediating mechanisms (or the failure of mediating mechanisms), minimal synthetic efforts, passivity of the ego before the onslaught of drive- and affect-charged fantasies, overruling of fragments of reality-testing efforts, and frequent inability to distinguish the line between fantasy and reality and between self and others. In varied forms, schizophrenic fluidity of the self-boundary is repeatedly evident. She sums up much of this analysis in her poetic statement on Card 14. "He will continue to look at the stars until he gets there."

Case 7

The following stories were told by a 23-year-old, single, Catholic, female college graduate who, more than a year before, had developed paranoid delusions of being talked about. At the time of testing she was occasionally able to recognize her delusions for what they were. The schizophrenic aspects of her stories parallel and complement those observed in the preceding protocol.

Card 5. Oh, this woman has a cat. It's a very fat, big, heavy cat. She keeps him in the cellar. One day she opens the door. She hears some scratching in the cellar and she opens the door to let the cat out of the cellar. When she opens the door she doesn't see the cat. He's downstairs. She sees a man downstairs. She is at first frightened but it turns out that the man is just an average—well, not an average but one of those bums that travels around different neighborhoods and asks her for food for lunch or dinner, whatever the case may be. And here, she might be—er—er—about, following such an incident she might be suspicious when she hears another sound from the cellar and she might be going from room to room to get to the cellar. That's all. [What does the current picture show?] She might have heard a subsequent sound again, if it were the cat. [How did the man get into the cellar?] Her cellar door was open because it was the summer. He wandered in the cellar. [What did she do when he asked for food?] She gives it to him and he goes on his way. It's based on people who used to come to our house occasionally and sit on the back step and ask for food and eat.

Temporal disorientation (the picture represents two points in time), frequent lapses in communication, weak or arbitrary synthetic efforts, or even the possibility of hallucinatory transformations of identity (the cat to the man), all stand out in these verbalizations.

> *Card 14.* Oh, let's see, this is a picture of a young man ready to commit suicide. Oh... let me see, what could he be committing suicide for? He has just discovered that his supposed future wife, his fiancée—let's put it that way—is dead. Did I say he was going to commit suicide? Let's change that and say he was contemplating committing suicide. He thought of—you know—in Romeo and Juliet fashion—wants to join his lover, you know, or his deceased lover. It also might be a picture of a young man looking at the view. That's about all, I guess. It looks like somebody sitting on the john too, reaching for the john paper [laughs]. [Outcome?] He does not commit suicide. [Thoughts and feelings?] He is extremely unhappy and anxious over the loss of his one and only girl [voice becomes sad here]. He's selfish because ..... [?] In that he feels he can never find anyone whom he can love as much. That's about it. [How is that selfish?] Well, it's, he is selfish in mourning the death of the loved one. He is concerned with himself, the loss to him. [Action in picture?] He is just sitting on the window sill thinking about whether he should jump. There's a river down below. It's in Europe. We could say it's the Seine River; I don't know why that should come into my mind.

There are three noteworthy aspects of how this story was told. First, the bizarre notion of the young man sitting on the john and reaching for the john paper: an intrusion of an inner fantasy that grossly violates the reality context even though it has fragmentary detail to "justify" it. Second, the inadequate verbalization when the young man is characterized as selfish because he is mourning the loss of the girl. It is not that the content of this idea is peculiar but that it is taken for granted that the connection between mourning and selfishness is self-evident and not to be developed according to a particular psychological point of view. Third, the patient's perplexity concerning one of her thoughts: her thinking of the Seine River. This perplexity is of a sort frequently encountered in the records of schizophrenic patients who have to some degree sealed over a psychotic break or are conspicuously fluctuating in their position as regards maintaining reality testing and a sense of control over their functioning. Perplexity concerning one's thoughts is different from the perplexity of the brain-damaged or toxic such as was noted in the case of the addictive woman above (Case 3). There the patient was perplexed about the nature of the external situation with its—to her—contradictory fragments. The present perplexity is also to be distinguished from the careful observation and reporting of one's thoughts characterizing the communications of certain obsessive persons. A variant of the perplexity in this story is evident in the first sentence of the next story.

> *Card A* (old man on shoulders of old man). At first I thought it was somebody giving somebody a haircut—but we won't use that because it looks a little too demoniacal. Let's see, the action is murder. The murderer is standing, the victim is seated, in front of a fire. This is way out in the woods someplace. Two men who are former partners.... Let's see.... One is guilty of embezzlement. To cover up his embezzlement he is burning some letters which his partner has seen and which definitely, I could say they definitely led, would lead to his punishment by the law. Let's say the man in the background has summoned the police but of course gets to the culprit first, and, instead of waiting for the police, he murders the friend. And in the picture he is thinking about or hovering over his victim, thinking about the murder or hovering over his victim. He has just—let's see—the man who was trying to perform the murder, his passion gets the best of him, his desire to be righteous, to see the right thing done; in other words he thinks and feels at this time that in murdering his former partner he will have justified the crime. This also might be a man who catches another man who has murdered his wife and was disposing of the body in a big hole—the man in the foreground, that is. I guess that's it.

The quick switch from haircut to murder in the beginning of the story is accomplished with enough poise to suggest that the patient is capable of achieving some distance from her disordered thoughts. There are, however, such peculiar verbalizations as "he of course gets to the culprit first," and "in murdering his former partner he will have justified the crime." Most striking is the near-contamination of thought and act in the repetition concerning the man's thinking about the murder or hovering over his victim. By all indications the theme is that of hovering over his victim and not thinking about it. It is the *patient* who is thinking about it, but she projects her subjective processes onto one of the characters in the story. It is not rare in schizophrenic records to find contaminations or near-contaminations of this sort. Thus, a patient not knowing what to think about the thoughts of one of the characters will say "he doesn't know what to think" in a manner that transparently transposes the problems from within to a figure in the story. The previous patient on Card 1 had the boy who looked like Yehudi Menuhin (an internal comparison) aspire to be like Menuhin (an external referent). A further aspect of disturbance of self-boundaries is brought out in the next stories.

Card 12 F. Oh dear! This is ... oh ... a mother and grandmother who are terribly distraught over finding out that their daughter has become pregnant. The mother is sort of indignant and disappointed. The grandmother simply smiles wisely and says nothing. The baby is eventually born and given up—oh no!—and taken home and cared for by the grandmother and mother. The daughter in the meantime dies [sigh], I guess. Let's see. Oh, you wanted to know the events leading up to that. I guess I told you that: their unhappiness after learning their daughter has just become pregnant. [Tester points out shift of affect attributed to older figure.] Well, let's say the grandmother is disturbed in that she knows what her own daughter's feelings are, having had a daughter of her own. But say that she has had experience with such things before, more experience than her own daughter and is therefore more tolerant of the incident. The picture of course takes place prior to the daughter's death. [Led up to daughter's death?] In childbirth.

Card 18 GF. Oh, this is a woman who is just helping her mother up from a fall. The mother has fallen down the stairs, is somewhat bruised and the daughter is sympathetic and unhappy to see her mother in pain. The mother recovers. That's it. [How did the mother fall down?] Oh, she was old and she slipped and fell. [How does the mother feel?] Sympathetic. No, you asked me how the mother feels? Oh, she is in pain. She is pleased that her daughter is solicitous of her health.

In these two stories a variety of indications of confusion between the mother's identity and the identification figure's identity are present. First, on Card 12 F the granddaughter is referred to several times as "their daughter" as if mother and daughter were one and not separated by a generation; second, they take the granddaughter's child so that they become its mother; third, in the inquiry she says that the grandmother knows what her own daughter's feelings are "having had a daughter of her own"—as if the merging of the two women pictured is so far-reaching that a separate daughter figure from the one portrayed must be implied; fourth, on 18 GF she reverses the usual relationship of generations in this picture—it is a daughter looking down at her mother; and fifth, the patient's slip of hearing during the inquiry when she first states what the daughter was feeling after having been asked what the mother was feeling. She spontaneously corrects this slip, indicating again (see beginning of Card A) a little capacity for self-observation and self-correction.

Case 8

One story from the protocol of a 19-year-old girl in an early phase of schizophrenia further illustrates the self-boundary problem.

Card 12 F. This girl—er—she has a lot of things on her mind. She's been having a lot of things on ... her mind, and—er—right now—er—something behind her or inside her—something evil—is trying to tell her what to do. And she's trying to look away, tries not to look at it! [Patient's voice is angry.] And at the time she's very confused and—er—sick, but she's going to overpower this thing in the background, somehow. [What evil to do?] Evil things, things she shouldn't do. [For instance?] Get even with people. [In what way?] Cause trouble. [Example?] Well she [old woman] knows that—er—this girl who's going out with a boy she likes very much, well, her parents don't want her to, so she's going to call them and tell them when the girl is going to go out and meet the boy someplace.

The patient is uncertain whether the young woman is dealing with an evil introject or an evil person. Magically, she hopes to combat the influence by "looking away." The patient obviously loses distance, that is, loses the storytelling orientation, and becomes angry and upset. During the inquiry the evil figure is fluidly re-externalized and is now informing on her rather than exerting evil influence directly. Psychotic confusion between the patient's self and a hostile mother figure is clearly implied, not because of the content alone, for that could be produced by a nonpsychotic (this picture does encourage symbolic or fantastic themes), but because the content is communicated with heated and dismayed affect and with fluid, perplexed development of the narrative.

Case 9

The following stories were told by a young man of 18, intelligent, imaginative, aspiring to be a writer or artist, and, diagnostically, somewhere within the ill-defined realm of borderline schizophrenia. Considering the way the stories are told, as well as certain aspects of their content, we find many indications of the regressive, restitutive, or reintegrative shifts of the level of psychic functioning that characterize the clinical picture of such patients.

Card 1. This little boy's brother is a great violinist and—er —just before this picture the brother was a great success at a concert. He came home and left his violin and went off to a party. And the boy is now sitting next to the violin, and, of course, he—er—kind of wonders how his brother did it, how his brother can make this piece of wood react so beautifully. But after the picture the boy doesn't try to play the violin. He feels that he couldn't do it. The boy feels, as he is watching the violin, a wonder and frustration and pain and yet pleasure because he loves his brother.

The story is rich in thematic implications. For purposes of this analysis I will refer only to the subtlety and complexity of feeling ascribed to the boy. Such treatment of TAT figures is most commonly encountered in the records of intelligent and sensitive subjects who are relatively normal or else are neurotic but not badly decompensated. As neurosis, character disorder, or psychosis increases in severity, such features tend to disappear from the stories. This parallels the generally observed greater subtlety and complexity of affective experience that goes with the attainment of higher levels of maturity. In the present instance, despite abundant indications of regressive modes of response in other parts of the TAT, and in the entire battery of tests, this articulated treatment of emotional experience will stand as an indication of ego assets which elsewhere are obscured or temporarily unavailable to the patient. We see a higher level of functioning this patient is capable of attaining. In reflecting on his treatment of affect, one must consider too that he has literary aspirations; however, by themselves, such aspirations do not guarantee a successfully subtle treatment of an emotional situation. It may well be that his literary aspirations are part of his restitutive efforts.

> *Card 5.* This happened in Germany. Before the picture the woman was out shopping and it was just after the war and she was bringing home a great assortment of fine foods for a dinner. She comes in the door. She has been thinking about what it would be like to finally prepare a meal like this. Then she opens the door and finds that her husband is dead. He died naturally. And after the picture she leaves the food in the house and she goes out and buys herself dinner. During the picture she feels almost anger at her husband which quickly wears off and then she feels a deep sorrow—and shame. [Shame?] Ashamed of her anger.

Again there is subtlety and complexity in the treatment of the woman's emotions. Equally impressive, however, is the rapid shift in the story from enthusiastic anticipation to dismal discovery and abandoned activity. The patient's abrupt introduction of this abruptly discovered event strongly suggests that he is familiar with internal experiences of this nature, that is to say, of marked and sudden alterations of his inner state. The woman's behavior following her discovery is, as stated by him, inappropriate.

Card 15. Before this picture this man has been told that he must go to the graveyard to find his grave. And as he goes in he finds that many, many people have died. He can't, he can't think of when he should have died, where his grave should be. He can't find his grave. And now he stands in the middle of his grave—among the graves—and he feels a sense of hate for the people who have died and complicated his own death. And after the picture he goes away from the graveyard and he avoids the people who told him to find his own grave. During the picture he feels, as I say, hate, and—er—he looks at the graves and he is envious of all the people who are safely put away and they are no more bother to anybody, while he is still standing there and it seems to be a great annoyance to some people that he is not underground.

We find another abrupt change of emotional position from hatred to envy of those dead and buried. In the way he words this story, he does not appear to be elaborating a complex set of feelings, as he had in his first two stories; he appears simply to have switched in midstream to a different orientation to the situation. Also striking is the very weak synthesis of detail and attention to requirements of adequate communication to the tester: he does not rationalize, fill in, or connect such elements as being told to go find one's own grave; fusing the time of death with the place of death; implying but never stating that the identification figure, rather than merely doing the bidding of others, is seeking death and therefore is hateful; and his subsequent avoiding of the people who sent him to find his grave after he could not find it. The view of existence expressed in the content is, of course, despairing: others want one to die, one feels a bother and that one should die, one envies the dead, etc. But again we must regard the story from the standpoint of the patient's literary aspirations. There is a trend in modern writing toward a "dream consciousness" rather than "stream of consciousness" approach; attempts are made, by shocking, startling, inexplicable events and changes, as well as by disruptions of narrative continuity, to develop dramatic power and perhaps to give form, in a way, to severe disruptions of the organization of psychic functioning. This patient may be "a little in love with death" and attempting to say so artfully. Experience with the TAT suggests, however, that mere striving for literary effect or style of this sort does not sufficiently explain very weak synthesis and inadequate verbalization. Subjects not in the toils of schizophrenic trends remain sufficiently related to the tester and the test situation to take cognizance of the requirements of ordinary social intercourse, if by no other means than indicating in a word or a tone that they are contriving an *avant-garde* type of story. Borderline schizophrenics frequently tell stories filled with perverse, sadistic, supernatural, and otherwise shocking and baffling morbidness, but close analysis suggests that they are not free to take this course or leave it alone; at most they may be free to manipulate the degree of bizarreness they introduce into their stories, but more or less bizarre stories they must tell. It is more than likely that they are, in one respect, trying to shock themselves so as to experience affect and a feeling of being alive and in contact. The concern with the beautiful reaction of a piece of wood on Card 1 appears to be a high-level version of this problem. The next three stories told by this patient support these last assertions and are representative of the remainder of the protocol.

Card 14. Before this picture, this man felt very, very happy. He was in bed and he felt, he felt so happy that he wanted to get up and look out and see if anybody else felt happy. And, and, he, in the picture, he opens the window, looks out and he couldn't see anybody around. Nothing there. Just the sky, which you could hardly say was there. And his happiness wears off and he stands there looking out and wondering why he wasted his happiness, got up [patient's voice breaks]. And after the picture he went back to bed. During this picture he feels merely a sense of loss.

There is considerable emotional incongruity in saying "merely a sense of loss" following the very poignant "he wasted his happiness." The treatment of the theme again introduces the abrupt shift of emotional experience referred to in discussing Cards 5 and 14; here he shifts from great happiness to the miserable experience of nothingness, isolation, and waste of feelings. Note, however, that both types of emotional experience—happiness and nothingness—occur in social isolation, essentially in a regressed context. It is further implied that the attempt to bridge this isolation, if only in the remote way of looking out of the window to see if others are happy, threatens one's feeling life—not just one's happiness but one's feelings in general. The (regressive) solution is to return to the encapsulated, isolated position in bed. The search for objects must be given up.

Card A (old man on shoulders of old man). Before this picture these two old men had all the power there ever was and they didn't know each other and they used their power wisely. Then, unfortunately, they met and became friends, and as friends they felt the urge to give to each other, and the only thing they could give was advice. And as soon as they began exchanging suggestions, while this corrupted their power, and —er—it was a long time before they finally got around to blaming each other for the—er—deterioration of, of their own worlds. And in the picture they seek to destroy each other. They seek to remain as the whole picture with no part of the other showing. And after the picture they destroyed each other and they had destroyed each other's worlds.

From one point of view he is telling the same story as he did to the previous picture except for exchanging a sense of omnipotence for a sense of great happiness. The message seems to be that attempts to establish object relations destroy any sense of inner feeling, satisfaction, or existence—"unfortunately they met." In addition, mutual destruction of objects is now introduced. Further, we find a remarkably illuminating statement of a problem frequently encountered in the psychotherapy of such patients as this one: the therapist's intent to help —by support, reassurance, clarification, or interpretation— is experienced by the patient as a destructive invasion of his inner world. This invasion is felt to destroy the possibility of a relationship as well as any sense of power, however regressively this sense of power may be founded. Finally, and of considerable interest as regards schizophrenic style of thought and communication, there is the weaving of perceptual detail into the story in such a way as to eliminate the effectiveness of the frame of the picture as a boundary between it and surrounding reality: the observations that only parts of the figures are showing, especially of the lower figure, and that the upper figure is pushing down on the lower figure, are regressively translated into the theme of being pushed out of the picture. The word "picture" is used to refer simultaneously to the picture before him and to psychological life-space. Again, viewing this regressive translation as a literary device aiming at increased drama cannot adequately account for its occurrence and its content. It must also be assumed that the boundaries between fantasy and reality cannot be consistently maintained, that the boundaries of the self that demarcate the inner from the outer world are fluid. We may reflect back on his unusual and repetitive use of the word "picture" in the previous stories: he says "before the picture" and "after the picture" rather than using a more fitting word like "situation." We are now in a position to assume that picture and real situation are not consistently differentiated in his inner experience.

Card 10. Before this picture, these two people—er—hated each other. And then they were accidentally thrown together in some situation and just before this picture a miraculous change took place which I can't describe. In the picture they, they feel as if they are a picture, a complete thing, and they are aware of their limits and they accept them. And after the picture they leave each other. Hmm, a bad picture. [What are their limits?] The boundaries of the picture. [Were you making some reference to the people?] No.

We have here an even more extensive disappearance of boundaries than the one just discussed. To say that they feel as if they are a picture and a complete thing and that they are aware of their limits is not just a metaphoric device for literary effect, i.e., a verbalization issuing from a high level of psychic organization. It is easily conceivable that a clearly nonschizophrenic subject might use such a device, but then we could expect him to signal the tester through words, tone of voice, or gestures that he was being fanciful; we would also expect him to tell a more coherent story and to establish meaningful continuity for the events of the story. This patient refers first to another abrupt ("miraculous") change of inner state, a transformation from hate to some indefinable sense of union, and then, with no further explanation, he has the people leave each other afterwards as if this sense of union could be thought of or tolerated only for a moment. In other words, this is hardly a narrative; it has all the signs of being a narratively undeveloped, almost direct representation of puzzling and fluid internal experience. It is more than likely that the patient tried to maintain awareness that this is a picture, and therefore an unreal union or intimacy (previous evidence indicates how frightening the prospect of union or contact is to him). However, this awareness does not remain within the boundaries of the self; it becomes the awareness of the characters in the picture: it is not the patient who feels they are a complete thing, they feel it; it is not he who regressively utilizes the edges of the picture to indicate that his tolerance of this experience is limited, they are aware of their limits; and it is not the patient who leaves this scene (and discredits it) through such devices, they leave each other. His concluding remark that it is a bad picture more than likely expresses the threat and dilemma he encountered in dealing for the first time in this test with two persons in direct contact and apparently not attacking each other. The picture can be construed as a fight but usually it is not; that he did not so construe it is reminiscent of the man's reaching out to share happiness on Card 14, the woman's pleasant anticipation of dinner with her husband on Card 5, the boy's vicarious gratification through his beloved brother on Card 1, and the articulated treatment of affect in the first two stories. That is, the patient appears still to be experiencing yearnings toward intimacy and shared pleasures even though he repeatedly indicates that he cannot tolerate these yearnings. He indicates this intolerance through regressive disruptions of communication and thought organization and through content concerned with withdrawal, emptiness of feeling, death, and non-existence.

IV

In the remainder of this paper, I will consider three different types of protocols—phobic, depressive, and hypomanic—in order to illustrate, even though briefly, analysis of *content as verbalized* in three frequently encountered clinical contexts.[1]

Case 10

The following TAT communications illustrate one way in which phobic trends in a predominant hysterical character setting may manifest themselves. The patient is a 24-year-old woman with two young children; she has completed some graduate work in ancient languages.

> *Card 1.* This looks like a boy who is discouraged about his music lessons. [Make up a story.] He has probably been told to play and doesn't want to. [What's going to happen?] He probably won't play and eventually will give up lessons.
> *Card 5.* Looks like a woman who is frightened. . . . Looks as if she heard something and came rushing in to see what it was. I can't tell what she sees. [Make up something.] . . . Maybe something is broken or. . . . [What will happen?] She will just go in and straighten whatever is wrong.

That the woman is seen as frightened would have no bearing on the presence of phobic tendencies: fear is commonly apperceived in this figure. What is noteworthy is the verbalization of her "rushing in": this is somewhat out of keeping with her fright, for fright, as we usually find it handled in response to this picture, would restrict the woman to a cautious investigation. This unusual treatment of motility in connection with fear, this excited passage through space, is something to note,

---

[1] See the study of depressive TAT's by Welch, Schafer, and Dember (1961).

something the significance of which will become progressively greater and somewhat clearer as we go through the protocol.

> *Card 15.* It looks like a man in a graveyard. It looks like a ghost-story picture [nervous laugh]. You could take it as a ghost or as a man in despair . . . . He looks as if he can't move until he got over what he is thinking about . . . . [Thoughts and feelings?] I would guess that he is thinking about death and is in despair about it. It doesn't look as if he is able to pray. Until he can, he will be in the same situation. [Outcome?] . . . . Eventually he will be given comfort by God.

That the picture suggests a ghost story does not by itself imply phobic trends. Coming as it does, however, from a woman with graduate education, being accompanied by nervous laughter, being not freely elaborated but rather developed in a somewhat blocked, fragmented, and unintegrated way and left in an indeterminate position in her subsequent story, the ghost theme strongly suggests a fearful response to the picture. In addition to this consistency with the observations of the preceding story, there is consistency of an unusual emphasis on motility: she says "he can't move until he got over what he is thinking about." She introduces here, idiosyncratically, the theme of paralysis of movement. Her statement presumably is meant in a somewhat metaphoric sense; that is, he cannot move emotionally or psychologically, but the choice of spatial metaphor must be regarded as significant.

> *Card 14.* It looks like somebody waking up very early in the morning and looking out of the window and seeing that it is light and he will probably have to wait a while before going out of the room. . . . [Thoughts and feelings?] He is thinking that it is a good day out; looks like he'd rather be outside than inside.

Note again the implication of paralysis or inhibition of motility: he will have to wait a while before going out of the room—a notion rendered even more striking by its not being rationalized by her in any form. The movement tendency is centrifugal but it cannot be released.

Card A (old man on shoulders of old man). It doesn't look like anything real. It looks like some sort of nightmare or some sort of classical myth [spreads hands in hopeless gesture]. It looks like water in the background or it looks like Jupiter subduing E—[recording illegible here: "Enceladus"?]. E— is not happy about it. [What will happen?] Just thinking of the established story: E—will be put in a cave and still be angry.

As in the stories to Cards 5 and 15, there is a combination of phobic implications in her referring to it as a nightmare and introducing blocked or paralyzed motility (being confined in a cave). The confinement is also reminiscent of Card 14.

Card 10. [Extremely uncomfortable smile and puts hands to head.] Looks like a man and woman who haven't seen each other for a long time and they could be husband and wife or brother and sister [shrugs, sighs]. [Thoughts, feelings, outcome?] They are glad to see each other but can't say what they want because they haven't seen each other for so long.

Here it is emotional expression that is inhibited. In another context, this might refer to a general difficulty in communicating in interpersonal relationships, but in this context it is very reminiscent of the man who can't leave the graveyard, the man who can't leave his room, and the man who can't leave the cave.

Card B (Picasso's *La Vie*). This looks more like a painting than something from real life. It looks as if the baby is the man's and this woman's [older woman] and that this is the wife here [younger woman]. The man is only looking at the other woman and not comforting the wife at all. [Led up?] It looks as if the other woman is a much stronger personality than the wife. [Thoughts and feelings?] It looks as if everybody is unhappy. [Why?] The wife would probably be jealous: a standard reaction. The husband looks as if he preferred the other woman to his wife and the other woman is probably accusing the man because she has the baby to take care of.

The common triangle scene elicited by this picture is given an unusual treatment: the man is said to prefer the older, clothed woman and to be rejecting the younger, nude woman, and this despite the fact that the older woman is hostile to the man. Simply the fact of this unusual treatment of the triangle situation strongly suggests a special focus of conflict in the area of triangular sexual relationships and thereby a significant predisposition toward hysterical oedipal involvements.

Card 13 MF. These are weird pictures. Looks as if the woman just died [tone of voice is embarrassed and uncomfortable, as if she is asking for support]. And I suppose the man is the husband. [What led up?] Since she is not dressed, she is perhaps having a baby.

The use of the word "weird," provided that it is not embedded in a sentence that unemotionally characterizes the artist's intent, is one of the most reliable indicators in verbalization of phobic trends. This holds in the Rorschach test too.

Card 12 F. An old mother and daughter. The old mother is living with the daughter and she never lets the daughter go very far away or do much and the daughter looks as if she would like to go somewhere [smile]. This is a situation that continues. [Daughter's feelings?] She feels tied down. [Outcome?] There will be the same situation for a long time.

Inhibition of centrifugal motility is again central but now it emerges in the context of a hostile-submissive tie to the mother figure—a tie commonly found in phobic women.

Card 3 GF. It looks like a person very unhappy or very tired, one or the other. [Make up a story.] A girl, coming from work, absolutely exhausted. All she can do is rest and then go to work the next day.

She responds very strongly to the bodily stance of the figure. While confinement is not the central implication, the blocking of further vigorous action by a physical condition is outstanding.

Card 2. A girl who lives on a farm and is a student and she is interested in her studies, and her parents are interested in the farm. [Make up a story.] ... She will study and then either get married or stay on the farm. [Pick one outcome.] She'll prob-

ably get married and go to a farm and not get out of the community particularly.
Note the indecisiveness about whether the girl will accomplish her centrifugal movement, as well as the final "resolution" which involves making an abortive attempt to move out but only ending up just where she started from—restricted movement in a cemetery, a bed, a room, a cave, or away from a mother, and now from the home locale.

> *Card 18 GF.* It looks like a woman is murdering somebody but I can't even make out if it is a man or woman. [Make up something.] . . . . [Who is being murdered and why?] . . . . I don't know. [It seems as though any intellectual effort is a painful undertaking for this woman.]
> *Card 12 M.* It looks like a minister saying a prayer for a boy who is sick. [Outcome?] He'll get better.

Throughout the protocol, and perhaps somewhat more strikingly toward its end, the paucity of spontaneous response to the pictures is, of course, very conspicuous. Since this is a patient with a Verbal IQ of around 120 on the Wechsler Adult Intelligence Scale, a major repressive emphasis in her defensive functioning is unmistakably implied, especially since severe depression, organic incapacity, schizophrenic withdrawal, or rebellious noncompliance can all be ruled out. In summary, therefore, we may conclude that the repressive emphasis, the unusual treatment of the triangular situation, the ambivalent dependency on the mother figure, the references to ghosts and nightmares and things weird, and the repeated emphasis on inhibition of movement or, in one case, excessive excitement, all suggest not only that this is a predominantly hysterical disorder, but that in addition phobic trends are likely to be conspicuous, and even further that the nature of the phobia is likely to be centered in some way on movement in space. This analysis was originally carried out without knowledge of the patient's presenting problem. It turned out that she had a crystallized phobia of airplanes falling on her from out of the sky.[2]

[2] See Chapter 9 for comparable manifestations in Rorschach responses.

Case 11

The following stories, the first four stories told by a depressed 30-year-old man of average intelligence, illustrate depressive features not only in the thematic material but in the manner of taking the test.

Card 1. He's got a violin and he looks awful blue. . . . Whether he wants to play it sometime or not. . . . . Or he can't play it at all and wishes he could. I can't think of nothing. [What will happen?] I don't know. [Build a story.] I'm not much good at making stories. Gee, gee, I don't know. [Further pressure for outcome.] He probably will end up playing it.

Card 5. This one: the woman coming in the house . . . door. She don't look happy, looks more or less depressed, like something happened. Maybe somebody had an accident and they're in the hospital. . . . Hmm. [Patient chews edge of card.] There are something, I don't know, I can't . . . [What will happen?] This boy might die. [There is a boy in the hospital?] That I don't know. [Which boy?] Her boy. [What happened before?] I don't know.

Card 15. This looks like a man who lost his wife, somebody close to him, recently, and he goes to her grave every so often. And it looks like he is mourning over her. Outside of that I don't know. [What will happen?] Well, he will either forget about it or stay that way the rest of his life. [Which?] I don't know. [Thoughts and feelings?] I don't really know.

Card 14. This one I don't know. It looks like a man looking out at the sky or something. And there is no light in the room. Or he could be looking at something else. Hmm, I don't know what it could be. . . . . . . [Thoughts and feelings?] I don't know. [What happened before?] I don't know. These pictures, I really can't illustrate anything.

Inability to be productive could, as in the previous phobic protocol, refer to strong repressive trends; however, the battery of tests as a whole as well as a good deal of the TAT content strongly points to a depressive context. Of particular significance in these few stories are such events as the following. (1) On Card 5, the relatively unusual introduction of the theme of the child dying as a result of an accident; not only that, but his being in the hospital at this time; and even further the emphasis falling on the woman's looking depressed rather than, as is usual, concerned or apprehensive. These features strongly suggest that fantasy themes of death and depression are prominent in this patient's present condition. (2) Even more striking, however, is his chewing the edge of Card 5. This behavior manifests poorly controlled oral-incorporative tendencies. Ordinarily we find only very young children behaving so in the course of testing. (3) In his story to Card 15 he states that the man either has to forget about his wife's death or mourn the rest of his life. He implies the impossibility of accomplishing the work of mourning. This implication is particularly forceful because "the rest of his life" does not take cognizance, as subjects ordinarily do when they tell a sad story to this picture, that this is an old man and the rest of his life is not going to be very long. Implied is identification with this figure intense enough to eliminate the age differential. (4) In his story to Card 14, the simple verbalization "and there is no light in the room" must be taken as more than a description of the card: subjects will frequently comment that the man is in a dark room; however, when the darkness is something they can contemplate with relative detachment, they refer to it in the manner of setting the scene, perhaps in a subordinate clause or by implication; they then say that it is at night, or that he is waking up in the morning, or that he is looking out of a dark room into the light. His offering as a statement sufficient unto itself that there is no light in the room, and doing so in the context of an extremely meager story, can be taken to indicate a highly charged emotional reaction to the darkness as representing feelings of gloom, being lost, receiving no outside help—themes he dealt with frequently throughout his TAT. In this respect particularly, the study of verbalization illuminates something of significance in the patient's condition, whereas regarded simply as a narrative detail, the absence of light in the room could be bypassed as an insignificant, commonplace, and realistic description of the picture.

Case 12

The following stories have been selected from the protocol of a married, Jewish woman of 44, of average intelligence, with a manic-depressive history of long standing and currently in a hypomanic phase. The stories illustrate hypomanic reliance on the defense of denial, especially in the form of reversal.

> *Card 5.* The mother opened the door to—it seems to me that she is looking in to see what is going on.... Also looks to me as if there is something going on [laughs].... She is a pleasant person, but knows what she is doing, what's going on.... If they get spanked, I don't know....

"Pleasant" is an unusual characterization of this woman: it eliminates the apprehension, disapproval, inquisitiveness, and/or dismay customarily mentioned. This denial becomes more blatant when the patient emphasizes that the woman knows what's what. The denial does not altogether succeed, for the prospect of spanking emerges tentatively at the end—maybe she is a "bad" mother. Breakdown of denial is very frequently observed in the stories of psychotic hypomanics. It sometimes leads to repudiation of the picture and/or the story possibility that has intruded into awareness and subsequent rejection of the card. As one young woman said after recognizing the hostility in Card A, "You've got me. I'm not morbid. I happen to be gay and chipper. If I did make up a story about them, it could be nothing pleasant, due to the art work."

> *Card 15.* That's a tough one. Oh, it's a cemetery ... and ... looks to me as if he is praying.... He is very deep in meditation. Is that enough? [Make up a story.] If somebody came along he would scare them—because he has a vicious-looking face, because of his appearance, the way he is standing there. [Led up?] It seems to me like he is praying. [Outcome?] He is going to go home [laughs]. You mean, is he going to cry? He won't cry. He'll probably turn around and walk away.

At the beginning and end of the story she tries hard to deny

what is to her his "vicious" appearance. When this defense
fails in the middle of the story, she resorts to a different form
of denial, with the help of displacement: it is not she
who is "scared"; someone else would be—while in fact she is
the somebody who "came along," and her fright is evident
in her impoverished, poorly organized, archaically defended "story." Her difficulty in perceiving that it is a cemetery should also be noted: in this context, it is very likely that
the perceptual problem is another manifestation of her denial efforts. Note too that she interprets the "outcome" question to refer to crying—an emergence, via projection, of the
depression to be warded off by her denials.

> *Card 10.* [Patient looks puzzled.] Oh, this is a woman. She is
> getting kissed by this man or he is whispering to her. I can't
> tell if this is his mouth or his beard. She looks very contented
> and him too, whatever they are doing, talking, or he is
> kissing.... [Led up?] I have no idea. [Make it up.] Either...
> they don't look like two people that would argue. He might
> be going away and kissing her good-bye. [How does she feel
> about that?] She seems very contented...also a little lonesome.
> ...She doesn't look angry.... She looks perturbed, not per-
> turbed, concerned....I think I crossed my thought there.
> [What do you mean?] Because first I said she looked contented
> and then I said she is going to miss him and be lonesome....
> He looks like he might be sorry he has to leave her. I don't
> know whether he looks as concerned as she does. He seems to
> have the impression that that is the thing to do and it is for the
> best. Good-bye, my love, good-bye [laughs]. You want me to be
> dramatic [patient's tone very mournful]. I ought to give you
> P—[her daughter] here: she'd give you something. [Patient starts
> discussing the personal problems and psychiatric treatment of
> her children.]

(1) The piling up of negations—they do not look as if they
would argue; she does not look angry—is a common test manifestation of great reliance on denial. (2) Another such manifestation is minimization—"a little lonesome"; "not perturbed, concerned." (3) Still another such is egocentric reference to one's motherliness or motherly efforts, such as is
suggested at the end of the story. (4) The patient herself be-

comes aware that a denial has failed: contentment is fluidly superseded by loneliness. (5) Note the disrupted perception of the man's mouth: oral themata and disruptions commonly stand out in hypomanic protocols, as they do in hypomanic dynamics as observed clinically. Oral emphasis is not diagnostic of any one condition, but it is consistent with the present diagnostic impression and is to be expected in hypomanic records in general.

> *Card 2.* Oh this is a lovely girl! And this I can't figure out if that's her mother and if this is her father. And it seems as if they are living in a faraway place. The mother is daydreaming about what she would like to do, where she'd like to go. The father is working and looks contented, interested in his work. The girl isn't looking at her mother but she seems to be daydreaming too. She is the studious type. The girl looks wholesome. You know what I mean by wholesome? But she too seems to be yearning to go some place, but she doesn't seem to be getting it from her mother. Maybe she read about it. And the horse is a very nice horse and the farm has a nice crop.

The patient tries to build up a wholesome family scene, going to a pathetically absurd extreme when she includes the horse and crop (the latter an oral reference too). But the daughter "doesn't seem to be getting it from her mother"; as in Card 5, the denials do not quite succeed in eliminating the spectre of the bad, unnourishing mother, be it her own mother, herself, or, as is most likely the case in a psychotic context, a fusion of the two.

> *Card 18 GF.* It looks like he has got a hold of her and he's ... he's kind, he's not angry. Or is it a she? It's her mother, it looks like. A woman and another woman and the woman that is standing is trying to tell the other woman something. It is for her own good. And the one that is leaning over the banister doesn't look pleased about this, telling her what she is telling her. I don't know what she is telling her. She seems a little, the one that is leaning over the banister looks as if she might have been a little bit upset. She is not upset now. I can't see her face so it is hard to tell. The other woman looks as if she is telling her something for her own good. She has a very kind face ... her hands, the one that is leaning over, her hands

seem determined but her hands are very kind. The other one seems limp as if to say, I've had enough. That's all I can think of. [What's going to happen?] I really can't say. I don't know what they are talking about. This one leaning over the banister might come around because the one leaning over her is trying so hard, and seems to be pleading, to have a pleading expression on her face.

(1) This story is strewn with denials by reversal, negation, and minimization. And again the inexorable bad mother emerges: the lower figure is "limp . . . I've had enough." Of course, the patient's chaotic struggle to maintain the benevolence of the mother itself implies the image of the evil mother as well as the regressive search for a happy sense of union or fusion with a good mother—for immersion in the motherly woman. (2) The "nice horse" of Card 2 is paralleled here by "her hands are very kind." (3) Seeing the upper figure as a man, even if only briefly, is a severe enough distortion to suggest psychosis by itself.

> *Card 12 M.* This guy looks like he is hypnotizing her. He doesn't look mean, vicious. His hands are kind of skinny and you know, but so are mine, bony. She seems as if she is lying there very contented and I don't know if she is fully asleep. I can't tell. She has a pleasant expression on her face—or is it a he? Is it a she? Or can you tell me? The haircuts the girls wear today, you can't tell, and the haircuts the boys wear, the Elvis Presley, you can't tell either. I don't think she is asleep. If she is asleep he might also be waking her up. And what happens? I really don't know. [Make it up.] I think he is hypnotizing her and what was the name of the book—Murphy? And we read so much in the papers about hypnotism. It seems to be a fad now. My daughter went to a party. They had a hypnotist there. She didn't want to be hypnotized. All the other girls wanted to be and by the time she made up her mind, his time was up.

The denial of viciousness through negation at the beginning of the story is immediately followed by a self-reference, so that we hear the patient, in the same breath, deny and assert her hostility. Consciously, at the moment, she is obviously secure in her "innocence."

In summary, this TAT's language and content combine to indicate extreme reliance on denial in several common forms, and instability of denial resulting in the inexorable emergence of the bad, unnourishing, hostile mother image as well as of reference to depression, fear, and oral regression. The omitted stories are entirely consistent with these inferences. Obviously, other major problems may be inferred from these stories—the confusion of sexual identity, for example, is particularly striking. The trends discussed are those most distinctive of the hypomanic position.

V

My discussion of the previous stories was not meant to be complete; nor was it meant to minimize analysis of content. I have tried to show that content may be most accurately and most subtly analyzed by continuously bearing in mind that the TAT is a test of communication as well as apperception. If we analyze *content as verbalized,* if we are steadily guided by the question, *How was this story told?* we are in the best position to assess major themes in terms of their dynamic force, their representations in subjective experience, their regulation and limitation by psychic structure, and their manifest versus latent disposition.

8

BODIES IN SCHIZOPHRENIC RORSCHACH RESPONSES

Of the many ways in which the schizophrenic Rorschach record may be approached, starting from one or another of the basic concepts advanced in dynamic psychiatry to define and organize the varied phenomenology of schizophrenia, that concentrating on the disruption of the body ego is one of the most fascinating. Its value in Rorschach research has already been demonstrated in some respects in the extensive series of studies by Fisher and Cleveland (1958). These investigators have concentrated on two variables, the definiteness and the permeability of ego boundaries, and have studied the manifestations of these specifically in the test content. Zucker (1958) has made a related, significant contribution, although she was particularly concerned with the broader issue of ego boundaries and explicitly avoided going into the manifestations of disturbed body ego as such in Rorschach responses. The range and definition of variables in her study is broader and more clinical than that of Fisher and Cleveland; she included analysis of some aspects of Rorschach scores, verbalization of responses, and indications of thought disorder, as well as content.

These reports do not, however, constitute an exhaustive treatment of the problem. On the one hand, other phenomenological aspects of body-ego disturbance may be investigated, such as the body ego's inner organization, vitality, and coping with stimulation, and, on the other, additional aspects of the Rorschach record may be brought into the analysis of dis-

First published in the *Journal of Projective Techniques*, 24: 267-281, 1960.

turbed "ego boundaries" to give it fuller meaning. It is my aim in this paper to extend the study of body-ego disturbances manifested in the Rorschach records of schizophrenics and to link the resulting observations to the broader issues of impaired ego boundaries and object relations.

I must first set forth certain generalizations about the relation of Rorschach responses to subjective experience, and then, more specifically, to certain aspects of schizophrenic subjective experience. Subsequently I shall analyze a Rorschach protocol in order to illustrate the application of these generalizations.

RORSCHACH RESPONSES, THE INNER WORLD, AND THE BODY EGO

Outstanding aspects of subjective experience, of the "inner world," are expressed in the imagery language peculiar to the Rorschach record. By "inner world" I do not refer to the general organizational principles of a given personality as customarily emphasized in basic Rorschach texts. I refer instead to the quality of existence, however dim, known to the patient. The inner world comprises a multitudinous population of conscious and unconscious, partial and total images of oneself and others. Some of these images are fleeting and variable, others fixed and unchanging. Some are embedded in proliferated fantasy constructions, others are fragmentary and isolated. Some are pale and soft-spoken, others are vivid and loud. Some are possessed of great force of a benign or hostile nature, while others are neutral records of the facts and the tools of living. Affects color this inner world and are best understood when seen in relation to its imagery.

The body ego is part of this inner world and also defines its boundary. It comprises the objectively discriminable, the distorted, and the fantasied sensations, positions, capacities, and interrelationships of the skin, bones, muscles, organs, and functions of the body, their movement or change in space and time, and their apartness and difference as a unity from other bodies in the environment, however similar and however close. Developmentally, the shaping and unifying of the body ego is greatly influenced by identifications, that is, by the (mostly unconscious) taking over of properties of other bodies and experiencing them ultimately as one's own in a deep and abiding fashion. The fruits of identification are to be distinguished from the ravages of aggressive and libidinal introjections and reintrojections of projected images; the latter (mostly unconsciously) assault the unity and integrity of the body ego, and they tend to restrict it to the role of tool, extension, or conglomeration of other bodies. It is the latter we discover in relatively stabilized form in neurotic symptoms, and, most of all, usually in fluid fashion, in the bizarre body experiences of schizophrenics (Erikson, 1956; Federn, 1952; Fisher and Cleveland, 1958; Pious, 1950; Schafer, this volume, Chapter 6; Winnicott, 1958; Zucker, 1958.)

In Rorschach records of all sorts we find colorful and revealing expressions of the subjective experience of the body in one or more of its key aspects.

THE BODY EGO IN SCHIZOPHRENIA AND ITS RELATION TO THE RORSCHACH TEST STIMULI

In schizophrenia there is a blurring, sometimes to the point of virtual disappearance, of the boundaries and articulation of the ego.[1] It must be recognized, however, that except in the most rigidly stabilized schizophrenic conditions, there occur continuous fluctuations in the patient's level of organization, and corresponding fluctuations in the type and degree of organization of his body ego. It is therefore not accurate to speak of *the* body ego or *the* body image of a particular schizophrenic, for where boundaries are blurred and in flux there is no defined and enduring ego to which to refer experience

---

[1] Fisher and Cleveland (1958) and Zucker (1958) have provided a detailed summary of the pertinent literature. Federn's formulations (1952) are especially relevant to the formulations in the present paper. The concept "body self" might be conceptually more desirable than "body ego," but it raises problems in its own right which I prefer to bypass at this time.

that, from the standpoint of a highly organized and differentiated observer, is internal to that patient. Rather, one can
speak only of "bodies," as I have done in my title. This eerie
title reflects the eerie experiences in question. At any given
moment, the schizophrenic may note aspects of external reality only by way of transformed subjective experience of his
own body, just as he may note aspects of his own body only
by way of apparent or real changes in external objects. This
is often conspicuous in therapeutic interactions where the
schizophrenic may report a change in his subjective state that
is actually an oblique recording of a change in the therapist's
state and vice versa. A heightening of the therapist's unconscious irritation, for example, may be "perceived" by the patient only as an "emptying out" of his own interest and motivation. Or the patient's feeling wooden may be "perceived"
by him as unresponsiveness of the therapist. Thus, on the regressed levels of organization on which the schizophrenic often functions, especially when his restitutions are not well established, it is not possible to designate with certainty the
body in question at any given moment. The patient is not a
reliable communicant of his source of cues and of their original content.[2]

We may also question whether it is correct or useful to assume that it is the disturbance in his body ego that is primary
to his disturbed perception of external objects. There are advantages to thinking in terms of regression to a level of organization of such a nature that the differences between inner and
outer that are so important on higher levels of organization
have no certain meaning any longer. It is this *level* of organization that is important, and the disturbed experiences of
one's own body and of other bodies perhaps should be seen
as concomitant manifestations of this level. Accordingly, for
purposes of Rorschach analysis, we may regard as pertinent
in this connection references to the boundaries, inner artic-

---

[2] With progress in treatment, the patient communicates more reliably and
the therapist translates more exactly. In the Rorschach situation some indeter-
minacy is inevitable.

ulation, and interaction of *all* entities, be they persons, objects, or things in nature. Formed and formless, articulated and diffuse, they all count. Also pertinent are many subjective attitudes conveyed through modes of verbalization and expressive movements during the response process.

If we turn to the test stimuli in the light of the preceding discussion, we may consider the blots themselves to be equivalent to bodies. Their treatment as stimuli, that is, the use of their colors, shadings, and forms, and the scores reflecting this usage, then can be seen to be additional related avenues of expression of the subjective experience of bodies. The relative formlessness, meaninglessness, and lack of inner articulation and relatedness of the areas in most of the inkblots act as forceful external realizations of, or parallels to, the schizophrenic's subjective experience of all bodies as having just these uncertain properties much or all of the time. That is to say, the blots are a kind of objectification of the schizophrenic's body-ego regression. (The same appears to be true, though not in the same way, in the case of the organic patient, whose blurring and fragmentation of the inner world and of external reality is realized or paralleled in the inkblots.) The schizophrenic patient in therapy reveals to us that ego regression is extremely threatening to him; correspondingly, so may the inkblots be, although the dangers signified by them are usually experienced in a microcosmic manner with small quantities of anxiety or other affect (Schafer, 1954, pp. 74-113). Of course, in the case of certain schizophrenics, borderline schizophrenics, and manic-depressives, the affects experienced may begin to become macrocosmic and contribute to the sometimes observed gross disruptions of the test relationship.

I am following here, in some respects, a suggestion of Alcyon Baer de Bahia (1950) to the effect that the Rorschach stimuli represent a "loss of objects" and that the test responses are restitutive efforts, that is, efforts to "restore objects." This author seems to assume that this loss of objects is experienced equally by all persons taking the test, whereas I would submit that it is particularly those patients already overwhelmed by actual or imminent loss of objects, such as psychotics and near-psychotics, who have this (usually implicit) experience in the Rorschach situation. The crucial loss must be seen to be in the inner world, that is, in the capacity to experience lifelike internal representations of persons. It is his fate in the inner world and not his actual presence and availability that determines whether the object is "lost" to the patient. The neurotic or character-disordered patient probably experiences such loss little, if at all, because his hold on objects is relatively secure. Like the Boston Brahmin matron who, upon being asked where she got her hats, haughtily replied, "I have my hats," he has his objects; their existence in his inner world is stable even if their dynamic significance is not. Consequently, his subjective experience of the Rorschach situation and stimuli will be qualitatively different from the schizophrenic's; coping with fantasy, mess, initiative, impulses to look and be looked at, and the like will figure far more prominently in his response to the stimuli than coping with object loss (Schafer, 1954, pp. 6-73). Thus, the schizophrenic's Rorschach responses and responsiveness, *including his scores* along with his content and test behavior, may be viewed as manifestations of the type and degree of restitutive effort or restoration of objects of which he is capable at the time of testing, as well as of his tolerance for the anxiety entailed and his inner resources for this work. Ordinarily, the examiner as "object" will be vague, and sometimes even basically unrecognized as a separate being.

Loss of objects is intimately related to our particular theme, the experience of bodies. "Object" is a more comprehensive psychological term than "body," for it includes a good deal of content in the way of motivation, affect, and anticipation. It is also to be noted, however, that what one says about bodies expresses a great deal about the contents of objects, doing so in the special language of wholeness, intactness, splitting or fragmentation, injury, deterioration, etc. Similarly, what one says about objects in the broader sense expresses a great deal about the state of bodies in the inner world. A therapist properly attuned to his schizophrenic patient cannot miss hearing his frequent and particular emphasis on depletion of energy, devitalization, and bodily fragmentation and disorientation in space, time, and interpersonal contact. Of course, "loss of objects" is best regarded as a limiting concept, useful in defining a hypothetical ideal case. In therapy, we find all degrees of loss of objects and of restitutive efforts, and the same must be held for the experience of the Rorschach situation.

Thus, in the following discussion, it will be assumed that there is a continuous flux of actual or threatening loss of objects in the schizophrenic's inner world, accompanied by attempts to regain and revitalize objects in order to restore higher levels of organization and function. Further, a prominent expression of the loss of objects will be seen in dedifferentiation of the patient's own body ego and its intermingling with internal representations of bodies in the environment. This occurs in a manner that makes it very difficult to localize and define bodily cues, and perhaps essentially meaningless to localize them in extended time. It will also be assumed that the patient's experience of bodies corresponds to or expresses in many respects his total problem with objects on the one hand (his concerns with their contents, their stability, their motives, and their availability) and with inner organization on the other (his concerns with the stability of defenses, sublimations, values, the self, etc.). Finally, it will be assumed that not just test content specifically and explicitly dwelling on boundaries and permeability, but all aspects of the Rorschach performance, including the traditionally emphasized scores, the test behavior, style of verbalization, and the other aspects of content, are pertinent to an investigation of this question.[3]

[3] Certain aspects of response to projective-test stimuli *qua* stimuli have been discussed by me elsewhere (Chapter 9); also, some of the TAT manifestations of bodies in schizophrenic subjective experience (Chapter 7). See also my discussion of the role of normal and pathological regression in projective-test responses (Chapter 6).

CASE STUDY

The following is the Rorschach record of a young man of 18. Upon initial psychiatric appraisal he appeared to be a borderline schizophrenic. He was referred for testing to help assess his suitability for admission to a small, private, open mental hospital; particular concern had been expressed regarding his capacity for impulse control. He wished to be admitted to this hospital rather than a closed hospital, and understood that the test results would play a part in the decision. He is the son of a physician and nurse, which fact adds greatly to the significance of bodily integrity in his case; moreover, his father essentially neglected his family in favor of his practice. Also, he is the child of a mixed marriage (Catholic father and Protestant mother), which, on the identity level, must further heighten his concerns with wholeness and unity. He was born and reared in New York City. He has an older brother and sister, a younger brother, and two younger sisters. He did not complete his first year at a small college in California and told the examiner that at college he had had no major subject or career in mind: "I had a lot of aspirations once but I ... " (shrug). His protocol is particularly rich in body language and is of interest as a model.[4]

The patient arrived ten minutes late for his first appointment during which the Rorschach test was administered. The examiner's first association on seeing him was "the wild boy of Aveyron" (Itard, 1932). His appearance was wild and slovenly. His hair was uncombed, shaggy, and hung over his eyes. His clothes were old and torn. He wore no socks and one shoe had no tongue or lace. In posture, movement, and speech he displayed the same disorderliness—mumbling, fumbling, and slumping forward most of the time. He scratched himself frequently and at one point drew a little blood. He conveyed a quality of great intensity with an element of ferocity. Equally noteworthy was the effortfulness

---

[4] See also my analysis of body experience in the Rorschach record of a hysterical woman (Chapter 9).

with which he responded, as if almost all looking and thinking were strenuous and hard to keep in focus.

Card 1. Reaction time 55″ Total time 2′30″
1. [Patient peers under hair hanging over his eyes.] In detail or in general? [Up to you.] It doesn't seem to resemble very much. I suppose we could, it might be three dancers, two on each side [usual side figures], one in the middle with her head back [usual middle detail]. Some sort of weird ballet—not so weird but. . . . That's about all. Female, three females. [Anything else?] No . . . I could go into more detail about the figures. Do you want that? [I mean any other possibilities.] From this angle? [Up to you.] ∨ < > [Sigh.]
Inquiry 1.[5] [What made it look weird?] Primarily a ballet with sort of a hint of a gypsy sort of thing as compared to more classical ballet or something like that; perhaps an Indian ballet or Mexican [patient trails off into mumbling]. [Gypsy?] If you try to put any apparel on them, I mean clothing, they seem not like ballet dancers; more of a Spanish feeling.

The quality "weird" stands out in this response. It refers directly to the patient's uncertain shifting between, and contaminating of, the classical ballet and the ethnic dance. Inner confusion is experienced in terms of a weird outer reality: the bodies and movements of others are experienced as unnatural. In its content the response poses, in one respect, the antithesis of the elegant existence versus the primitive, perhaps disreputable and "rock-bottom" existence. This antithesis is underscored by his saying "apparel" and then shifting to the down-to-earth "clothing." Shall he be the scum of the earth or an aristocrat? In another respect, the antithesis is between stylized, disciplined action versus exotic, voluptuous action. One can read the response on the level of conflicting social identities *and* on the level of clashing modes of bodily expression and differences in vigor and abandon (Erikson, 1956). Especially because it appears so early in the test, his confusion—he cannot give two distinct alternatives

───────────

[5] The method of test administration followed has been described by Rapaport, Gill, and Schafer (1945-46); it includes inquiring after the patient completes each card, and, except for establishing locations, inquiring with the blot out of sight.

—indicates the body to be a significant locus for expressing fluidity of both social identity and inner vitality.

This disturbance is also evident in formal aspects of the response. On the one hand he is concerned with completing (restoring the wholeness of) the central figure, and inventively assumes the head to be thrown back out of sight. In so doing he indicates noteworthy synthesizing interest and capacity (Prelinger, 1958). On the other hand he splits the concept of the dancers into their bodies and their clothing, indicating thereby a breakdown of synthesizing capacity; this may be said because we usually encounter automatic blending of these figures with their clothing. The dynamics of this split are likely to include exhibitionistic-voyeuristic interests; note in this regard his choice of words—"if you try to put any apparel on them"—with its intimation of nakedness. Again, however, we may shift our level of analysis and see in this perceptual splitting and its suggestive wording the uncivilized representation of the body and the implied resistance to be overcome in civilizing it, or, in other words, a savage identity fragment reminiscent of the ethnic emphasis in the response content. His mumbling, his physical appearance, and his stripping off of clothing during the test, as noted below, are obviously pertinent to the themes here formulated.

Card II. Reaction time 2'15" Total time 3'20"
1. [Sigh.] ... ∧ ... ∨ ... < ... > ∧ ... Do I have to find something for each one or ...? [No, but give it a chance.] ... [Have you thought of any possibilities?] No, none ... [Patient's eyes almost covered by his hand as he seems to try to limit the area under consideration in this way rather than, as is more usual, by covering parts of the inkblot with his hand.] In a way it kind of resembles a cartoon, or some sort of thing, of a couple of animals, two bears perhaps, with a red cap or some stupid thing like that! I don't know what they are doing! I can't think of anything they'd be doing in such a pose ... with their paws together up here!
Inquiry 1. [What did you have in mind about the red caps?] Just a cap, a long cap. [Patient points out that the head would be in the white space between the upper red and the dark area.]

As on Card I, and as will recur throughout the test, after first blocking and then expressing inadequacy, the patient produces a more or less vivid M. It is as if the alternatives for him are nonresponsiveness in a static, empty world versus rich body experience and interaction with others. This inferred opposition would partly parallel that between the classical ballet and the ethnic dance on Card I. Continuing conflict in relation to bodies is also evident in his irritability concerning the dress and position of these figures; the confusion experienced as external weirdness on Card I is now expressed in his own affective disruption. Also, this response is sapped of its inherent vitality by his seeing it only as a cartoon and as animals in humanlike movement. His previous M clearly shows him to be capable of the easier vital M on Card II, so that we may infer at this moment a falling off or ebbing of body representations in his inner world.

On a higher level of functioning, there may be defense against the suggestion of sexual or aggressive interaction that, empirically, appear to be inherent in this visual gestalt. On a regressed level, there may be archaic anxiety concerning human contact of any sort, perhaps embodied here in the "paws together" that he cannot cope with. I would emphasize the latter inference, partly on the basis of the entire foregoing analysis, but most of all on the basis of his expressive movement of covering his field of vision close to his eyes. This action seems to express how oriented he is toward the inner world and transformations therein, and how little he undertakes active, adaptive, physical manipulation of the environment, such as covering parts of the card with his hand as many subjects do. Thus, in the setting of an abstracting difficulty, he transforms his body rather than the object, and only then can he sort out details and focus well enough to respond.[6]

Card III. Reaction time 3'15" Total time 4'

1. ... > ... ∨ ... All I can think of here is an odd painting. You know, not... an actual thing but an odd version of two Negro women, say, with very odd-shaped bodies and ... hold-

---

[6] Compare Rapaport (1957, especially pp. 181-193) on other, related aspects of such disruptions in the response process.

ing something, some sort of scepter or some kind of thing [the dark areas, seen upside down, the scepter being the lower leg of the popular response.]

Inquiry 1. [What did you have in mind by the odd shape?] They were very deformed, that's all. [In what way?] [At this point patient takes off his sweater exposing a torn sport shirt with only one button and a good deal of his torso.] In what way? Her mid-section was... just sort of squeezed down and went out laterally [reference to lower back of popular figure]. Everything was just sort of as if they had brought something down on their head, and their neck was broken, and her legs were all squeezed into one hunk [legs are upper torso and head and neck of popular]. [What suggested a painting?] Because it looked hardly natural. [Anything else?] No, merely their forms together. [Negro?] Their hair and shape of their faces. [Anything else?] The profile of the face mostly and the appearance of the hair. [What about the hair?] It appeared to be rather short and for some reason it looked like it could be curly and yet they didn't look like men.

This M is of poor form quality in essential respects. Initially he describes this quality as "odd-shaped." In doing so, he is in one respect taking critical distance from his response, while in another he is experiencing as external an internal difficulty of integration. When he goes on to describe the figure as squeezed, broken, and compressed into partial amorphousness, he continues his efforts to test external reality and work out adequate syntheses of apparently external properties; however, these adaptive efforts are altogether dominated by obviously implied fantasies of violent persecution of bodily integrity. This combination of M minus, confabulation, and bizarrely morbid content leaves no doubt that bodily experience of delusional and/or hallucinatory quality is familiar to him, at least in its transitional or borderline forms. In particular, his saying "*they* had brought something down" suggests the presence of ideas concerning external persecutors. In final analysis, however, this may all be body language expressing regressive experiences of splitting and fusing in many respects; and very possibly the destructive content introduced shows how he tries to fill in and make sense of the experience of inability to cathect his body and its interpersonal contents as a differentiated whole. Yet, a crippled body —a fragmented ego—remains: it is the one that can say, "I can think," "I can't think," "It resembles," and, later (Card V) "Every way I looked at it," etc.

It must also be noted that he sees the figures as female, and that, during the inquiry into the hair texture, he indicates that it has been a problem for him to make this sexual differentiation; also, that there is particular emphasis on the area that would be a protruding abdomen on the woman. Considered together, these items hint at bizarre, frightening fantasies concerning pregnancy in the mother and, through the patient's implied feminine identification, in himself. More evidence will be needed, however, to establish this theme. In any case, the woman-self is violated in this response at the same time as, in striking contrast, ruling power is ascribed to her through the scepter (see also Card IX). And again, he introduces an ethnic emphasis with low caste *and* vigorous connotations.

Card IV.   Reaction time 4' Total time 4' 50"
1. . . . ∨ . . . < ∧ . . . This doesn't look like very much. [Any possibilities?] No. Once again it sort of resembles feet, these [lower side details] and it looks as if it could sort of be a person [W] bending way over and his head is between his legs [head is lower middle detail facing the viewer].
Inquiry 1.   [Did anything beside the head make it look bent over?] The form of what was there; you saw his legs going up to here and his head between his legs. [?] No.

The application of levels of analysis is clearly exemplified in the understanding of this delayed, vivid, and distorted M. Obviously, the position implies an anal-homosexual presentation of the body; this implication is continuous with that of feminine identification on Card III. If, however, we shift our viewpoint to that of regressed ego experience, we observe that this figure is seeing the world backwards and upside down; in addition, in consequence of its contorted organization, it cannot safely be said to be either coming or going. All this despite the fact that it is comparatively easy and common for subjects to see the blot as an erect figure approaching or moving away, or as an extended figure lying down. In this instance, a subjective sense of disorientation in space and life appears to be expressed. The patient's long delays throughout the test before responding with M's, the mixed plus and minus form quality in these M's, and his odd way of covering his field of vision close to his eyes, may all be seen as manifestations in time and motion of this disorientation and of his difficulties in achieving orientation.

Card V. Reaction time 1' 55" Total time 2' 40"
1....... It could be a bird lighting on the water [left half of blot] and this could be its image [right half]. A big billed bird ... and large winged ... a large bird! [Anything else?] No. Every way I look at it it reminds me of a bird in one form or another. [The bill is one half of lower middle projection.]

With all its intense and delicately poised motility, this response also reflects both splitting of the body and fusion of bodies. With regard to splitting, the bird's largeness evolves from fragmented impressions of the bill first and then the wings; only afterwards, with an air of discovery, is the bird's size achieved. (There is a naïve realism or concreteness of thought in the "large" concept, as well as indication that size is an especially important component of body experience.) On Card IV there was a similar (Do-like) progression from the legs to the whole figure. As Rapaport, Gill, and Schafer have pointed out (1945-46), it is warranted to assume that the normal response often evolves in just this way, but with the important difference that its development usually goes on silently, easily, and almost automatically, so that only the final synthesis appears in consciousness and does so quickly. In contrast, synthesis is here typically a late, labored, and uncertain accomplishment. Splitting is also suggested by the nonattainment of the popular winged creature on this card: the dividing mid-line of the inkblot dominates the response process, and only in the concept of reflection is the ordinarily easy synthesis of the entire inkblot accomplished. (This delayed, secondary synthesis is attained on Card VI in the same way; there too he does not attain the popular response.) From a formal point of view, reflections are adequate syntheses only if they are accompanied by evidence of capacity to subdue the mid-line and accomplish single-bodied integrations of the blots as well.

Of course, the mid-line is a region of contact as well as a divider. In the present response, reflecting the patient's increasing efforts to resynthesize what has been split, that is, to make restitution to higher levels of organization, the mid-line appears as a region of self-contact through the outside world, in the same sense as any mirror might be for a person whose inner world does not include a steadily felt, bounded, and articulated body ego. Perhaps this patient's saying "image" rather than "reflection" hints at just this process of trying to find an image of himself through reflections from the outer world.[7] In some records the mid-line as divider is bizarrely accounted for by notions of bodies literally being split or torn in half.

With regard to fusing of bodies, once the bird is recorded in his experience it contaminates his perception of other birds: "a bird in one form or another" is for him the same as the first bird. It is not that it looks like the same bird from any position of the card. In this instance, one body is also several.

Card VI.   Reaction time 1′ 45″ Total time 2′ 15″
1.   < . . . ∧ . . . < . . . This, I suppose . . . ∧ . . . < . . . This could be some sort of raft with some men on it, a few men, four or five. This one could be pointing and this one is just standing in despair and the rest of them are probably sick.
Inquiry 1. [Patient is asked to show the edge of the raft.] I don't know. [What did you have in mind?] Around here [vaguely indicates the length of the mid-line of the large lower detail] and this were perhaps land or something [upper detail]. [Patient points out that the upper side projection of the large

[7] We may venture this far not on the strength of this response alone but only in the interest of following through a point of view about responses and with the caution of doing so with careful attention to the context of the total record; the same is true for all aspects of the analysis of this record.

lower detail is the hand of the pointing figure and the small
bump further down the outside edge is his head; the despairing figure is the lower side projection facing toward the top
of the card "with his head down"; the rest of the figures are
vague, the patient uncertainly pointing out the small projection below the lower side projection as the head and arm of
another figure.] [What made you say they were probably sick?]
The over-all look of everyone: the man standing looked rather
ill or . . . sort of . . . suggests . . . they all seem sort of . . . without
life; they appear to be lying down or ready to slump down;
everyone was lying down except this one who was sitting down
[lower side projection] and he looks ready to fall down.

This response is a stunning illustration of the main thesis of
this paper. With almost disorienting effect, it encompasses
undifferentiated, disproportionate, and blended bodies. Its
end result is a confabulated jumble of humanity. And it is
dying humanity—diseased, precariously upright or fallen,
sapped of vitality, and dead. The raft image itself suggests
drifting in an uncharted area with no connection to larger,
secure, sustaining bodies, such as land or ship. Note in the
formal aspects of this response how even the boundaries of
the raft are uncertain, not to speak of the boundaries of the
separate bodies aboard it. These then are the fast-fading sur-
vivors of a wreck. The reference to land, and, by implication,
the pointing to this land, while signs of hopefulness, are pa-
thetic, for the land in question is disproportionately small
and spiky in contour; furthermore, it is mentioned only during the inquiry and then it was stimulated by the examiner's
need to define the boundaries of the raft and not by the patient's inner processes. What is more hopeful about this response is the patient's sensitive attention to postural expressiveness: he has already indicated this asset—for example, in
the bird lighting on the water on Card V. It must be recognized, however, that this asset, with all its empathic potential, is mostly in the service of sensing and communicating
disorientation, decomposition, and death. Such is his world.
Intensified but morbidly narrowed empathy of this sort is
often seen in schizophrenic functioning. We may well wonder

too if this young man is not signaling fearful anticipation of
further, extreme regression, of being "ready to fall down,"
and manifesting his readiness to grasp at any straw, any little
bit of land, to prevent his drowning in regression. (A report
from the closed hospital in the Midwest in which he was hospitalized not long after this testing described pronounced regressive manifestations shortly after his admission.)

 Card VII. Reaction time 3′ 30″ Total time 4′
1. > ∧ [Patient has been handling cards with increasing
roughness. At this point his feet are out of his shoes and, since
he is wearing no socks, it can be seen that they are filthy.] . . .
∧ . . . ∨ . . . < . . . > . . . These just look like, yes, like. . . maybe these are just faces, one on top of another. . .
 Inquiry 1. [Patient points out popular face in upper third,
a vague face on the inner edge of the middle third, and the
clear face on the outer upper edge of the lower third. He characterizes the first two as "Negro" and points out their hair, and
the lowermost face as "Indian."] [Negro?] Their features. [Any-
thing else?] No. [What did you have in mind when you said
"one on top of another"?] Just the way they were represented
there, as if they were just one drawn on top of the other: three
of them, no bodies, placed one on top of the other.

That there are no bodies, only faces, seen here, especially
when he sees the profile of the popular figure and does not
even make out the relatively easy and common complete head
or head plus torso, further indicates the splitting of bodies in
his inner experience. (These may be the disembodied faces
he feels he presents to the world—what we, on our own levels
of organization, often carelessly call "fronts.") The response
also underscores the come-and-go nature of his experience
of bodies, for in review we see he experienced them strongly
on Card I, uncertainly on Card II, passively on Card III
(where he also missed the easiest M of all), topsy-turvy on
Card IV, strongly on Card V, and jumbled and fallen on Card
VI; and now we have a precariously balanced, meaninglessly
thrown together heap of faces. It is also instructive to note in
review of Cards III-VII how much the direction of movement
of his bodies is explicitly or implicitly downward: the down-

ward force, the head down, the lighting on the water, the fall
ing, and the implicitly tottering heap. His rough card handling is especially evident to the examiner at this point; very
likely it is his reaction to the accumulating, anxiety-arousing
plastic representations of downward, regressive experience;
perhaps the terrible impact of Card VI is most important in
this respect.

His Negro and Indian references are reminiscent of the
gypsy, Indian, Mexican figures on Card I and the Negro women on Card III. The former body vitality and the ruling
power are now gone, however, like the vanishing Indian.

Card VIII. Reaction time 2′ Total time 2′ 30″
1.   . . .   I don't see anything in that. This looks like an
animal [popular]. . . a body and four . . . just a quadruped
[stumbles over this word], along the line of a bear maybe or. . . .
Inquiry [Did you have something more in mind?] No.

It is surprising that he now virtually escapes from his dismal
world of bodies. If nothing else, he could easily have seen the
animals hanging on or falling or being pushed down by the
upper gray-green extensions. Other patients with similar problems often do so. It seems that he has momentarily regained
an adequate level of integration and is successfully warding
off his inner world with the help of the area in question, for
of all the inkblot areas in the test this is the one most nearly
pictorial in quality, in addition to being almost completely
separated from the rest of the inkblot. In these respects it
poses no special problem of splitting or fusing bodies. But be
that as it may, we must still note a speech disruption when he
tries to elevate himself, i.e., his language usage, from "animal" to "quadruped." (See Card I for a similar change of
wording.)

Card IX. Reaction time 50″ Total time 1′ 25″
1. . . . ∨ . . . This is like looking through some kind of painted
door and there is a woman in a dress, more like a robe, a regal-
looking woman. The person is very close to the door, looking
through; can see her coming toward. . . .
Inquiry 1. [Patient points out the entire colored area as the

door, and while doing so refers to it as "painted flowers." The woman is the middle space with the head vaguely indicated in the center of the lower red; the arms are seen between the middle space and the lower red, in the brownish area.] [Did you mean it looked like painted flowers?] No, it had flowerlike colors; it was painted with flowerlike colors. [Regal-looking?] She just seemed to, let's say, stately-looking, partly because of her dress and her posture, the way she carried herself, a superior kind of a feeling, a self-confident one.

The visual position of the observer described in this response corresponds in a crucial respect to the one he expressed through his own body on Card II. Then he covered his field of vision close to his eyes in order to define a figure; now he introduces into the response content an obstruction close to the eyes—the door—again defining a figure thereby. It is as if he must narrow down his field of vision to have a definable experience. It is a way to focus, to counteract perceptions that are fluid, without contour and articulation. In this respect it is a process of structuralization to remedy a defect, the defect being closely linked with intrusions of the primary process. It may be, however, that he is expressing a different though related experience, that of having to see around himself or his body periphery as around a physical obstruction like his hair. His body ego in this case would be shrunken within his depersonalized physical frame.

In this case, as on Card III, it is a ruling woman who is discovered. This time, however, it is an idealized figure and one who is approaching. In the context of his schizophrenic disturbance in ego experience and object relations, we may infer that perhaps he is expressing a wish for a strong maternal figure with whom enlivening contact may be possible, and, as the necessary counterpart to that, a wish for a regal self capable of inner confidence and the bodily vitality that goes with it. That this response content can be read as expressing noteworthy voyeuristic interest is obvious, but by attending to the archaic ego experience implied we gain the advantage of recognizing provisionally the significant growth-need aspects of his voyeuristic interest. That is to say, to see and to be rec-

ognized, in the sense here discussed, is to live. However negative in form, his dramatic flair for motion, dress, and undress
compels his being seen and felt; he fills the room the way a
great dramatic star fills the stage. The response is another
hopeful sign in a mostly bleak record.

Yet, even this response has its share of schizophrenic hope-
lessness and confusion. It is not just that the woman's head is
vaguely and arbitrarily seen, thereby impairing the full-
bodied potential of the image. More important is his essentially artificial use of color. He could not attain "a flower" or
"flowers" on this card, those not infrequent uses of color that
could bespeak vitality of emotional and sensory experience.
For him it is only paint on a doorway, a put-on thing without fragrance, soft texture, or fecundity. He approaches a
"flower" response in his transient contamination, that is, in
his reference to "painted flowers," though, of course, even
that image is still at a significant distance from real flowers.
Thus, at best, the warmth and feel are on the door and in
neither the observer nor the woman, and we find, in his inability to use color freely and substantially, a formal Rorschach
counterpart of the devitalization of his world. This congru-
ence enables us to proceed with the basic theme so far developed with added confidence.

Card X. Reaction time 4′ Total time 5′
1. < ∨ ... ∧ > ∧ ... < ∨ ... < ∨   [Patient looks
at back of card.] ... These look like animals, animals of the sea,
many of them, some with the characteristics of people, sort of
. . . [W].
2. This looks like a paper boy [lower outer orange].
Inquiry 2. [What made it look like that?] I don't know, it
just looks like what people think paper boys look like. [Try to
describe it.] No, just like a little boy, not too little, with a hat
on [patient mumbles] ... [Patient points out a peaked cap and
a vague face on the lower outer edge.]
Inquiry 1. [Did you make out any specific animals?] I remember a turtle [side sepia]; it looked like it was very fatigued.
And it seems I remember a couple of crabs somewhere [upper
gray] ... [Did you make out any others?] ... I can't remember.
[What did you have in mind about the characteristics of peo-

ple?] Just like, they didn't walk like animals but the way people do, one when tired and the other just in a very careless way; they seem to be lying down in a human kind of way [the crabs]. [While the patient points out locations he adds the following:] And these are sea horses up here [lower green] and this [side blue] is something, I don't remember what, it looks like something, maybe something like ... some kind of a ... sort of a spider crab kind of thing and yet like kind of human too. Maybe they have polio or something. [Polio?] It just looks like it. [How?] The legs and everything seem to be ... they just don't seem natural and yet they seem as if they are all there and yet warped or bent or something. [Kind of human?] In that way. [What made them look like sea horses?] They ... sea horses look like something and that resembles what this something is: it just resembles a sea horse. [Can you say what the quality is?] No, just the body, the shape. [What made the turtle look fatigued?] The way its arms and legs were. [What made it look like a turtle?] The body form, shape. [Anything else?] No. [What made the other ones look like they were lying down?] The position of the arms and legs, a very unusual crab. [Patient points out the usual legs on the upper gray as arms and the usual antennaelike projections as legs.]

In the inquiry into the "paper boy," and later, into the "sea horse," the patient is unable to define his own perceptual experience directly. In the former instance he can do so only through the experience of others ("what people think paper boys look like"). In the latter instance the boundaries between inner processes and outer objects is lost ("that resembles what this something is"). And in both instances he is annoyed with the examiner. The annoyance accounts, however, only for the place of occurrence or expression of these ego failures and not for their quality, for obviously there are many ways to feel and express annoyance without such drastic decline of one's ego level. A related disturbance occurs during the inquiry, just before he establishes the spider crab response: even while looking at the area in question, his response is momentarily unavailable to him except as a memory —"This is something, I don't remember what..." The implied impairment of the ego's recognition function also reflects the split between what he sees outside and what he makes of it—or has made of it—inside.[8]

Returning to the paper boy, three additional aspects of this response are noteworthy. First, in switching from "little" to "not too little" he again indicates sensitivity to body size (see Card V). At the same time he flounders in concreteness. Second, a paper boy is one of our "all-American boy" or Horatio Alger stereotypes, and may express a preadolescent, conventional, self-reliant, enterprising identity fragment (Erikson, 1956). Like some previous responses, this is another slight sign of hope. At this time, however, we see in the patient's clothing, in his body movements, in his response's poor form elements, and, most of all, in his test responses in general the virtual unavailability of this identity fragment for genuine development or employment. Third, in this total context, "paper boy" may also be read as a pun, that is, a boy of paper, not of flesh and bone, that is, a lifeless imitation. This inference would correspond to the fact that the "all-American boy" stereotype, such as we find on slick magazine covers, has itself become a common model for a slick cover over human confusion, anxiety, passion, and emptiness.

The large-scale drama on Card X lies, however, in the contamination of human and animal qualities, and in particular, in its development in terms of fatigue and lying down, and, finally, in terms of polio. He introduces increasingly severe, deadening disruptions of body integrity and vitality. In the spider crab with polio we see a threatening creature immobilized, its biting and tearing parts crippled. Spider crab, like octopus and spider, has malevolent connotations. In line with the theme of this paper, it would appear closest to the quality of schizophrenic experience to regard this as an aspect of the way he sees and experiences bodies—his own in relation to the mother's and the mother's in relation to his, or, put in

[8] Rapaport (1957) has clarified the altered states of consciousness such responses imply.

the most consistent way, the two of them in an undifferentiated, "warped" unity.

		Scores[a]			Summary of Scores
I	W	M+	H		R 12
II	W	FM,[b] FC+	A	(P)	Average Reaction Time 2′35″
III	W	M∓	H		Average Total Time 3′15″
IV	W	M±	H		W 9 (75%)
V	W	F+	A		D 2 (17%)
VI	W	M∓	H,N		S 1 (8%)
VII	W	F∓	Hd	(P)	sum M/sum C 6/0-1
VIII	D	F+	A	P	F%[c] 33/100
IX 1.	S	M±	H		F + %[d] 50/50
2.	W	F/C—	Arch		A% 33
X 1.	W	FM∓	A,H	(P)	H% 58-67
2.	D	F∓	Hd		P 1 + 3 (8%-33%)

[a] See Rapaport, Gill, and Schafer (1945-46) for criteria and rationale of scoring.
[b] FM is used for weak M or animals in humanlike movement, and counts .5 in sum M; it is not used for animal movement.
[c] The numerator is $\frac{\text{all F} \times 100}{R}$; the denominator is all responses scored for form level $\frac{}{R} \times 100$, that is, the % of responses with strong form components.
[d] The numerator is $\frac{F+,F\pm \times 100}{\text{all F}}$; the denominator is all responses scored $+, \pm \times 100$; the latter is the more significant all responses scored for form level measure.

Turning now to the summary of scores, we find an abun-
dance of human movement impressions. This is especially
striking in the setting of a comparatively low R. Relatively
many of these M's are more or less poor in form quality. Jux-
taposed to these data is a virtual absence of color responses.
Although he gives two FC responses, indicating efforts toward controlled emotional contact with others, he is disturbed by the redness of the hat on Card II and refers only
to *painted-on* colors on Card IX. The quantitative and qualitative poverty of emotional experience expressed in the color

scores is a formal indication of what is inferrable from the disrupted form and content of his M's that is, from the distortion, fusing, fatigue, loss of vitality, falling over, etc. Thus, these various aspects of the movement-color distribution suggest general impoverishment and distortion of the body ego and a trend toward regressed body experience. The quantitative and qualitative aspects of M and C also indicate, of course, the extent of his immersion in his inner world of fantasy and delusion, and they imply the predominance of introjective and projective mechanisms in his functioning with but little note being taken of the outer world *recognized as such*. More than likely, what he can usually recognize of the outer world are fragments of it encountered as inner reverberations, though even these he may notice only upon reprojection into the outer world. His generally low form level (F+%) further indicates severe impairment of reality testing. His related limitation of interest in conventional reality is indicated by his producing only one solid popular response, though he comes close to a few more.

Yet it is particularly noteworthy how large a percentage of his responses pertains to human content or to animals with humanlike qualities. This indicates the retention of a very lively interest in human experience. His other scores indicate, however, that this experience is regressively conceived for the most part and dulled by the devitalizing aspect of his regression. In the intensive therapy of schizophrenics, it is commonly observed that they have by no means lost their interest in human affairs. It is a question of the level on which they carry on and express this interest, of the predominance of primary processes in this inner world, and of the depletion of psychic energy available for sustained interest and restitution. Only in a limited sense, therefore, may we speak in this case of a turning away from the environment or from relationships.

It is also not to be thought that his scores show him to be incapable of emotional discharges onto the environment. In general Rorschach analysis, the virtual absence of any determinant other than form expresses a major effort rather than a secure accomplishment, or else a major impairment rather than a total loss. Also, this patient's dramatic appearance and test behavior speak against total withdrawal. In the context of a couple of very weak FC and the absence of substantial color responses, the likelihood is that tenuous adaptive efforts and nonresponsiveness will be sporadically disrupted by intense discharges. This conclusion would hold for a neurotic patient too, but is particularly likely in this case in view of the indicated regression to primitive levels of ego organization; on these levels the capacity for delay through defense or ego control is greatly diminished. Thus, as regards subjective experience of his own body, we might expect brief moments of intense vitality, or at least brief moments of intense activity as a restitutive measure through which he is seeking to find his energy or deny its loss.

The very high W% points to extreme synthesizing efforts, and, in context, to megalomanic propensities. The latter would be the counterpart to the persecution ideas suggested in the content (Card III). Yet, considering the slow and effortful manner in which he ground out his responses, it would appear that he even has difficulty keeping in touch with processes and contents in his inner world. And the relative speed with which he gives up each card after giving one response indicates either how little comfort he experiences in the process or how quickly he may become depleted in the process of trying, or both.

The internal consistency of the protocol *in all its aspects* allows us to accept it as valid and representative of the patient, and not artificially slanted or exaggerated in order to influence the decision about hospitalization. In any case, we are in no position to assume that he was of one mind in wanting to get into an open hospital. Only in intensive therapy might it be learned how he saw his test performance in relation to the question of disposition, and how, if at all, he *tried* to slant it.

In summary of this analysis, this patient's subjective experience of bodies appears to emphasize the following themes:

as regards their *direction*, they are seen primarily as moving downward and possibly turned upside down or backwards as well; as regards their *differentiation*, they merge with each other and become amorphous in their inner detail; as regards their *stability*, they are precarious, and either about to fall or fallen; as regards their *vitality*, they are weak, sick, tired, crippled, and dying, although in an uncertain and not sustainable fashion their size, vigor, integrity, and dignity may also be experienced; as regards their *relationships to the environment and to each other*, they are isolated, drifting, disoriented, obstructed, merged into a jumble of humanity, or else grandiose and/or persecuted by crushing forces. As regards *subjective awareness* itself, it is blocked, fragmented, sometimes inaccessible, and may require for its definition radical transformations of his self and body ego or discernment of these through projection into the experience of others. The trend of experience is steadily regressive. There is marked dedifferentiation within the body ego and loss of boundaries of his body ego in relation to others. There is continuing emphasis on depletion, disease, and destruction. The same conclusions are suggested by the slow, labored, artificial, distorted, fragmented, arbitrarily and expansively synthesized, and relatively colorless formal aspects of his record. In the end, we can be only astonished at this instrument, the Rorschach test, which can stimulate and support a very sick young man to expose the horrors in his mind with so little evident pain.

SUMMARY

I have presented formulations concerning the schizophrenic's disturbance of body ego and its relation to his loss of objects in the inner world, and have illustrated with a case study how these phenomena seem to appear in the Rorschach record. I have made special use of three general principles of test analysis. The first is that of pursuing a compelling hypothesis exhaustively, empathically exploring every aspect of every response for pertinent implications, and seeing what total picture ultimately emerges. In this regard, I believe that, as with any data, what Rorschach data tell us depends on what questions we put to them. The second principle of analysis is that of seeking convergence and patterning of implications of test scores, content, behavior, and mode of verbalization, without being partial to any one type of data. These are all vital materials for building a test report. The third principle is that of interpreting these data as being significant on more than one level of organization of functioning. This is especially important in dealing with schizophrenic material because from one response to the next we commonly encounter flux in level of functioning as well as multilevel significance within the single communications. With the help of these principles, the examiner may discover whole worlds of subjective experience expressed in Rorschach results. In the present context, the world considered has been that of unstably bounded, poorly differentiated and integrated bodies, or, more concretely, bodies which repeatedly split, inflate, get crushed or crippled, die, or get lost in each other or in undefined and topsy-turvy space.

9

REPRESENTATIONS OF
PERCEIVING AND ACTING IN
PSYCHOLOGICAL-TEST RESPONSES

In the psychological-test situation, we expose the subject to a great variety of stimuli about which he must do something. In the Rorschach test these stimuli include forms, spaces, colors, shadings, connections and separations, and figure-ground qualities; in the TAT, men, women, and children, alone and together and in various postures, moods, and settings; in the Wechsler Adult Intelligence Scale (WAIS) up to 287 items involving words, pictures, geometric symbols, numbers, and objects. To cope with these varied stimuli, in addition to those stimuli emanating from the person of the tester and the context of testing (Schafer, 1954), the subject must attend and concentrate, survey and abstract, remember and anticipate, organize and judge, create fantasy and test reality, move and talk. We may well ask, therefore, *How does the subject represent his inner experience of and attitudes toward being thus stimulated, as well as his strategy and tactics in coping with this stimulation?*

In answering this question, we shall define more clearly than we might otherwise the subject's dominant modes of perceiving and acting. In other terms, in addition to asking how he characteristically structures the world about him and

First published in *Festschrift for Gardner Murphy*, ed. J. G. Peatman and E. L. Hartley. New York: Harper & Row, 1960, pp. 291-312. Copyright 1960 by John G. Peatman and Eugene L. Hartley. Reprinted by permission of Harper & Row, Publishers.

within him (which is our most general and familiar question based on the projective hypothesis), we may now ask the closely related question: How does he experience the demand for structure and the process of creating structure? In so far as we are successful in this latter inquiry, we will be in a position to enrich our description of the subject's ego organization. And ego organization is what we are primarily concerned with in our test analyses (Rapaport, Gill, and Schafer, 1945-46; Schafer, 1954).

It should be noted that we are here engaged in an application of key aspects of Freud's ego psychology (Freud, 1920, 1923, 1926). In defining the ego, Freud emphasizes its perceptual and motor aspects. To begin with, the ego is a "body ego." It is the "perceptual cortex of the id" and becomes its executive agent. It scans the environment, and its thinking is experimental action in this environment. It develops under the considerable influence of perceptions of, and discharge into, the internal and external worlds. Ultimately it gains sizable energies of its own and more or less effective control over the internal and external conditions of stimulation and discharge. Some of the ego's energies are deployed in the perceptions and actions that establish and maintain the psychological boundaries between the inner and outer worlds—the stimulus and the response, the wish and the deed, the fantasy and the percept. Some of its energies are expended in the perceptions and actions that establish and refine adaptive and defensive signaling functions, as in the cases of anxiety and empathy (Schafer, 1959). In general, the ego's biological-adaptational function is secured and served by perceiving and acting. Traumatic situations are those which disrupt this function: they are defined by excitations too intense to be discharged adequately or worked over effectively in the mind; they result in marked impoverishment and dedifferentiation of function or in extreme expenditures of energy to master the trauma; the latter eventuality also brings about impoverished function in the total ego. Accordingly, it is first in the order of the ego's business to avert traumatic situations.

In what follows I will limit myself to detailed clinical examples of the test analysis of perceptual and motor experience. I will discuss the test results of two patients. I must forego a systematic and necessarily lengthy summary of the classes of pertinent events in each of the commonly used clinical tests; however, those readers familiar with complex analysis of test results should be able to infer the rationale of the various interpretations to follow, and to sense the organization of the implicit manual of interpretation. It will be obvious that I draw on many nuances of the responses—their scores, score patterns, and sequences; their formal organization; their content; the perceptual and verbal distortions in them; and the general style of verbalization and test-taking attitudes escorting them to expression and further defining their significance (see Chapter 7). The rationale and requirements of simultaneous interpretation of these varied facets of test responses have been discussed elsewhere (Schafer, 1954). Also, it should be noted in what follows that virtually all of the projective-test responses are treated as more or less pertinent to the theme of this article. This is a common consequence of applying a fresh hypothesis: suddenly all the data seem to become eloquent with respect to one's interest. In final analysis, the limits of profitable application of any point of view must be defined. For the time being, however, I consider it preferable to give this interest free rein and follow where it leads.

ILLUSTRATIVE CASE MATERIAL

Neither of the two patients to be discussed is psychotic. It is clinically well established that virtually every set of psychotic test protocols is replete with more or less dramatic representations of disturbance in the body ego.[1] My intent here is to show that neurotic and character-disordered protocols also often express such disturbance, although in other terms and on other levels of organization. The same can be demonstrated in the case of normal test protocols. The psychotics

[1] See Chapters 7 and 8.

have helped alert us to the phenomena in question; it is now our burden to learn the expressive language of the body ego in superficially less dramatic material.

Patient A

This is a divorced man in his early 40's who has had numerous brief hospitalizations over the 15-year period since his neuropsychiatric discharge from the Army during World War II. Exposed to repeated bombings, he had developed incapacitating anxiety and insomnia. Since then he has been a heavy drinker, using alcohol to help overcome his persistent insomnia and nighttime anxiety. He has been unable to stick to a job; once his talents are recognized by his being given more responsibility, he is compelled to leave the job.

Rorschach Test. He fails four cards (II, III, VII, IX), and gives only seven responses in all to the rest. He produces no Human-Movement responses, one Color-Form response that is almost a Pure Color response, no shading responses, a high percentage of pure Form, animal, and popular responses. Form level is adequate. Four of his responses are relatively insignificant in content: IV, a bear rug [W]; V, a flying bat [W]; VIII, rodents [D 1]; and X-1, crawfish [D 1]. His three significant responses are: I, "A moth" [W], and in the inquiry, "A little battered. [?] Frailed ends of the wings"; VI, "A skinned cat" [W], which verbalization remains unchanged during the inquiry, even though he obviously means the skin of a cat; and X-2 [W], "All the coloring looks like something you find down in the tropics.... All different.... The varied colors of coral.... of coral. I really don't see the pink, the yellow, and the brown: like you can get out of those [other colors]. Just looks like coral and shells ... like you see in the tropics. They don't satisfy my nerves.... They make me nervous!" His card rejections were irritable and externalized the responsibility for the difficulty: he said, "Nothing here," or "Not a darned, damned thing!" Otherwise he appeared mostly indifferent and as if "going through the motions."

Wechsler Adult Intelligence Scale. He obtains the following scores: Comprehension, 10, Information, 11, Digit Span, 7, Arithmetic, 15, Similarities, 14, Vocabulary, 11, Picture Arrangement, 10, Picture Completion, 13, Block Designs, 10, Object Assembly, 7, and Digit Symbol, 7. His IQ scores are Verbal 108, Performance 101, and Total 105. The following excerpts of his verbalizations are striking. On the *lost in the forest* item of Comprehension: "You know, people get so far out they can't get back, like me and my being nervous . . . you get lost"; *city land:* "[Land in the country] was undeveloped like nature left it"; *shallow brooks are noisy:* "Somebody that does a lot of babbling hasn't got a brain"; *eye and ear* in Similarities: "They are all senses"; in Vocabulary, the definition of *regulates:* "Like when you regulate a motor, tune it to the best you can"; of *obstruct:* "Is to barricade, hold off in some way or another"; of *hasten:* "To get a good pace up"; of *fortitude:* "A party that has a lot of spunk and go, to go out and get it, a hustler, wears his clients down." In doing the last four designs in the Block Designs subtest, he characteristically starts with the center block, and when the peripheral blocks are correctly placed and the center one not, he destroys the entire arrangement in his struggle to get the center correct.

While the impoverishment of the Rorschach test might suggest organic brain damage or depression, the high scores on Arithmetic, Similarities, and Picture Completion, and the absence of pertinent qualitative signs, tend to eliminate this suggested diagnosis. Some decline of his over-all intellectual level may be inferred from the scatter of the verbal scores and may be a result of his heavy drinking over a long period. Neither test raises the question of schizophrenia.

The Rorschach content suggests feelings of injury and hypersensitivity at the periphery, and irritable and anxious responses to such stimulation as he cannot avoid (he does reject four cards) and to which he is apparently very vulnerable. This state of affairs is powerfully expressed in his image of "a skinned cat": a creature that is all exposed nerve endings. Against this painful sensitivity he raises a protective barrier of indifference, though not very successfully. The strikingly high Arithmetic and Picture Completion scores in the WAIS strongly suggest a steadily maintained hyperalertness, and his slowing down on the visual-motor subtests (relatively low scores), as well as his mode of approach in Block Designs, suggests that something has in fact been disrupted between the center and periphery (capacity versus execution) and that he senses the disruption. The WAIS verbalizations quoted emphasize the brain, the barricade, *all* the senses, the natural and undisturbed state of affairs, getting disoriented, firing yourself up energetically so that you have speed, push, power, and endurance: these themes too appear to cluster around a marked feeling of sensorimotor disruption and feebleness. The relative impoverishment of functioning evident in the Rorschach test suggests a strong response to trauma as a likely basis for this disruption. The TAT stories of this patient fill in this aspect of the total picture in an illuminating fashion. They will be presented in full and then discussed.

Thematic Apperception Test. 1. 10″ Well, it's a kid who probably heard someone playing, could be the father or someone else ... or someone bought him a fiddle ... could he ever make a sound like the one he heard ... anticipating trying it and wondering how long it could or would take him to make that thing talk. 65″

2. 12″ I'd say in the picture a girl apparently just came from school ... the father here has been plowing in the field all day, all morning ... he's got his shirt off and is still working ..... mother is resting there having brought him his lunch ... the old man will continue on with his plowing ... the daughter will go home and mother will linger on a bit ...... that's all here in that picture. 80″

3 GF. 15″ Well ... a girl standing at a door ... either she is barring it or it is barred from her ... could be that she probably had an argument with her husband and he left and she's standing there full of remorse and hysteria, with her head on her arm and one arm on the door ...... that's all I see in that [big sigh]. [Tired?] No, just weary ... this is a tedious task. .... maybe we can get through in time to get coffee at the canteen? 85″

6 BM. 25″ It looks like the young fellow has just come home ... he's got something heavy on his mind and doesn't want to look at his mother ... he is worried ...... possibly could have done something that upset her ... that is how that looks to me

...... he's trying to tell her and he doesn't know how ......
that's it! 65″

4. 10″ It looks to me like the background has a picture on
the wall ...... well, the man in the picture looks very mad ...
maybe he did something to the girl ...... she's holding him,
pleading for him not to go ...... that's all I see in that. 55″

5. 20″ Well, all I see here is a woman opening a door with
surprise on her face ...... what is beyond the picture is the
cause of the look of shock on her face ...... that's all you can
see there. ......what she came upon after she opened the door
was very shocking to her ... something she didn't expect ......
[What might that be?] A burglar, for example, looting her house
...... or her husband kissing the maid ...... there's a lot of
things beyond the door. 105″

7 BM. 17″ Looks like to me an old man talking to the
younger one ... whether he is giving serious advice or coun-
sel ... the young man looks worried at something he has done
...... he is really in for it ... that's it. 45″

8 BM. 12″ This is a boy ... dreaming, probably has an ambition to be a doctor or a surgeon or else he's thinking he
doesn't know much about a hospital and maybe his Dad is in
the hospital and all he can think about is the operation, that
they are going to cut him up ... or his ambition to be a surgeon ...... I don't think much of the artist that did this one.
65″

10. 12″ This looks like a man and a woman ... and ah ... he
just came back from somewhere and she has her head on his
chest close to him ...... he's probably whispering in her ear
"I'd come back." With her eyes closed she's content to just be
close to him ... that's all I see in that. 55″

12 M. 20″ Looks like to me like this woman is dead or asleep
and her old man is either coming or going ...... unless it is
somebody asleep and he's a thief in the night walking towards
her ...... well, that's all I see in that! 58″

13 MF. 12″ Well ... this looks like to me ... I don't know
whether that girl is dead or unconscious ...... the man is facing away from her, his hand on his brow ...... I don't know
whether he's harmed her or did her in ... he's shook up ......
whether she's dead or alive ...... that's all I see in that. 72″

18 GF. 24″ This picture here ...... at the bottom of a stair-
case, it looks like as if one woman is choking the other
one ...... she's got a mean look on her face ...... that's all I
see in that. 60″

18 BM. 20″ It looks like this guy doesn't ... don't want to have his picture taken ... like these are hands from the rear holding his head up to the camera ...... that's all I see in that. 55″

16. 2″ Well, I see two people sitting opposite each other, on opposite sides of the desk ...... ah ...... one is sitting ... ah ... one writing is working and the other one is a patient ...... he doesn't want to be there ... he'd rather be getting coffee ...... ha ...... that's all there. 25″

In the first story his emphasis on having heard someone play immediately calls attention to strong response to *sensory stimulation;* then, when the boy wonders whether he could ever make a sound like the one he heard and how long it could or would take him to make that thing talk, it is as if the question is whether, with respect to sensory stimulation, he can *convert passivity to activity* and thereby achieve some responsive discharge. In the second story, *no stimulation* passes between any of the three figures and the mother needs *rest* after a light chore. In the third story a severe *disturbance at the threshold* is represented in his vagueness about whether one is controlling the entryway by barring it (his superficial indifference) or whether one is passively shut out (the assumed underlying traumatization and helplessness). It is significant that at this point a disruption of test-taking attitude occurs, and it is possible that his reference, immediately preceding the disruption, to remorse and hysteria points to components of the initial traumatic state. His unusual concern with who is barring the door and who is barred suggests a relatively undifferentiated sensorimotor state. Looking ahead in the record to 12M, such a state is again suggested by the unusual question about whether the older man is *coming or going.* We may assume that, in both of these stories, he is implicitly conveying that he thinks of himself as someone who does not know whether he is coming or going.

In the third story, notice the way thoughts are described as *heavy* and how special emphasis is put on *avoiding the stimulation of looking* at the mother as well as on the *inability to express,* both of which are reminiscent of themes discerned in the first two stories. Skipping over Card 4 and going on to Card 5, we find the emphasis building up from surprise to *shock;* shock is a comparatively strong description of this woman's appearance and again calls attention to traumatic sensory experience. Her *unpreparedness* is in accord with this inference, and his final verbalization that "there are a lot of things beyond the door" again points to a sense of *disturbance at the threshold* (see the second TAT story, the "frailed wings" in the Rorschach test, the "barricade" definition of *obstruct* in the WAIS). In 7 BM an anticipation of a heavy (emotional) *bombardment* is suggested in his concluding verbalization. In 8 BM there is a suggestion of his identifying with the father in the passive position of being *traumatized* and then *converting this to activity* in the role of the surgeon; the surgery scene itself implies *violent entry by external stimuli or agents.* In Card 10 he appears to emphasize *soothing stimulation.* In 12 M, in addition to the already mentioned dedifferentiation of coming and going, there is again an *unexpected intruder* (see Card 5). In 13 MF the themes of *unconsciousness* and *being shook up* and *turning away from stimulation* stand out. In 18 BM there is a suggestion of the traumatic effect of being *immobilized* in the face of external stimuli (an only apparently paradoxical reaction to a camera) and possibly an implication of *fright* at being exposed to a flash bulb. Very likely, he is also referring to the disturbing effect of the test situation itself—a close look at him being taken while he is immobilized, so to speak. This disturbing effect is rather strongly suggested in Card 16, where he is interested only in obtaining some fluid that is simultaneously *soothing and energizing* (see the low soft stimulation in Card 10). Also, in this way he would end his immobilized state in the test situation.

In the light of this *partial analysis,* it is therefore compelling to think of this man as being consistently and almost totally preoccupied with shock and the avoidance of shock (notice how frequently his characters are asleep, unconscious, turned away, etc.). He craves gentle, soothing stimulation; he quickly considers how passive stimulation may be converted into active mastery and discharge; and he reacts with consternation to a subtle confusion around the borders of the body ego. There is only an apparent paradox between this conclusion and the inference of hyperalertness from his WAIS scores: his hyperalertness would be in the service of a protective screen of avoidance and indifference; it would not be a free, adaptive alertness predicated on a sound ability to assimilate varieties of stimulation. In other words, his hyperalertness appears to express relative perceptual and motor impotence rather than mastery. He scans all too well because he has to limit carefully what he allows himself to see fully. A normal degree of relative autonomy from the environment has thus been drastically reduced. In all these respects he appears to fit Freud's description (1920) of the energic and structural disruption of the ego in traumatic neuroses.

Patient B

This patient is a married, childless woman in her late 20's. After a few years of college education, she worked as a secretary and technician in a physiology laboratory. She had more than a year of psychotherapy a few years ago and is now seeking psychoanalysis. Phobic and conversion symptoms stand out in her presenting complaints. The essentials of the test analysis to be presented were worked out by Dr. Cynthia Dember and the author with no knowledge of these symptoms. The analysis will center on her Rorschach record.

Rorschach Test. I. 1. 5″ A butterfly or a bat or some winged animal [W] ...... Oh, am I supposed to go on talking? It still looks like a butterfly or a bat. [Anything else?] Can I turn it another way? [Up to you.]
2. ∨ If you really look at it, it could look like an Indian statue or something [lower part of Dd 24]. ([?] There is a little spot that could be the eyes. [?] No.)
3. ∧ ... An airplane [W].

II.   1. 2″ Looks like two elephants kissing, or two dogs. They always look like animals [D 1].

2. < ∨ It looks like two elephants this way too [D 1]. ([?] The same sort of thing either way. It seems similar. [?] Trunk. [?] Of course it is grayish, the same color. [?] The head.) > ∧ 1′10″.

III.   1. 5″ It looks like a mobile, sort of modern sculpture ... like something you'd see in the Museum of Modern Art [D 1]. ([?] The thin wire carvings that they have, very narrow wire statues. Mobile is not the right word for it. Very narrow. [?] No, except they do look like figures and they are very thin and they don't have too much of a lifelike effect.)

2. It also looks like two of those dogs that they clip— poodles—sort of each of them balanced on a ball [D 1]. ([?] They seem to have a very thin neck and puffy thing around. I mean those poodles that are clipped. That more than anything I think. [?] I can't remember anything else.)

3. < ∨ This looks like two old men with beards looking in opposite directions [D 4]. ([Beards?] I don't think I mentioned it but that is what I was thinking of [patient blushes]. They look like beards, that is all. They jut out. [?] It's just the general shape of a beard.)

4. And a tree branch up, on the side [D 5].

5. ∧ I suppose the red is supposed to mean something but it seems irrelevant. This looks like a bow here [D 3] ([?] The shape of a bow pulled in the middle, like a kid wears in her hair. [?] No.)

6. These look like kidneys hanging on something [D 2]. ([?] The shape of kidneys. [?] No.)

IV.   1. 25″ That one doesn't look like much. That way it looks a little bit like a bat again [W].

2. < ∨ Well, it looks sort of like the skull of an animal you'd see in the ... museum [W]. ([?] The total picture looked like a skull. I think it was particularly the white spots on each side that looked like blank areas [Dds 24] about where the sinus is. [Blank areas?] Spots where the sinuses are. In the skeleton there are spaces. [Kind of skull?] Some large animal, a buffalo, something like that.)

3. All of these, by the way, look something like X rays, I think [W]. [The others too?] Yes, I thought of that for the others. I really don't see anything here. ([?] I think it is the color, the shading more than anything. [?] The lines. [?] Various lines

or stripes, which is really practically the same thing as shading.)

4. This top part looks like a blossoming flower [D 3]. ([?] The way it was sort of going out on the side. [?] No, just the general shape.)

5. This part looks like a candle with the wax dripping down [D 1].

6. These here look like dog's ears [D 4].

7. ∨ This looks like some kind of an insect [bottom of D 1]. ([?] Oh, I remember, there were little sort of tentacles sticking out the top. [?] There may have been but I don't remember.) 4′25″

V. 1. 4″ It looks like an eagle . . . . . . or a hawk [W] . . . . . . ([?] The things that look like talons hanging down on the bottom. [?] No.)

2. ∨ . . . . . . ∧ I think this means I don't have a very creative mind because I don't see anything else . . . . . . [Covers half of card.] . . . Well, if you look very hard at either side you might see a lion sort of lying back like he was on a chaise lounge [D 4] . . . . . . ([?] The things sticking out on either side look like the legs of a lion and they are a sort of dark area and the general shape of a lion's mane. [?] No. [Mane?] The general shape. [?] Mostly it is just a general impression. [Patient doesn't see chaise, but explains that it is as if lion were at the appropriate angle.])

3. It looks like a wishbone on top [D 3]. 3′30″

VI. 1. 10″ The bottom doesn't look like anything much off-hand. The top looks again like a butterfly [D 8]. ([?] A general sort of winged effect but on a small scale. [Winged?] It seemed to me there were things on either side in the shape of wings. [?] No.)

2. The very top looks like, well, it doesn't really look like a cat but it is like the face with whiskers sticking out on the side [D 7].

3. . . . . . . ∨ . . . . . . [Smiles.] It looks like two people being burned at the stake [W]. It doesn't really look like people [D 1] but vaguely the top part does. The bottom looks like fire [D 3]. ([?] The bottom part didn't look like people but the top part looked like arms sticking out and what could have been a stake in the middle [D 5]. Obviously it would have to be two of whatever it was. It looks like a face in profile, arms . . . reaching out. The bottom part doesn't look like a person. [How much of a person?] Most of the person but the bottom didn't look much

like it from what could have been the waist down. I don't remember the waist really. [Fire?] It looks like flames leaping up. It was sort of the shape of flame. [?] No.)

4. . . . . . It looks like a bear rug, a bearskin rug [W]. [No inquiry by oversight.]

VII. 1. 12″ Again this one looks like some sort of modernistic sculpture, these things poised up here [D 2]. ([?] Because it doesn't look like much of anything and it's all things lying sort of crosswise on each other. [?] No.)

2. Like driftwood [W]. ([?] Because it looks like driftwood. It just looks like driftwood. [?] It looks like branches on driftwood. [?] No, because I don't even remember it very well now.)

3. ∨ ... Well, it looks like it could possibly be a very peculiarly shaped woman with a large derriere and one leg and a very large head perched on her back and an arm reaching out [W]. ([Perched on her back?] Well, it is not coming on straight to her body, it is sort of coming out behind her as though it were stuck on at one spot there.) ∧ . . . [Covers half of card.] . . . . . . 2′35″

VIII. 1. 15″ Umm, well, the two things on the side look like two rodents, two pink things [D 1].

2. ∨ . . . . . . < ... It looks like a pink and green rocketship [W]. ([?] It looked like a sort of nose cone [D 4]. Do you remember how I held it?)

3. . . . . . . This part here looks like slices of tangerine; probably the color more than anything [D 7]. ([Anything beside the color?] Yes, it was the shape of one slice of tangerine or orange, except the color was tangerine.)

4. Well, the whole thing gives you the effect you might see if you were lying on the beach in the sun and closed your eyes [W]. ([?] Well, it is the colors, of course, more than anything. It is a pattern, colors in a pattern that doesn't make too much sense. [?] . . . . . . No . . . no . . . just the brightness of it after seeing the gray.) . . . . . . 3′15″

IX. 1. ∨ 28″ We have a mushroom cloud from an atom bomb [D 6]. ([?] The shape. [?] Well, it is not the color and you can't exactly say it is the texture but it is the effect, sort of a smoky effect. Just this pink cloud. [Smoky?] No, just the general effect.)

2. A couple of boiled lobsters down here [D 3]. ([?] There is a claw effect and part of it is the color of the lobster and my husband had lobster the other day.)

3. ∨ [Covers half of card with hand.] ... Well, it could, by a stretch of the imagination, be some sort of a plant in a flower show although, of course, the colors don't go [W]. ([?] Well, it is a flower arrangement. This is the holder down here [D 6] and the rest of it is the flowers.) 2′30″

X. 1. This is pretty. 10″ These look like spiders [D 1].

2. This really looks like the Museum of Modern Art: it just looks like a modern painting [W]. ([?] The lack of relation as far as I could see of the things to each other ... modern painting. It looks a little bit like Salvadore ... Dali. [?] The colors. [?] No.)

3. Oh, we have an old-fashioned coal stove here [D 11]. ([?] Well, I grew up with a coal stove for one thing and it is sort of the shape of one and there is a thing sticking up that looks like the smokestack or pipe or whatever you call it. [?] Just the one part on top that looks that way.)

4. And a man from Mars on the bottom [D 7]. ([?] Oh, there was a little picture, a little face in the middle and long green ears hanging down. [?] I always associate green people with Mars. [?] No.)

5. And a couple of crabs on the side here [D 7]. ([?] Well they just have the general shape of soft-shelled crabs. [?] Color. [?] No.) ∨ ...... Well, it is very hard to see the thing as a whole. You sort of have to take it piece by piece. The spider and the crab look like they did the other way ...... [Covers part of card.] ...... ∧ ... I don't, I can't relate the things in the picture to each other. [?] I am trying to take the whole picture in and see it as one thing and you really can't see it as one thing. 3′25″

From the standpoint of perceptual and motor experience, the most expressive response in this record is VIII 4 (the sun through closed eyes). It conveys a preference for screening out or blurring external stimuli impinging on one—by closing the eyes (repressing and denying) and by immobilization of the body (lying on the beach). At the same time, the pleasant context of the sun's rays suggests the fantasy of exposing oneself to the father (symbolized by the sun) and basking in his warmth. (In the WAIS Information subtest she explains that dark clothes are warmer than light-colored clothes because they "attract the sun's rays"; in the Word Association Test her response to *money* is "Clothes. [?] I always liked clothes.")

Thus, at one and the same time, according to these hypotheses, she defends herself repressively by blurring, immobilization, and obliteration of conscious mental content, and gratifies herself by a passive, self-exhibiting, incestuously toned contact. Rorschach responses I 2 and V 2 also express the effortfulness of looking; and responses VI 1 and VI 2 suggest specific inhibitions of looking at the lower part of the body (the labial or vaginal area of the card, and the lower half of the body respectively). Further, III 3 has people looking in opposite directions. Note also the late and muted appearance of movement and color in the record, and her dismissing an early impact of color (Card III) as "irrelevant" in III 5: these suggest, in this context, further restriction on her capacity for looking and acting.

We must necessarily suppose a link between activity and clarity in perceptual functioning and the success of the information-gathering functioning of the ego, although the latter is, of course, also mediated by factors of memory organization (Rapaport, Gill, and Schafer, 1945-46). Thus, in the Information subtest of the WAIS, which tends to present special difficulties to subjects with marked repressive, ego-restrictive inclinations, this patient is relatively frequently unsure of correct responses and sometimes rejects them; she relatively often gives near-correct responses; in addition, she gropes for words and mixes up opposites, confusing, for example, the freezing point and the boiling point of water. A veneer of sophistication over this naïveté is suggested in the Word Association Test where she associates "Freud" to *masturbation* and uses the indecorous word *lousy;* the same veneer is suggested during the Comprehension subtest of the WAIS when she drags in a comment about modern real-estate trends while explaining why land in the city costs more than land in the country, and when she challenges the question *Why should we keep away from bad company?* Very likely she is also trying by these means to appear to be a promising, "enlightened" candidate for treatment.

With specific regard to the motoric components of ego

functioning and self-definition, we encounter further evidence of significant conflict and splitting in the patient's Rorschach test content. There the body and its parts tend to be portrayed, directly or in terms of external objects, as on the one hand lifeless (I 2, III 1, IV 2), hanging limply (III 6, IV 5, IV 6, V 1, V 2, X 4), lying down (V 2, VII 1), soft (VIII 3, X 5), thin (III 1), clipped (III 2), bound (VI 3) smoky (IX 1), artificially arranged (III 2, VII 1, VIII 4, IX 3, X 2), poorly connected or drifting (VII 1, VII 2, VII 3, end of X), and on the other hand actually or potentially protruding (II 2, III 4, IV 7, X 3), burning (IV 5, VI 3, IX 2, X 3), exploding or ejecting (VIII 2, IX 1), predatory (I 2, V 1, V 2), growing and expanding (IV 4), and moving or capable of moving fast and forcefully (I 3, II 2, IV 2, V 1, V 2, VIII 2). Combinations of these contrary trends are seen in a number of responses such as V 2, which is perhaps the second most striking in the present context—the lion on a chaise. This content has potentially powerful, destructive, phallic aspects and yet it is represented in an inert, limp, immobilized form. Moreover, the perceptual organization of the figure is poor (head and legs too close together) and involves a failure to achieve the not unusual human-movement response that is implicit in the content given (a reclining figure). Similar combinations of the two conflicting trends occur on Card III in the mobile that is immobile and on Card VIII in the rocket that is pink and green. These responses are neurotic patchworks: inappropriate juxtapositions and arbitrary fusions predominating over sensible and forceful synthesis (Prelinger, 1958).

The splitting and the reduced synthesizing capacity may also be inferred from her relatively low number of human-movement responses, as well as her missing some such responses or else seeing them late (e.g., cards II, III, and V), and even then integrating them poorly (e.g., VI 3 and VII 3); and the same for her missing (III 5, IX 1, IX 3) and forcing (VIII 2, X 4) Form-Color responses. A weakness of affective integration is also suggested by her apparently responding strongly to color and shading and yet tending (1) to give color responses late (she gave none to II and III), and (2) to be relatively unproductive on Cards VIII, IX, and X. In addition, the suggestion of docility in her color responses (marked preference for FC) and in her response content stands alongside a comparatively high emphasis on whole responses; the latter suggests high ambition, which, in turn, considering the total context, very likely expresses the intellectual side of the phallic aspirations that are evident in other aspects of her response content.

Pertinent responses in the WAIS include:

(1) Picture Completion item 16: "The arm seems to be missing" in reference to the missing *reflection* of an arm; (2) an unusual error on Picture Completion item 20: "I don't see a way to open the barn door," where the correct response is the absence of snow on top of a woodpile; (3) Information item 23: the boiling point of water is "32° . . . . . . is it Fahrenheit or Centigrade? I always get them mixed . . . [?] Centigrade. [Question repeated.] It freezes at 32°. [?] I don't know, 120 I'll say"; (4) Comprehension item 14, *What is the meaning of "One swallow doesn't make a summer?"*: "I think that's the sort of thing mothers say to their daughters when they're jilted by suitors; there are other fish in the sea"; (5) Similarities item 9, *How are an egg and seed alike?* "They're . . . well . . . [laugh] . . . both the same sort of . . . [?] Both the beginning of life."

These WAIS responses again suggest an impaired body ego. They introduce themes of incompleteness, obstruction at the periphery, and affective (thermal) confusion in the interior. They also point to defensive reliance on repression in this regard and associated naïve, girlish dependence on "mother."

In summary, *as seen from this selective standpoint*, the following picture emerges of this woman: she is characterized by disturbed perceptual and motor functioning. Strict repressions appear to predominate against a hysterical-oedipal-phallic configuration. Concomitantly she suffers a significant restriction of imaginative processes, affective responsiveness, perceptual and bodily (including sexual) differentiation, synthesis, and sensitivity. Her body image emphasizes that all is not well in the body as regards its integration, tonus, liveliness, and receptiveness (the barn door, the closed eyes). A kind of hysterical curtain appears to hang about this woman: it is not so much an iron curtain as a smoky curtain which renders the patient and the world hazy, diffuse, and half-asleep. This curtain serves the repressed impulses as well as the defenses against them. In front of it there is a superficial enlightenment and warm receptiveness; behind it there is repressive ignorance and frigid door-locking. Actually, her initial communication was coming for the testing without her glasses: in the light of the test analysis, this was very likely a condensed behavioral expression—a charade—of the major problems discussed above; in effect, she said thereby, "My trouble is that I can't allow myself to see—and move—well." There is enough accuracy of perception in most of her responses to suggest that not having her glasses facilitated the expression of her disturbed perceptual and motor functioning rather than artificially caused it.

In conclusion, it should be noted first that this approach has potential value for the psychotherapist, for it may sensitize him to the elusive, yet so often central psychopathological communications conveyed through perceptual and bodily modes of function; also, it may help him understand in what way and to what extent he will be allowed to impinge on his patient in the therapeutic process. Second, as suggested by such recent publications as those of Fisher and Cleveland (1958) and Zucker (1958), the clinical research potential of this approach is manifold. And third, there is a current of psychological investigation emanating from or fed by Freud's ego psychology within which this mode of analysis has developed; this current includes studies of perception and motility in the treatment situation, personality-in-perception experiments, and studies of stimulus deprivation in children and adults. All these investigations progressively clarify how and to what degree the ego expresses its needs, its organization, and its relative strength in the way it perceives and moves in space and time.

BIBLIOGRAPHY

Alexander, F., & French, T. M. (1946), *Psychoanalytic Therapy: Principles and Application*. New York: Ronald Press.

Baer de Bahia, A. (1950), Le Test de Rorschach Interprété du Point de Vue Analytique. *Revue Française de Psychoanalyse*, 14:455-503.

Balint, M. (1950), On the Termination of Analysis. *Int. J. Psycho-Anal.*, 31: 196-199.

Bellak, L. (1950), Thematic Apperception: Failures and the Defenses. *Trans. N.Y. Acad. Sci.*, 12:122-126.

——— (1954), A Study of Limitations and "Failures": Toward an Ego Psychology of Projective Techniques. *J. Proj. Techn.*, 18: 279-293.

Bergler, E. (1944), A Clinical Approach to the Psychoanalysis of Writers. *Psychoanal. Rev.*, 31:40-70.

——— (1945), On a Five-Layer Structure in Sublimation. *Psychoanal. Quart.*, 14:76-97.

Brenman, M. (1952), On Teasing and Being Teased: And the Problem of "Moral Masochism." *The Psychoanalytic Study of the Child*, 7:264-285. New York: International Universities Press.

Carr, A. C. (1949), An Evaluation of Nine Non-Directive Psychotherapy Cases by Means of the Rorschach. *J. Consult. Psychol.*, 13:196-205.

Eissler, K. R. (1950), The Chicago Institute of Psychoanalysis and the Sixth Period of the Development of Psychoanalytic Technique. *J. Gen. Psychol.*, 42:103-157.

Erikson, E. H. (1950a), *Childhood and Society*. New York: Norton.

——— (1950b), Growth and Crises of the Healthy Personality. *Psychological Issues*, 1 (1):50-100. New York: International Universities Press, 1959.

——— (1956), The Problem of Ego Identity. *Psychological Issues*, 1 (1):101-164. New York: International Universities Press, 1959.

Federn, P. (1952), *Ego Psychology and the Psychoses*. New York: Basic Books.

Fenichel, O. (1938), Ego Strength and Ego Weakness. *The Collected Papers*, 2nd Series. New York: Norton, 1954, pp. 70-80.

——— (1941a), The Ego and the Affects. *The Collected Papers*, 2nd Series. New York: Norton, 1954, pp. 215-227.

——— (1941b), *Problems of Psychoanalytic Technique*, trans. D. Brunswick. Albany, N.Y.: Psychoanalytic Quarterly.

Fisher, S., & Cleveland, S. E. (1958), *Body Image and Personality*. Princeton, N.J.: Van Nostrand.

Freud, A. (1936), *The Ego and the Mechanisms of Defence*. New York: International Universities Press, 1946.

Freud, S. (1900), The Interpretation of Dreams. *Standard Edition*, 4 & 5. London: Hogarth Press, 1953.

215

———— (1905), Jokes and Their Relation to the Unconscious. *Standard Edition*, 8. London: Hogarth Press, 1960.

———— (1907), Creative Writers and Day-Dreaming. *Standard Edition*, 9:141-153. London: Hogarth Press, 1959.

———— (1911a), The Handling of Dream-Interpretation in Psycho-Analysis. *Standard Edition*, 12:91-96. London: Hogarth Press, 1958.

———— (1911b), Formulations on the Two Principles in Mental Functioning. *Standard Edition*, 12:213-226. London: Hogarth Press, 1958.

———— (1915), The Unconscious. *Standard Edition*, 14:159-215. London: Hogarth Press, 1957.

———— (1920), Beyond the Pleasure Principle. *Standard Edition*, 18:7-64. London: Hogarth Press, 1955.

———— (1921), Group Psychology and the Analysis of the Ego. *Standard Edition*, 18:69-143. London: Hogarth Press, 1955.

———— (1923), The Ego and the Id. *Standard Edition*, 19:12-59. London: Hogarth Press, 1961.

———— (1926), Inhibitions, Symptoms and Anxiety. *Standard Edition*, 20:77-174. London: Hogarth Press, 1959.

———— (1937), Analysis Terminable and Interminable. *Standard Edition*, 23:216-253. London: Hogarth Press, 1964.

Fromm, E. O., & Elonen, A. S. (1951), The Use of Projective Techniques in the Study of a Case of Female Homosexuality. *J. Proj. Techn.*, 15:185-230.

Fromm-Reichmann, F. (1950), *Principles of Intensive Psychotherapy*. Chicago: University of Chicago Press.

Gibby, R. G. (1952), Examiner Influence on the Rorschach Inquiry. *J. Consult. Psychol.*, 16:449-455.

Gill, M. M. (1954), Psychoanalysis and Exploratory Psychotherapy. *J. Amer. Psychoanal. Assoc.*, 2:771-797.

Gitelson, M. (1952), The Emotional Position of the Analyst in the Psychoanalytic Situation. *Int. J. Psycho-Anal.*, 33:1-10.

Glover, E. (1931), The Therapeutic Effect of Inexact Interpretation: A Contribution to the Theory of Suggestion. *Int. J. Psycho-Anal.*, 12:397-411.

Haimowitz, N. R., & Haimowitz, N. L. (1952), Personality Changes in Client-Centered Therapy. In: *Success in Psychotherapy*, ed. W. Wolff & J. A. Precker. New York: Grune & Stratton, pp. 69-93.

Hamlin, R. M., Berger, B., & Cummings, S. T. (1952), Changes in Adjustment Following Psychotherapy as Reflected in Rorschach Signs. In: *Success in Psychotherapy*, ed. W. Wolff & J. A. Precker. New York: Grune & Stratton, pp. 94-111.

Hammer, E. F., & Piotrowski, Z. A. (1953), Hostility as a Factor in the Clinician's Personality as It Affects His Interpretation of Projective Drawings (H-T-P). *J. Proj. Techn.*, 17:210-216.

Hartmann, H. (1939), *Ego Psychology and the Problem of Adaptation*, trans. D. Rapaport. New York: International Universities Press, 1958.

———— (1950), Comments on the Psychoanalytic Theory of the Ego. *The Psy-*

choanalytic Study of the Child, 5:74-96. New York: International Universities Press.

—— (1956), Notes on the Reality Principle. *The Psychoanalytic Study of the Child*, 11:31-53. New York: International Universities Press.

—— (1964), *Essays on Ego Psychology*. New York: International Universities Press.

——, Kris, E., & Loewenstein, R. M. (1946), Comments on the Formation of Psychic Structure. *Psychological Issues*, 4 (2):27-55. New York: International Universities Press, 1964.

Hertzman, M., & Pearce, J. (1947), The Personal Meaning of the Human Figure in the Rorschach. *Psychiatry*, 10:413-422.

Hoffer, W. (1950), Three Psychological Criteria for the Termination of Treatment. *Int. J. Psycho-Anal.*, 31:194-195.

Holt, R. R. (1951), The Thematic Apperception Test. In: *An Introduction to Projective Techniques*, ed. H. A. Anderson & G. L. Anderson. New York: Prentice Hall, pp. 181-229.

—— (1954), Implications of Some Contemporary Personality Theories for Rorschach Rationale. In: *Developments in the Rorschach Technique*, Vol. I, by B. Klopfer, M. D. Ainsworth, W. G. Klopfer, & R. R. Holt. Yonkers-on-Hudson, New York: World Book Co., pp. 501-560.

—— (1956), Gauging Primary and Secondary Processes in Rorschach Responses. *J. Proj. Techn.*, 20:14-25.

——, & Havel, J. (1960), A Method for Assessing Primary and Secondary Process in the Rorschach. In: *Rorschach Psychology*, ed. M. A. Rickers-Ovsiankina. New York: Wiley, pp. 263-318.

Itard, J. M. G. (1932), *The Wild Boy of Aveyron*, trans. G. & M. Humphrey. New York: Century.

Jacobson, E. (1954), The Self and the Object World: Vicissitudes of Their Infantile Cathexis and Their Influence on Ideational and Affective Development. *The Psychoanalytic Study of the Child*, 9:75-127. New York: International Universities Press.

—— (1964), *The Self and the Object World*. New York: International Universities Press.

Klatskin, E. H. (1952), An Analysis of the Effect of the Test Situation upon the Rorschach Record: Formal Scoring Characteristics. *J. Proj. Techn.*, 16:193-199.

Klein, G. S. (1951), The Personal World Through Perception. In: *Perception, an Approach to Personality*, ed. R. R. Blake & G. V. Ramsey. New York: Ronald Press.

Knight, R. P. (1952), An Evaluation of Psychotherapeutic Techniques. *Bull. Menninger Clin.*, 16:113-124.

—— (1953), Borderline States. *Bull. Menninger Clin.*, 17:1-12.

Kris, E. (1952), *Psychoanalytic Explorations in Art*. New York: International Universities Press.

Levey, H. B. (1939), A Critique of the Theory of Sublimation. *Psychiatry*, 2:239-270.

——— (1940), A Theory Concerning Free Creation in the Inventive Arts. *Psychiatry*, 3:229-293.

Loewald, H. (1960), On the Therapeutic Action of Psychoanalysis. *Int. J. Psycho-Anal.*, 41:16-33.

MacAlpine, I. (1950), The Development of the Transference. *Psychoanal. Quart.*, 19:501-539.

Muench, G. A. (1947), An Evaluation of Non-Directive Psychotherapy, *Applied Psychol. Monographs*, Monograph 13.

Nunberg, H. (1931), The Synthetic Function of the Ego. In: *Practice and Theory of Psychoanalysis*. New York: Nervous and Mental Disease Pub., 1948, pp. 120-136.

Oberndorf, C. P. (1948), Failures with Psychoanalytic Therapy. In: *Failures in Psychiatric Treatment*, ed. P. Hoch. New York: Grune & Stratton, pp. 10-20.

Olden, C. (1953), On Adult Empathy with Children. *The Psychoanalytic Study of the Child*, 8:111-127. New York: International Universities Press.

Piaget, J. (1928), *Judgment and Reasoning in the Child*. New York: Harcourt, Brace.

——— (1929), *The Child's Conception of the World*. New York: Harcourt, Brace.

——— (1930), *The Child's Conception of Physical Causality*. London: Routledge & Kegan Paul.

——— (1932), *The Language and Thought of the Child*, 2nd ed. London: Routledge & Kegan Paul.

Piotrowski, Z., & Schreiber, M. (1952), Rorschach Perceptanalytic Measurement of Personality Changes During and After Intensive Psychoanalytically-Oriented Psychotherapy. In: *Specialized Techniques in Psychotherapy*, ed. G. Bychowski & L. Despert. New York: Grune & Stratton, pp. 337-361.

Pious, W. L. (1950), Obsessive-Compulsive Symptoms in an Incipient Schizophrenia. *Psychoanal. Quart.*, 19:327-351.

Prelinger, E. (1958), Identity Diffusion and the Synthetic Function. In: *Psycho-Social Problems of College Men*, ed. B. M. Wedge. New Haven: Yale University Press, pp. 214-241.

———, Zimet, C. N., Schafer, R., & Levin, M. (1964), *An Ego-Psychological Approach to Character Assessment*. Glencoe, Ill.: Free Press.

Rangell, L. (1954), Panel Report, Annual Meeting, 1953. *J. Amer. Psychoanal. Assoc.*, 2:152-166.

Rapaport, D. (1950a), On the Psychoanalytic Theory of Thinking. *Int. J. Psycho-Anal.*, 31:161-170.

——— (1950b), The Theoretical Implications of Diagnostic Testing Procedures. *Rapports, Congrès International de Psychiatrie*, 2:241-271. Paris: Hermann & Cie.

——— (1951a), The Autonomy of the Ego. *Bull. Menninger Clin.*, 15:113-123.

———, ed. (1951b), *Organization and Pathology of Thought: Selected Sources*. New York: Columbia University Press.

——— (1951c), Consciousness: A Psychopathological and Psychodynamic View. In: *Problems of Consciousness*, Trans. of the Second Conference, March 19-20, 1951. New York: Josiah Macy, Jr. Foundation, pp. 18-57.

——— (1953a), On the Psychoanalytic Theory of Affects. *Int. J. Psycho-Anal.*, 34:177-198.

——— (1953b), Some Metapsychological Considerations Concerning Activity and Passivity. Unpublished manuscript.

——— (1957), Cognitive Structures. In: *Contemporary Approaches to Cognition*, J. S. Bruner et al. Cambridge: Harvard University Press, pp. 157-200.

——— (1959), The Structure of Psychoanalytic Theory: A Systematizing Attempt. *Psychological Issues*, 2 (2). New York: International Universities Press, 1960.

———, & Gill, M. M. (1959), The Points of View and Assumptions of Metapsychology. *Int. J. Psycho-Anal.*, 40:153-162.

———, ———, & Schafer, R. (1945-46), *Diagnostic Psychological Testing*, 2 vols. Chicago: Year Book Publishers.

Reich, A. (1950), On the Termination of Analysis. *Int. J. Psycho-Anal.*, 31: 179-183.

Rickman, J. (1950), On the Criteria for the Termination of an Analysis. *Int. J. Psycho-Anal.*, 31:200-201.

Rioch, M. J. (1949), The Use of the Rorschach Test in the Assessment of Change in Patients under Psychotherapy. *Psychiatry*, 12:427-434.

Sanders, R., & Cleveland, S. E. (1953), The Relationship between Examiner Personality Variables and Subjects' Rorschach Scores. *J. Proj. Techn.*, 17:34-50.

Schachtel, E. G. (1945), Subjective Definitions of the Rorschach Test Situation and Their Effect on Test Performance. *Psychiatry*, 8:419-448.

Schafer, R. (1945), A Study of Thought Processes in a Word Association Test. *Character & Pers.*, 13:212-227.

——— (1948), *The Clinical Application of Psychological Tests*. New York: International Universities Press.

——— (1949), Psychological Tests in Clinical Research. *J. Consult. Psychol.*, 13:328-334.

——— (1954), *Psychoanalytic Interpretation in Rorschach Testing*. New York: Grune & Stratton.

——— (1959), Generative Empathy in the Treatment Situation. *Psychoanal. Quart.*, 28:342-373.

Schur, M. (1953), The Ego in Anxiety. In: *Drives, Affects, Behavior*, ed. R. M. Loewenstein. New York: International Universities Press, pp. 67-103.

Sharpe, E. F. (1935), Similar and Divergent Unconscious Determinants Underlying the Sublimations of Pure Art and Pure Science. *Int. J. Psycho-Anal.*, 16:186-202.

Sullivan, H. S. (1947), *Conceptions of Modern Psychiatry*. Washington: William Alanson White Psychiatric Foundation.

Watkins, J. G. (1949), Evaluating Success in Psychotherapy. *Amer. Psychologist*, 4:396 [abstract].

Welch, B., Schafer, R., and Dember, C. F. (1961), TAT Stories of Hypomanic and Depressed Patients. *J. Proj. Techn.*, 25:221-232.

Werner, H. (1948), *Comparative Psychology of Mental Development*, rev. ed. New York: International Universities Press, 1957.

Winnicott, D. W. (1958), *Collected Papers: Through Paediatrics to Psychoanalysis*. New York: Basic Books.

Zucker, L. J. (1958), *Ego Structure in Paranoid Schizophrenia*. Springfield, Ill.: C C Thomas.

APPENDIX

For the reader's convenience, this Appendix lists in sequence all the partial and full clinical test analyses included in this volume. Each entry specifies the diagnosis, the tests discussed, and the page numbers of the discussion. Brief references to test patterns are not listed; they may be found through the Index.

1. Incipient schizophrenia: Rorschach Test and retest; 42-44.
2. Schizophrenia: Rorschach Test and retest; 44-45.
3. Schizophrenia: Rorschach Test and retests; 46.
4. Narcissistic character disorder with borderline psychotic trends: Rorschach Test and retest; 46-49. Retest report of battery of tests; 54-56.
5. Phobic, infantile, demanding state with borderline psychotic trends: Rorschach Test and retest; 49-50.
6. Schizophrenia (adolescent): Rorschach Test and retest; 71-76.
7. Paranoid schizophrenia (late adolescent): Rorschach Test, Thematic Apperception Test; 100-103.
8. Hypomanic and paranoid state: Rorschach Test; 103-106.
9. Normal: Rorschach Test; 106-108.
10. Narcissistic character disorder with alcoholism: Thematic Apperception Test; 115-128.
11. Depression: Thematic Apperception Test and retest; 128-130.
12. Addiction (barbiturate and Benzedrine): Thematic Apperception Test; 130-133.
13. Delinquency with developing psychopathic trends (adolescent): Thematic Apperception Test; 133-135.
14. Delinquency with developing psychopathic trends (adolescent): Thematic Apperception Test; 135-140.
15. Schizophrenia: Thematic Apperception Test; 140-146.
16. Paranoid schizophrenia: Thematic Apperception Test; 146-150.
17. Schizophrenia: Thematic Apperception Test; 150-151.
18. Borderline schizophrenia: Thematic Apperception Test; 151-158.
19. Anxiety hysteria (phobic): Thematic Apperception Test; 158-162.
20. Depression: Thematic Apperception Test; 163-164.
21. Hypomanic phase of manic-depressive psychosis: Thematic Apperception Test; 165-169.
22. Schizophrenia: Rorschach Test; 177-196.
23. Traumatic neurosis, chronic, with alcoholism: Rorschach Test, Wechsler Adult Intelligence Scale, Thematic Apperception Test; 200-206.
24. Hysteria with conversion and phobic symptoms: Rorschach Test, Wechsler Adult Intelligence Scale, Word Association Test; 206-214.

Name Index

SUBJECT INDEX